THROUGH THE GREAT CANADIAN WILDERNESS

READER'S DIGEST

Travels & Adventures

THROUGH THE GREAT CANADIAN WILDERNESS

Published by The Reader's Digest Association Limited
LONDON • NEW YORK • SYDNEY • CAPE TOWN • MONTREAL

♦ COVER:
Main picture: **The still, blue waters of Moraine Lake, high in the Canadian Rockies, reflect the surrounding landscape of mountains and forest.**

Smaller pictures, from top to bottom: **David Halsey (left) and his companions on the Trans-Canada Expedition: Peter Souchuk and Ki. A grizzly bear watching over his territory in the Rockies. Typical 19th-century transport into the interior, as painted by Frances Anne Hopkins (1838–1919), one of the passengers in this birchbark canoe. An elk, or wapiti, with an impressive pair of velvet-covered antlers. Warm lamplight glows between the joins of this Inuit hunter's igloo.**

Spine: **This splendid carved and painted head comes from a West Coast Indian totem pole.**

♦ FRONTISPIECE:
The wilderness in winter: a cluster of ramshackle log cabins, perhaps still used by hunters and trappers, nestles beside a stream in a remote woodland clearing.

♦ TITLE PAGE:
This red squirrel, eating a spruce cone, is building up its fat reserves before the onset of winter.

♦ OPPOSITE:
Canada geese, such as this devoted couple, pair for life, which may be as much as 20 years.

♦ CONTENTS PAGES:
Left: **A lone fisherman on a tranquil mountain lake savours a glorious sunset.**

Right: **David Halsey (left) and his companions on the Trans-Canada Expedition: Peter Souchuk and Ki.**

♦ PAGES 8–9:
With the onset of autumn, vegetation around Vermilion Lakes, Alberta, takes on a variety of dramatic new colours.

♦ PAGES 42–43:
A group of Inuit hunters setting out in winter with their teams of huskies to cross the wide, open expanse of a frozen Arctic landscape.

THROUGH THE GREAT CANADIAN WILDERNESS was edited and designed
by The Reader's Digest Association Limited, London.

National Library of Australia cataloguing-in-publication data:

Through the great Canadian wilderness.
Includes index.
ISBN 0 86449 017 8 (series).
ISBN 0 86449 018 6.

1. Halsey, David, 1956-1983 - Journeys - Canada.
2. Canada - Description and travel. I. Halsey, David,
1956-1983. Magnetic north. II. Title: Magnetic north.
(Series: Reader's Digest travels & adventures).
917.1

Contributors

Consultant Editor: Donald Payne
Special Advisers: Dr John Davis, James Wilson

Editor: David Scott-Macnab
Assistant Editor: Charlotte Rundall
Associate Editors: David Blomfield, David Compton
Copy Editors: Caroline Arthur, Caroleen Conquest
Researcher: Julia Bruce
Designer: Louise Dick
Assistant Designer: Stephen Strong
Picture Researchers: Caroline Hensman, Diana Morris
Assistant Picture Researcher: Joe Hedges
Additional material by:
John Ellison Kahn, Martin Leighton, Tim Locke, James Wilson
Watercolour illustrations: Mark Entwisle
Cartography: Malcolm Porter
Index: Brian Amos

◆ The publishers and project team would like to express their gratitude to the Royal Geographical Society for its ongoing help and advice. They would also like to thank Peter Souchuk and the many individuals who have contributed to the preparation of this volume.

Contents

PART 1 AN EVOCATION

A LAND OF WOODS AND WATER

PART 2 AN ADVENTURE

ACROSS THE WILD CONTINENT

A condensation based on MAGNETIC NORTH by David Halsey with Diana Landau

PART 1 AN EVOCATION

A LAND OF WOODS AND WATER

A Land of Woods and Water

THE HEART OF CANADA is an untamed wilderness: a frontier-land of frozen plains, silent forests, tranquil lakes and multitudinous rivers, all fashioned on a huge scale.

Canada is the world's second-largest country, surpassed only by the gigantic Russian Federation. Just one of its ten provinces (the Northwest Territories) covers an area ten times greater than the whole of the British Isles. Yet this vast country is populated by fewer than 30 million people, of whom the great majority—over 80 per cent—live in cities in a narrow strip of fertile land adjacent to the USA. To the north of this strip lie over three million square miles of territory wholly unsuitable for agriculture and therefore among the most sparsely populated on Earth. This is the heart of Canada: a wilderness of primordial woodland, patterned by a mosaic of rivers and lakes which contain nearly ten per cent of the world's fresh surface water. The further north one goes the more desolate this wilderness becomes, until in the Canadian Arctic it degenerates into a wasteland where the subsoil is permanently frozen and winter temperatures can drop to –60°F.

The sheer immensity and diversity of this beautiful but intransigent land can seem quite overwhelming, and newcomers to Canada invariably wonder just how so many contrasting environments came to coexist. The answers lie all around them in the landscape itself.

The Dividing Mountains

The Rocky Mountains, or Rockies as they are familiarly called, form a huge chain, extending from northern British Columbia all the way down to Mexico, nearly 3,000 miles to the south. And they divide Canada into two quite separate zones. To their west, in British Columbia, lie hills, valleys, rushing streams and, in a narrow coastal region bordering the Pacific Ocean,

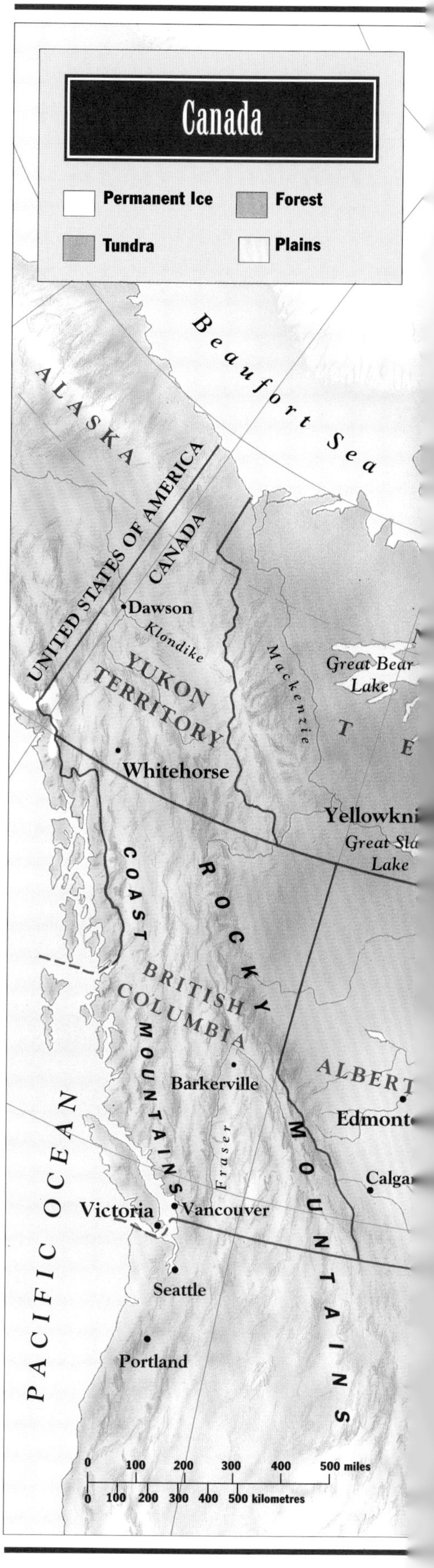

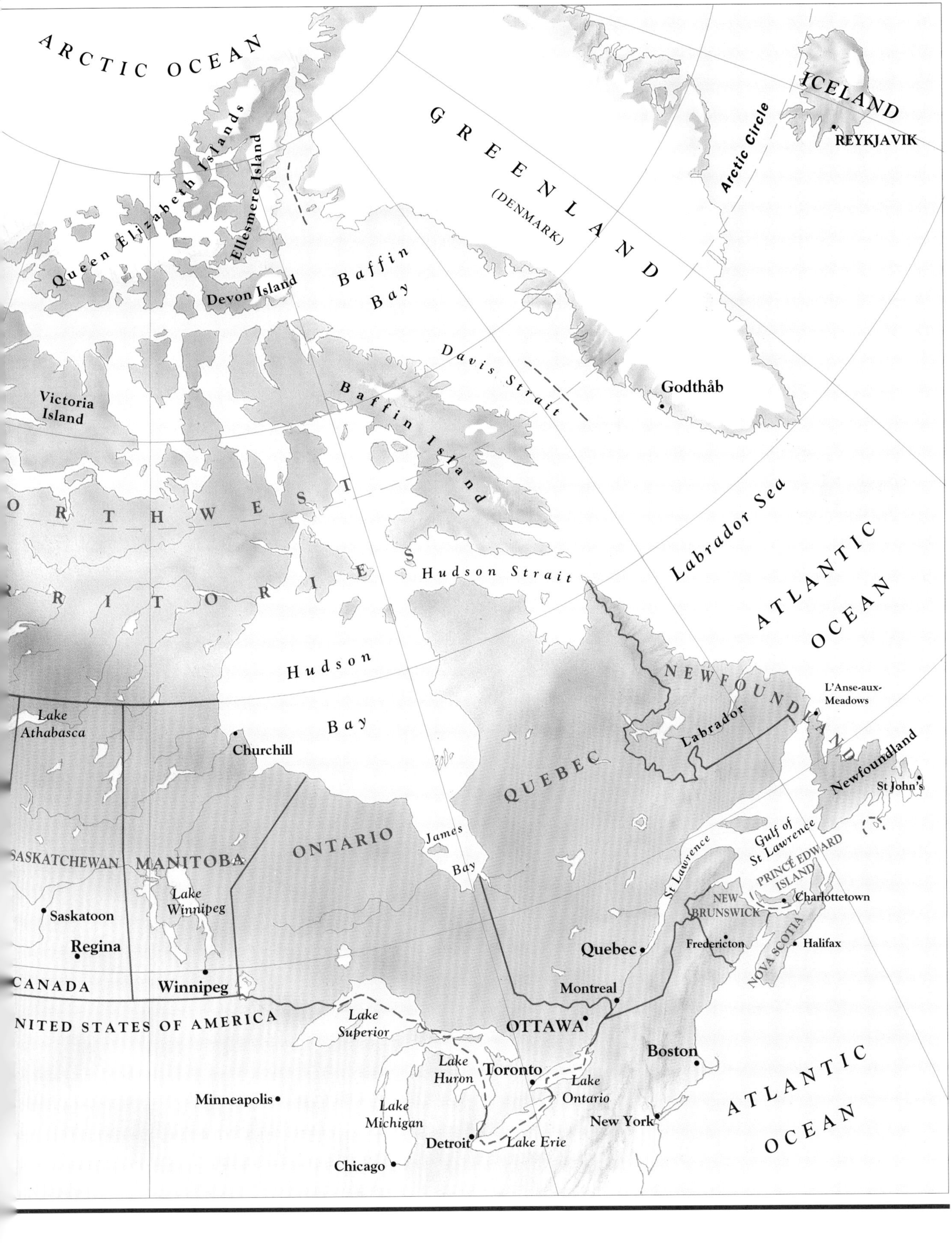
ARCTIC OCEAN
Queen Elizabeth Islands
Ellesmere Island
Devon Island
Victoria Island
Baffin Bay
Davis Strait
Baffin Island
GREENLAND
(DENMARK)
Godthåb
ICELAND
REYKJAVIK
Arctic Circle
NORTHWEST TERRITORIES
Hudson Strait
Labrador Sea
ATLANTIC OCEAN
Hudson Bay
NEWFOUNDLAND
Labrador
L'Anse-aux-Meadows
Newfoundland
St John's
Lake Athabasca
Churchill
QUEBEC
ONTARIO
James Bay
SASKATCHEWAN
MANITOBA
Lake Winnipeg
Saskatoon
Regina
Winnipeg
CANADA
UNITED STATES OF AMERICA
St Lawrence
Gulf of St Lawrence
PRINCE EDWARD ISLAND
Charlottetown
NEW BRUNSWICK
Fredericton
NOVA SCOTIA
Halifax
Quebec
Montreal
OTTAWA
Lake Superior
Lake Huron
Toronto
Lake Ontario
Boston
Minneapolis
Lake Michigan
New York
Detroit
Lake Erie
Chicago
ATLANTIC OCEAN

▲ **The prairies—Canada's breadbasket—where wheat fields stretch to a distant horizon.**

A Land of Natural Splendour

NO ONE CAN VISIT Canada without being awestruck by the magnificence of the country's landscape: by the colours and vistas—indeed, by the sheer scale and drama of Nature's handiwork. Every region and every season, it seems, has its own individual magic.

Perhaps best known of all are the Rocky Mountains and their adjacent ranges: the Purcell and the Cariboo Mountains, to name but two. Here is an imposing world of precipitous canyons and gentle alpine meadows; of glacier-clad peaks and shining lakes tinted in hues that defy belief.

Below the mountains' southeastern foothills roll the vast prairies—Canada's breadbasket—at harvest time, a sea of rippling, golden wheat. And northeast of them lies the huge Canadian Shield, an ancient geological formation exposed by glaciers during the ice age and covering nearly half of the country.

Even the austere northern tundra, known as the Barren Grounds, is vibrant at certain times of the year. Myriad plants burst into pink, white and purple blooms to take full advantage of the region's brief summer, and then glow a deep red or orange in autumn.

▲ **The normally bleak northern tundra, here clad in the vivid colours of autumn.**

▲ A breathtaking view across Moraine Lake in Banff National Park in the Rockies. Its turquoise colour and characteristic sheen are caused by sunlight reflecting off fine sediments deposited in it by glacial meltwater.

These stark granite cliffs, forming part of the huge Canadian Shield, were smoothed and rounded by one of the colossal ice sheets that covered the country during the last ice age. ▼

dripping temperate rain forests. The climate here is generally milder and the vegetation more lush than anywhere else in the country. Yet, strange as it may seem, prickly pears and other desert plants also thrive in the province, thanks to a smaller, though no less dramatic, range called the Coast Mountains. This acts as a great sponge, soaking up the moist air that drives in from the Pacific Ocean and creating in its lee a region of parched grasses and sagebrush.

Above this dry belt tower the Rockies themselves: a cataclysmic fusion of fast-flowing rivers, pellucid lakes, slow-sliding glaciers and huge, snowclad peaks. Remote, inaccessible and 'far from the madding crowd', this is an area of spectacular scenic beauty: one of the last redoubts of the natural world.

By contrast with the jumbled, tumbling topography of British Columbia, the eastern slopes of the Rockies give way to a flat, monotonous landscape stretching to the horizon. To the north is open tundra extending to the Arctic Circle; to the south, prairie grassland, which blends almost imperceptibly into the Great Plains of the United States; and, in between, lies a vast coniferous forest that finally ends only when it reaches the Atlantic Ocean, some 4,000 miles to the east. When the first European explorers entered this forest in the early 17th century, it covered most of the country. And even now, from the air, much of it looks like a roadless wilderness untouched by man. Indeed, few people have ever lived here, not because of the savage cold of winter, but rather because the area has an extremely shallow topsoil and is therefore useless for farming—a consequence of the dramatic forces that were at work during the last ice age, known as the Wisconsin Glaciation.

The Legacy of the Ice Age

About 70,000 years ago, the Earth entered a major cold spell. The temperature, in the Northern Hemisphere in particular, fell dramatically: to the point where all the seasons merged into one year-round winter. New falls of snow failed to melt, but accumulated, layer upon layer, until finally they formed enormous ice caps that covered most of Canada and Greenland, and much of northern Europe.

In North America, two vast ice sheets—the Laurentide and the Cordilleran—eventually stretched from the Arctic Ocean to the Great Lakes, and from Newfoundland to the Pacific. The larger of the two, the Laurentide, lying east of the Rockies, may have been as much as two miles deep. Its weight is barely imaginable and even today the evidence of its presence and power is everywhere. For not only did the ice sheet compress the ancient volcanic and sedimentary rocks that lay beneath it into a deep, saucer-shaped depression (part of which now contains Hudson Bay), it also flowed outwards under the force of gravity, gouging, scraping and bulldozing everything that lay in the path of its inexorable advance.

As a result, when the ice receded some 11,000 years ago, it left behind a reshaped landscape of gently rounded hills and shallow valleys filled with meltwater. These became the maze of streams and lakes that typify the heart of Canada today. The ice sheet also left a landscape stripped bare of topsoil and in which were revealed some of the most ancient rocks in the world: among them granite and greenstone formed up to 3,800 million years ago during the Precambrian era, when the Earth was in its infancy. This exposed, primeval bedrock is probably the most characteristic feature of the the great depression left by the ice sheet: an area covering almost half of Canada and known today as the Canadian Shield.

In time, lichens made a home in this unpromising environment, taking hold on the rock and breaking it down into a new topsoil, which even now, after 11,000 years, is often no more than ten inches deep. Grasses followed, then shrubs and finally trees: great forests of jack pines, spruce and conifers, which support themselves in the shallow soil with a web of horizontal roots. The forests grew until they covered more than 35 per cent of the land, yielding only in the north to the shrubs of the tundra and in the southwest to the grasses of the prairies.

Animals of the North

Animals followed the greening of the land, finding food and habitat in the burgeoning forests, grassland and tundra. They were not the same animals that had fled south in the face of the advancing ice sheets—elephant-like mastodons, sabre-toothed cats, camels and horses—but they were hardy and adaptable.

Nowhere is this more apparent than in the barren, high Arctic regions of Canada. This is the domain of the polar bear, which spends most of its life adrift on pack ice and floes, on which it stalks seals. Further south, on the bleak, treeless tundra, live other creatures that must cope with a cruel winter lasting three-quarters of the year: the Arctic fox, the Arctic hare and one of the largest animals in Canada, the musk ox—a survivor of the last ice age, whose long, thick coat enables it to survive in extremes of cold. Here too, during the short summer enjoyed by this region, are large herds of caribou feeding on herbs and berries, and over 100 species of migrant birds which use the tundra as a breeding ground. However, with the onset of

Canadian Wildlife

CANADA'S VAST WILDERNESS has been a haven for wildlife for many thousands of years. The golden eagle, with its wingspan of up to eight feet, is undisputed king of the skies, while on the ground a number of remarkable creatures have adapted to the harsh climate and varied landscape in their own particular ways.

On the west coast and in the Rocky Mountains lives the brown bear—also known as the grizzly, because its thick, coarse fur is often grizzled with grey. Usually committed loners, grizzlies tolerate one another on only two occasions annually: during the mating season and during the salmon run, when they gorge themselves on salmon returning in their millions from the sea to spawn.

Whereas grizzlies, like other bears, spend most of the winter asleep, wolverines are masterful winter hunters. Weighing only about 50 pounds, these animals are immensely powerful for their size. They also have broad, furry feet which act like snowshoes, enabling them to run at speed across deep snow and pull down moose or caribou up to twenty times their own size.

Equally well-adapted to winter are the mild-tempered musk oxen that roam the northern tundra within the Arctic Circle. They are protected against the cold by a shaggy coat of guardhairs hanging down to their ankles, and a dense layer of underwool, finer and lighter than any cashmere: a pound of it can be spun into a strand ten miles long.

▲ Musk oxen, which live in the Arctic, gather into a circle when threatened by their main predators—packs of wolves.

◀ Poised above a waterfall, this grizzly has nimbly caught a salmon in its mouth.

A wolverine stalks across the snow on its broad feet. Its indiscriminate appetite has earned it the nickname 'the glutton'. ▶

▲ A majestic golden eagle, whose powerful talons enable it to capture prey as large as young deer, cries its defiance to all who might hear.

◀ Moose feed on aquatic plants, and are therefore in their element in a land of so many rivers, pools and lakes.

Conquerors of the Arctic

UNTIL VERY RECENTLY, the people of Canada's frozen Arctic wastes were referred to universally as the Eskimo—a Cree Indian word meaning 'eaters of raw flesh'. Their preferred name for themselves, however, is Inuit, meaning simply 'the people'.

Unlike the Indians of more southerly regions, whose ancestors migrated to North America at least 25,000 years ago, during the last ice age, the Inuit are relative newcomers to Canada. Experts are not sure exactly how long they have lived here, but the evidence suggests that they probably arrived by boat between 2500 and 1000 BC. Like the earlier migrants, the Inuit came from Siberia; but unlike them, the Inuit did not move south, preferring to make their home in the cold, inhospitable north.

And here they prospered as nomadic hunters and fishermen, living much as the earlier ice-age migrants must have done. The mainstays of their diet were fat and meat; for caribou, walruses, seals, whales and fish are plentiful in the Arctic, while fruit and vegetables simply cannot grow in the frigid soil. Entire families, with all their belongings, would make at least two major journeys a year—from summer to winter hunting grounds and back again—often spending the whole winter in igloos made from hard-packed snow.

For all but a very few remote groups, however, the traditional Inuit way of life is now virtually a thing of the past. Electricity, television, snowmobiles and government schools have changed their outlook for ever.

▲ A handmade caribou-skin coat and hood keep this Inuit hunter warm, despite freezing Arctic temperatures.

▲ Warm lamplight glows invitingly between the joins of an igloo built from snow. Igloos offer better protection against fierce Arctic winds than any other temporary shelter.

Fishing through a hole in the ice requires limitless patience. This man, dressed in a white fox-fur coat, is harpooning fish as they rise to nibble at a baited line. ▼

◀ A colourfully dressed Inuit family on the move using traditional transport—a sled drawn by a team of huskies.

winter, merely a handful of birds remain: only a hardy few, such as the great grey owl, the grouse and the ptarmigan, will risk braving the icy blasts of a long Arctic winter.

South of the tundra lies the great boreal, or northern, forest, which supports most of the wildlife considered typical of Canada: moose, which can stand seven feet tall at the shoulder, lynx, beavers, wolverines and bears. Black bears, which live on a varied diet of leaves, insects and small mammals, are still spread widely over the country. Not so their larger cousin, the awesome brown or grizzly bear, which has been all but exterminated east of the Rockies. Grizzlies normally weigh about 800 pounds, but gigantic individuals can be twice as heavy, putting them on a par with polar bears as the largest carnivores in the world. They are not normally aggressive, which is just as well, since an angry grizzly is reputed to have killed five bison in a single charge.

For millennia, these wild creatures thrived in an unspoilt paradise because the people of the ice, the coast, the plains and the woods valued and respected them, killing only as many as they needed for food or clothing. So who were the people of the Canadian wilderness and where did they come from?

The Ice People

Ever since Christopher Columbus landed in the West Indies in 1492, Europeans and their descendants in the 'New World' have been puzzling over the origins of North America's native people. Columbus himself, convinced that he had reached Asia, called them 'Indians', while other early explorers believed that they must be a lost tribe of Israel, or survivors from the legendary vanished civilisation of Atlantis.

The Indians themselves have no such uncertainty: as far as they are concerned, they have always thrived on the coasts, plains, tundra and forests of North America. Many tribes, including the Inuit, call themselves simply 'the people', and tell elaborate stories of how their ancestors came to be created in the very places where European explorers first found them and where many of them continue to live to this day.

Modern historians and scientists cannot believe that these creation myths contain the whole truth. Their evidence indicates that modern Indians are descended from Mongoloid hunters who migrated by land from Siberia during the Wisconsin Glaciation, some 30,000 years ago. At this time, with much of the water of the oceans locked up in ice caps and glaciers, the sea level in the Bering Strait was at least 200 feet lower than it is now, turning today's seabed into tundra, and today's islands into mountains. In some places this bridge of dry land was almost 1,000 miles wide, allowing migrating herds of mammoth and caribou, and the Siberian hunters who followed in their wake, easy access to Alaska and the Yukon.

Here the early hunters settled and prospered, for at that time these territories were ice-free and abundant in animals. The great Laurentide and Cordilleran ice sheets lay to the south, stretching as far as modern-day California and New York, and totally blocking any further migration into the Americas.

Then, about 15,000 years ago, the earth's climate started to warm up. The ice sheets gradually melted, the seas rose and the migrants were cut off from their 'Old World'. At the same time, ice-free corridors began to open up to the south. These were quickly exploited by the hunters, who again started to migrate. Some pushed on as far as South America, while others fanned out to populate North America from west to east, all the while diversifying and adapting to the immense variety of landscapes they found in the continent.

The Worshippers of Salmon

All the regions of Canada are distinctive in their own way, but few are as different from all the others as the Pacific Coast—a lush, mist-shrouded region of islands, inlets and valleys, covered in dense evergreen forest and crisscrossed by fast-flowing waterways. Protected by mountains to the east and warmed by the Alaska Current to the west, the region has a temperate climate and high annual rainfall, which combine to make it one of the most bountiful parts of North America.

The West Coast Indians used this natural richness to create a unique culture and way of life. They hunted bear, deer and elk in the teeming forests, and killed seals and whales from large sea-going canoes. Most important of all, using weirs, nets, spears and traps, they harvested enormous quantities of salmon.

Each summer, tens of millions of Pacific salmon leave the ocean and swim up the turbulent Canadian and Alaskan rivers, returning to spawn in the very headwaters where they were born. At times they are so close-packed that it is impossible to see the riverbed through the moving curtain of their bodies. This is a mass migration that never fails: a source of food more reliable than any crop. And a grateful people believed the

Enormous wooden long houses such as these, decorated with paintings of symbolic plants and animals, were a typical feature of West Coast Indian settlements. Up to 160 feet long, they were used both as homes and as ceremonial buildings. ▶

salmon were a race of immortals, who in winter lived as men beneath the sea and in summer changed into fish to offer their bodies as food.

This harvest of the sea provided the stability needed to build a prosperous society. Instead of moving about in a constant search for game, the West Coast tribes were able to live in permanent villages and evolve complex societies with highly sophisticated arts, crafts and ceremonies. They built huge plank houses—some of them 160 feet long—wove beautiful baskets, blankets and even clothes out of shredded cedar bark, and developed an extraordinary style of wood-carving. Their intricate, brightly coloured totem poles, decorated with the figures of animals and supernatural beings, are perhaps the best-known and most recognisable images of North American Indian art.

Prosperity also had another side, however, for the West Coast Indians were obsessed with personal wealth and prestige, and their societies were strongly hierarchical. At the top of the social scale were chiefs or 'nobles' and their families; then came 'commoners' and, at the bottom, slaves, usually captured from other tribes. The nobles were constantly vying with each other to show off their property and status, especially in a remarkable ceremonial feast called the potlatch, when they would give away and even destroy their possessions in a flamboyant exhibition of wealth. Early Christian missionaries condemned the potlatch as 'pagan' and wasteful, but most anthropologists now argue that the ceremony had an important purpose in redistributing surplus food and goods to people at the lower end of the social scale.

East of the Rockies, the Indians led very different lives.

People of the Plains and Woods

The Rockies divide the Pacific coast from the rest of Canada so effectively that when you cross them you enter what seems to be a completely different world. To the southeast lie vast prairie grasslands, where gigantic herds of bison once grazed until they were all but exterminated by professional white hunters in the 19th century. Before this happened, the bison supplied the Indians of the plains with all their needs. Bison meat was dried, shredded and then pounded with fat and dried fruit to make small, long-lasting cakes called pemmican; buffalo hides and fur were turned into tents, blankets and clothes; bison bones became tools and toys. And because the buffalo were always on the move, so too were the Indians, with their many dogs dragging their baggage and belongings.

Elsewhere, in the great boreal forest, a few tribes were able to practise limited forms of agriculture close to the Great Lakes.

▲ Snowshoes allow this woodland Indian to hunt moose in the middle of winter—an undertaking for the fit and strong alone.

▲ A Plains Indian dressed in all his finery and wearing dramatic face paint for a powwow—a tribal get-together.

▲ **The traditional camp of a woodland hunter. The tepee, decorated with colourful designs, is built from branches draped with birch bark. In the background, animal pelts hang up to dry.**

The Nomadic Hunters

UNTIL RELATIVELY RECENTLY, the vast majority of Canada's native people lived as nomadic hunters—on the tundra and prairie grasslands, and in the great boreal forest that covers a great swathe of the country. A few tribes in the vicinity of the Great Lakes cultivated the earth to supplement their diet of forest produce; but the rest spent virtually their entire lives in an endless hunt for food.

On the plains, vast herds of millions of bison provided tribes such as the Blackfoot and the Sarcee with everything they needed: meat for food, hides for making clothes and shelters, bones for tools. But killing the bison was not easy: they had to be pursued on foot, or driven over cliffs such as the aptly named Head-Smashed-In Buffalo Jump in Alberta. The popular image of Plains Indians hunting bison on horseback became possible only in the 18th century, after the Spanish had introduced the horse to the Americas.

In the subarctic forest and tundra, the Cree, the Chipewyan and the Yellowknife, among other tribes, hunted animals such as caribou, moose, hare and beaver, usually by constantly moving to wherever game could be found. This type of existence can support only a small population: perhaps 25 or fewer individuals per 100 square miles. As a result, the subarctic Indians lived in small bands of, at most, a few families, with a single skilled hunter as their leader. These bands had little contact with each other, except for a few days each year, when related bands would get together to trade, socialise and find marriage partners. To early European explorers and traders, the Indians' lives appeared bleak and dangerous; their own myths and legends, however, view the world with cheerfulness and vitality.

▲ **In ceremonies such as this 'buffalo-calling dance', the Plains Indians celebrated their relationship with the bison that were so important to their lives.**

The Vikings in Canada

According to the well-known children's rhyme, Christopher Columbus sailed the ocean blue 'in fourteen hundred and ninety-two' on a momentous voyage that led him to the Americas, specifically the West Indies. There can be no diminishing Columbus's achievement, yet we now know that he was not the first European to set foot in the New World: credit for that must go to Leif Eriksson, a Viking explorer who landed in Canada in the late 10th century AD.

The Old Icelandic sagas tell us that Leif was the son of Erik the Red, an outlaw banished from Iceland for feuding and murder. Exile prompted Erik to sail the seas and eventually to settle in Greenland, where he founded a colony some time in the year 985 or 986. Six months later, a young Icelandic merchant named Bjarni Herjolfsson set out to visit Erik's settlement, only to be blown wildly off course. When he finally did make it to Greenland, Bjarni had a remarkable tale to tell: wooded country lay far to the west.

Inspired by Bjarni's discovery, Leif Eriksson set sail in about 990 with a crew of 35 to learn more of the mysterious land. Leif soon landed in eastern Canada, probably at Baffin Island, then Labrador, and finally Newfoundland, which he named Vinland, or 'Wineland', because of the grapes he found growing there. The Vikings soon realised that these new territories were far richer than those they had left behind, especially in salmon and timber. But their attempts to settle were thwarted. Several colonising expeditions set out from Greenland, only to meet with hostility from local Indians. Finally, after only a few years, Vinland was abandoned, becoming merely an evocative allusion in the sagas until it was eventually rediscovered by the Genoese explorer John Cabot almost 500 years later.

▲ In full Viking regalia, this man looks every bit the transatlantic adventurer.

◄ A reconstructed Viking longboat moored in a quiet Norwegian fjord. Such a ship would have been used by Leif Eriksson and his crew on their historic westward voyage.

▲ Ornate gold jewellery attests to the sophistication of Viking culture.

◀ A dramatic painting of Leif Eriksson sighting Canada by the Norwegian artist Christian Krohg (1852–1925).

▲ Reconstructions of the Vikings' turf houses at L'Anse-aux-Meadows on the northern tip of Newfoundland—the supposed site of their Vinland settlement.

But over most of the subarctic region, the long, severe winters and lack of topsoil made farming impossible. Game was often widely scattered, so the Indians had no choice but to maintain a more or less ceaseless quest for food, trapping beavers and hunting woodland animals such as deer and moose. In the north, most of them followed the huge herds of tens of thousands of caribou that migrate every year between the forest and the tundra.

Because of their nomadic existence, the subarctic Indians had few opportunities to develop strong artistic traditions, although clothing, bags and other essential items were often beautifully decorated. They did, however, have an immensely rich and imaginative inner world, expressed in long and complex stories about heroes, spirits and monsters that explained their relationship with the animals and the land.

Their lives were hard, but stable. Yet it was only a matter of time before new migrants would arrive to lay claim to their land.

The First Europeans

A thousand years ago, the waters of northern Europe were dominated by the Vikings—fierce mariner-warriors who were then at the height of their power.

The popular image of these great seafarers is of vicious, Dark Age barbarians pouring out of their longboats to loot a church and then going on to pillage a town and murder its inhabitants. Certainly, there is ample evidence that the Vikings were past masters of lightning-swift raids, but many of their voyages were intended as much for trade and settlement as plunder. Throughout the 9th, 10th and 11th centuries, Viking colonies sprang up in the British Isles, France and even the heartland of Russia; they also appeared in the Shetland and Faeroe islands, in Iceland, and then in Greenland. Moving ever westward, the Vikings even tried to settle in Canada.

According to the Old Icelandic sagas, an outlaw by the name of Erik the Red initiated the colonisation of Greenland, while his son, Leif Eriksson, led the first European expedition to set foot in the New World. In about AD 990, so the story goes, Leif set out to check the reports of a merchant called Bjarni Herjolfsson, who claimed to have sighted unknown lands west of Greenland. The sagas tell how Leif and his men soon sighted land and went ashore; but they found no grass, only 'great glaciers, and right up to the glaciers from the sea a single slab of rock'. Leif called this place Helluland, 'Flatstone Land'; it was almost certainly Baffin Island. After sailing south for a few days, they sighted another coast and again went ashore. In the words of the sagas, 'The country was flat and covered with forest, with

▲ **In this painting by Ernest Board (1877–1934), John Cabot bids the dignitaries of Bristol farewell before embarking on his historic voyage across the Atlantic in 1497.**

The Westward Search for Asia

WITHIN A FEW YEARS of Columbus's epic voyage across the Atlantic, explorers from all over Europe were planting flags wherever they could in the New World. England, too, staked a claim—albeit a tenuous one—in Canada. In 1497, John Cabot sailed from Bristol to Newfoundland, asserting on his return that he had reached Cathay (China) and the land of the great Khan. He was immediately sent back with five new ships, but was never seen again, and the English lost interest.

The French presently stepped into the vacuum. Their ships began fishing off the Newfoundland coast, returning with rumours of a vast waterway leading to the Orient. In 1534, Jacques Cartier was despatched by the king of France to investigate. Cartier sailed into the Gulf of St Lawrence, and the following year into the St Lawrence River, both of which he named. The great size of the river and the salinity of its water led Cartier to believe that he was on the right track; and when local Indians told him (or so he thought) that there were further great waterways to the west, leading to gold and spices, he was convinced. But Cartier had not reckoned with the ferocity of the Canadian winter, which put an end to both his exploration and his subsequent attempt to establish a colony.

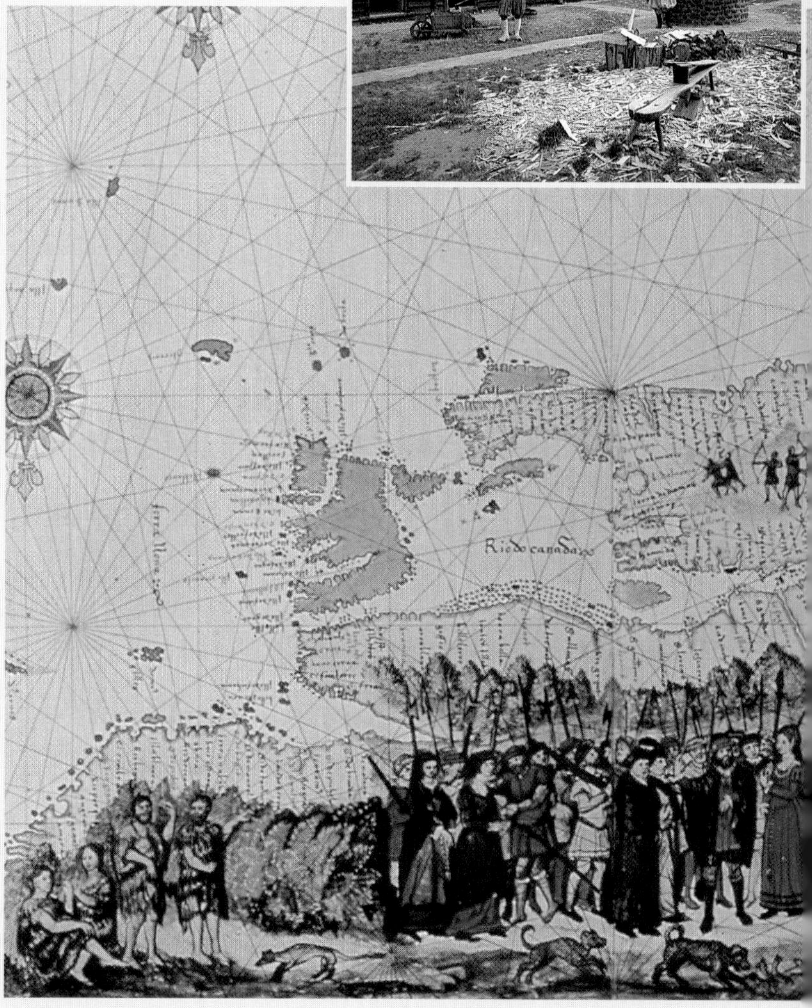

An early map (with north and south inverted) showing Jacques Cartier arriving in Canada. ▶

▲ **The vast St Lawrence River, 90 miles wide at its mouth, was easily mistaken by Jacques Cartier for a sea strait.**

◀ **A 'settler' in period costume strolls through a reconstruction of an early French colony in eastern Canada.**

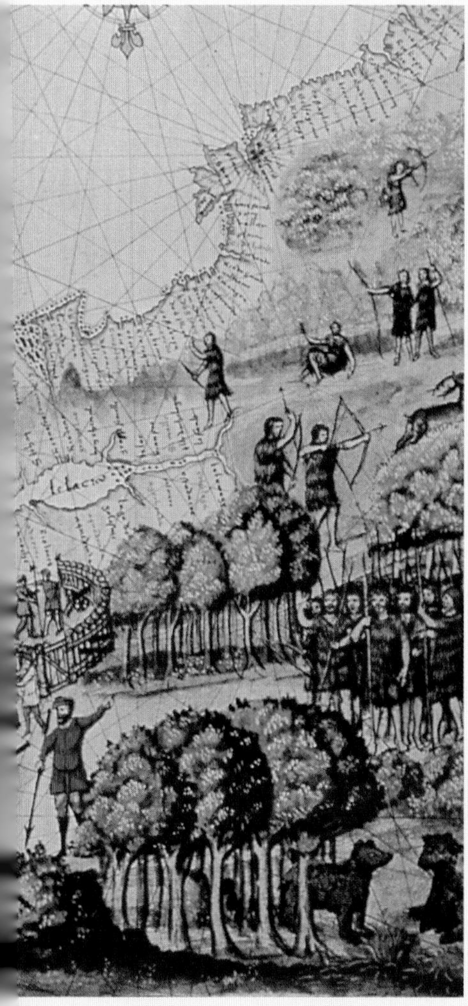

extensive white sands, and shelving gently to the sea.' Leif called it Markland, 'Woodland'; it was almost certainly Labrador.

Two days later they made another landfall in an idyllic place: the water was the sweetest they had ever tasted, and 'there was no lack of salmon in river or lake, and salmon bigger than they had ever seen before. The nature of the land was so choice, it seemed to them that none of the cattle would require fodder for the winter.' In exploring this new country, one of Leif's crew discovered grapevines, so Leif called it Vinland, 'Wineland'.

Vinland has been sought by many a scholar, and its most likely location is now thought to be L'Anse-aux-Meadows on the northern tip of Newfoundland. Here archaeologists have found the remains of several houses, a smithy and a charcoal kiln, all of which have been carbon-dated to about AD 1000. The design of the houses is Scandinavian, not Indian; and the presence of iron rivets suggests that this was a site for repairing the sort of vessels that the Vikings used on their great voyages.

Unfortunately for them, the Vikings never had much opportunity to enjoy their land of vines and salmon. At least three expeditions were sent to Vinland, but all were driven off by the hostility of the local Indians, or 'Skraelings' ('wretches') as the Vikings called them. For a few decades 'Vinland the Good' was eulogised in Greenland and Iceland; then it faded from memory, and almost 500 years were to pass before Europeans again made contact with the New World.

The Rediscovery of Canada

After Columbus's successful crossing of the Atlantic in 1492, powerful monarchs throughout Europe vied with each other to discover the riches of the New World, which many believed to be eastern China, or a country very near to it. The climate was ripe for adventurers, fortune-hunters and mercenaries of all sorts, eager to lay hands on the untold wealth of the East. One such adventurer was John Cabot, or Giovanni Caboto, an Italian navigator who managed to persuade England's King Henry VII and the merchants of Bristol to finance a journey into the northwest Atlantic in search of unknown lands. In June 1497, Cabot landed somewhere on Newfoundland, unfurled both the Venetian and English flags, and took possession of the territory in the name of King Henry. At that moment, the long-forgotten link which had been forged between Europe and Canada by the Vikings was re-established, and the land claimed for England.

Yet the English made no immediate effort to explore or settle their new possession, whereas the French did. In 1534, Jacques

Cartier sailed to Canada with a commission from King Francis I of France to discover gold, spices and a passage to Asia. Instead, he discovered the Gulf of St Lawrence and the mouth of the mighty St Lawrence River. Cartier was not especially pleased with what he saw; instead of wealthy Asian merchants trading in silk, he found only a few 'wild and savage folk' who went about 'clothed in animal skins'. As a result, he wrote with some disappointment, 'I am inclined to believe that this is the land that God gave to Cain.'

Nevertheless, he claimed the land for France and returned the following year to sail directly into the St Lawrence, which he still hoped might be a strait leading to China. At the end of a month of slow, hazardous progress, the estuary was still several miles wide; but it was narrowing, and Cartier eventually realised that what he was negotiating was not a strait, but a great river. His winter quarters proved equally disappointing, for the cold was far worse than he had anticipated. His ships became frozen in, many of his crew died of hypothermia and scurvy, and it was with some difficulty that he struggled back to France in the spring.

In 1541 he tried again, this time with several hundred would-be settlers. But the Indians were hostile, and once again conditions proved too harsh to be endured. Not surprisingly, half a century was to pass before the next attempt at settlement.

The French Colonists

Although Cartier failed to find a route to Asia, he did return to Europe with reports of forests abundant in fur animals, and waters teeming with fish and whales. He also took back a name for the new territory: 'Canada', from an Iroquois word meaning 'village'.

As a result, fleets of fishing boats were soon harvesting the seas around Newfoundland and Nova Scotia, and in the 1580s fur traders began negotiating with the Indians in earnest for large quantities of beaver pelts. The Indians, in turn, were quick to learn how to play rival merchants off against one another, and so make the most of a competitive market. Indeed, they were so successful that European merchants soon complained that there was no longer any profit in the trade.

In 1608, the French decided to act. Samuel de Champlain and 32 men were sent to establish a fortified colony on the St Lawrence River, from where they could exercise some influence on the fur trade. Champlain chose a site called a *kébec* by the local Indians—meaning 'a place where the river narrows'—precisely where the modern city of Quebec stands today.

He could not have arrived at a more dangerous time: the warlike southern Iroquois were expanding their territory and so

▲ Pioneering journeys into the interior were made by French *coureurs de bois* such as this valiant pair, depicted here with their escorts by Frederic Remington (1861–1909).

An engraving, also by Frederic Remington, showing Indian traders paying a visit to their dandified French counterparts in Montreal. ▼

▲ A gruesome portrayal of an Iroquois warrior scalping an enemy.

As their mission burns behind them, French Jesuit martyrs stoically endure the cruellest tortures. ▼

The French Settlers

BY THE EARLY 17TH CENTURY, a thriving fur trade had been established along the St Lawrence River, with ships from all over Europe stopping to collect beaver pelts from local Indians. The French, however, decided to take control of the trade, both for commercial reasons and in the hope of building an American empire.

In 1608, Samuel de Champlain founded a fortified colony on the St Lawrence and established friendly relations with the Huron Indians. At the same time, he made the mistake of clashing with the warlike Iroquois, the Huron's great enemies—thereby provoking the Iroquois into a deep and long-lasting enmity towards the French.

Within a few decades, French settlements, trading posts and forts were dotted all the way along the St Lawrence and Ottawa rivers to the Great Lakes. Intrepid young men called *coureurs de bois* were moving ever further into the interior to find fresh trapping grounds and new tribes with whom to trade. And French Jesuit priests, called 'blackrobes' by the Indians, were braving a precarious existence in the most remote areas to establish their missions. One of the largest of these missions was Sainte-Marie-among-the-Hurons, run for ten years by the popular Father Jean de Brébeuf. In 1649, however, the hazards of pioneer life were reconfirmed when a massive Iroquois army swept over the area. Brébeuf and a fellow Jesuit, Gabriel Lallemant, were captured and cruelly tortured to death, their teachings parodied as they were 'baptised' with buckets of boiling water. Both men would later be canonised as two of the first martyr saints in North America.

The Quest for a Northwest Passage

THE STORY OF THE SEARCH for a navigable route to the Orient through the frozen seas of the Canadian north is one of remarkable courage, stoicism and perseverance in the face of extreme adversity.

In 1576, Sir Martin Frobisher led the first major voyage to the Canadian Arctic, where he was attacked by Inuit. He also discovered what he thought was gold, and this instantly distracted his sponsors from the Northwest Passage. They sent him back twice more to bring back hundreds of tons of ore, which shortly after was found to be worthless iron pyrites—fool's gold.

When Henry Hudson sailed into Hudson Bay in 1610, he was sure he had found open waters to the East Indies. However, at the bottom end of James Bay his ship, the *Discovery*, was trapped by winter ice and released only the following June. Hudson then announced that he would not return to England for fresh supplies—at which the crew mutinied, abandoning Hudson, his son and seven loyal crew members to certain death in an open boat.

Perhaps most tragic of all was John Franklin's voyage of 1845. A fatal error in Franklin's map led his two ships into a field of virtually permanent ice, where they remained trapped for two whole years. Forty search parties from England failed to find any survivors, but did come across their remains, which included evidence that the starving seamen had resorted to cannibalism in their plight.

It was only in 1906 that the Norwegian explorer Roald Amundsen finally found the elusive Northwest Passage. The hazards of the route are such, though, that few have dared follow in his tracks.

▲ In this poignant painting by John Collier (1850–1934), Henry Hudson has the look of a man who knows a horrific fate awaits him.

A small modern ship cuts through ice that would have defeated many early explorers. ▶

◀ A 16th-century illustration of the fateful encounter between men from Sir Martin Frobisher's expedition and hostile Inuit.

HMS *Investigator*, one of the many ships sent to find Franklin, was itself trapped by ice. ▼

▲ **Looking determined and efficient, Roald Amundsen, discoverer of the Northwest Passage, is pictured here on one of his later Arctic expeditions.**

coming into conflict with the Algonquin Indians and their allies, the Huron. Champlain promptly formed an alliance with the Huron and even took part in a raid on an Iroquois village—a rash action which created a highly dangerous enemy for the French. Never again would French traders, missionaries or settlers be safe from Iroquois attack.

On the other hand, the raid cemented friendship with the Huron, with the result that Huron trappers and traders were soon flocking to Champlain's settlement. At the same time, bored young Frenchmen began leaving the colony to live among the Indians as trappers. Wearing buckskins and speaking Indian dialects fluently, these *coureurs de bois*, as they were called, pushed ever further into the interior, making contact with new tribes and so enlarging the fur trade.

For a time it looked as if Champlain's mission would be an overwhelming success—and in many ways it was. Champlain founded several new colonies and was eventually appointed administrator of Quebec, or New France as it was then known. But further to the north another great power was expanding its sphere of influence: the British were beginning to take a keen interest in Canada's lucrative supply of furs.

The Elusive Northwest Passage

At first, British interest in the New World was limited to searching for a Northwest Passage through the Arctic Ocean to the Orient. For sailing ships, this passage was to prove a dangerous and costly chimera. Sometimes blocked by ice for 50 weeks out of 52, the straits between Canada's northern islands are so tortuous that 400 years would in fact pass before a passage between them was found. Nonetheless, the search for a Northwest Passage helped shape the course of Canadian history: it focused British attention on the far north, from where there was open access to the strategic heart of the country.

First to lead a major expedition to the Canadian Arctic was Sir Martin Frobisher, one of the ablest seamen of the 16th century and a licensed privateer who preyed on French shipping. In 1576 he crossed the Atlantic to Labrador and Baffin Island, where several of his crew were killed by hostile Inuit. Frobisher responded by kidnapping one of their attackers: he rang a bell, which so intriuged the Inuit that one of them paddled up to the ship, only to be hauled on board, kayak and all. The unfortunate man was taken to London as proof of Frobisher's discoveries, but died shortly after arriving from a cold caught at sea.

A far more attractive voyager was John Davis, who sailed north up the Davis Strait between Greenland and Baffin Island in three voyages between 1585 and 1587. He made every effort to befriend the Inuit, who were at first terrified at the sight of the Europeans. Hearing them shout and scream in the distance, Davis ordered his ship's musicians to disembark and play some music. Before long, ten kayaks had drawn up and friendly embraces were being exchanged between Inuit and Englishmen.

In July 1610, Henry Hudson sailed into the bay that now bears his name, convinced he would see China before Christmas. Instead, he was beset by ice and survived a miserable winter, only to freeze to death after being cast adrift by mutineers the following June.

The search reached its climax in the 19th century, when the British Admiralty had men and ships to spare following the end of the Napoleonic Wars. From 1818, successive expeditions under Edward Parry, John Ross and John Franklin searched for a possible route between the Atlantic and Pacific oceans, but made little headway, except with scientific observations. Many were iced in, sometimes for several years, yet suffered no major calamity. Then, in the 1840s, Franklin achieved tragic notoriety by getting lost with two ships and perishing with all hands.

The passage was eventually discovered by the Norwegian Roald Amundsen, who entered Baffin Bay in 1903 and emerged from the Bering Strait in 1906—his voyage, like his later conquest of the South Pole, a triumph of meticulous planning.

On the face of it, these voyages achieved little. They did, however, create an awareness of the Canadian north, and they led to a realisation of its potential and wealth. First to exploit this wealth was the Hudson's Bay Company.

'Caesars of the North'

Hudson Bay is a remote and rather awesome place. It is covered much of the year with drift ice and its shore is made up of a mixture of tundra and swamp. There is a lot of swamp here because a great number of Canada's rivers drain into this huge inlet: a fact that helps explain the success of the world's oldest and largest conglomerate, the Company of Adventurers of England Trading into Hudson's Bay—usually called the Hudson's Bay Company, or the Company, or HBC for short.

Ironically, this manifestly British company came into being because the French governor of Quebec and the authorities in France refused to support a proposal by two of their best *coureurs de bois* to establish a fur-trading route via Hudson Bay. In high dudgeon, Médard Groseilliers and Pierre Radisson then approached the English court with a simple proposition: if the British would send ships into Hudson Bay, Groseilliers and

▲ The moment of victory: a large tree succumbs to the chisel-sharp teeth of a beaver. The animal could easily be killed if the tree fell the wrong way.

▲ Safe in the dry, central chamber of her lodge, a mother beaver suckles her young, called kits.

◀ The remarkable handiwork of the beaver: a dome-shaped lodge in the middle of a tranquil pond, created when the beaver dammed up a stream with a sturdy wall (right foreground) of branches, sticks and mud.

Indian trappers haul a load of beaver pelts, and a fresh carcass, to European traders waiting at a riverbank. ▼

The World of the Beaver

FIVE HUNDRED YEARS AGO beavers were common throughout continental Europe and Asia. But they were mercilessly hunted for their meat, scent glands and luxurious, thick pelts, and by the 17th century they were all but extinct across much of the Old World. At the same time, demand for felt hats in Europe had never been greater, and by common consent no animal's fur produced better felt than the beaver's. Consequently, for European furriers and the merchants who supplied them, the discovery of some ten million beavers in Canada was little short of miraculous. The Hudson's Bay Company, in particular, was to grow fabulously rich on these animals.

The beaver itself is one of Nature's most ingenious creatures—an engineer and a builder of the first order. Equipped with two pairs of constantly growing, chisel-sharp teeth, and fore-paws that are almost as dexterous as a human hand, the beaver sets to work felling sizable trees by gnawing through them. It then gnaws off the trees' branches, and slowly but surely weaves them together across a stream to make a dam wall, behind which a large area soon becomes flooded. In the middle of the pond so created, the beaver then builds its lodge—an impregnable fortress as well as a family home, with a central, dry chamber, ventilation shafts and secret underwater entrances. And here, summer and winter, this remarkable rodent is secure from all predators except man—the most rapacious of them all.

Radisson would persuade their Indian friends to bring beaver pelts down the rivers that drain into the Bay and exchange them for trade goods.

Their scheme had everything going for it. The Indians were just acquiring a taste for European goods, especially those made of steel; and the Europeans had an insatiable craving for 'the most lustrous coat of the beaver'. To the south and west of Hudson Bay stretched the kingdom of the beaver: more than a million square miles of untapped wealth.

Under the terms of its 1670 charter, the Company was given control of the entire catchment area of the rivers that drain into the Bay; and over the next 200 years it gradually extended this domain to embrace the whole of Canada's arctic and subarctic regions—an area more than ten times larger than the Holy Roman Empire. The Company's wealth and power were stupendous: revenue from its furs eventually accounted for more than a third of the value of all British imports—little wonder then that someone should joke that the initials HBC probably stand for 'Here Before Christ'. 'We were Caesars,' boasted one of its founder members, 'there being no one to contradict us.'

It would be difficult to overstate the importance of the role played by the Company in pushing back the Canadian frontier. For as regions around the Bay were cleared of beaver, fresh trapping grounds had to be found further afield. The search led Company men like Alexander Mackenzie and Samuel Hearne to trace Canada's great north-flowing rivers; it led Antony Henday to discover the Canadian prairies; and it led Thomas Simpson and John Rae to delineate Canada's arctic coastline. There is hardly a town in northern Canada that hasn't grown up around a Company store.

Anglo-French Rivalry

There was always likely to be friction in Canada between the British and the French, as rivalries from the Old World spilled over into the New. Competition for furs soon created grounds for further rivalry in Canada itself.

In 1689 England and France began a succession of wars which flickered on and off for 125 years. At first, neither nation showed much enthusiasm for fighting outside Europe, although in Canada the French did raid a number of British settlements, as well as send a fleet that destroyed Company ships and outposts in Hudson Bay. Yet in 1713 the Treaty of Utrecht overturned all French gains, with the result that the Company was left with its domain intact in spite of the fact that the British had lost every important battle in the hostilities.

▲ Sentries dressed in 18th-century costume guard a drawbridged entrance to Fort Louisbourg, Nova Scotia, built to defend France's Canadian colony.

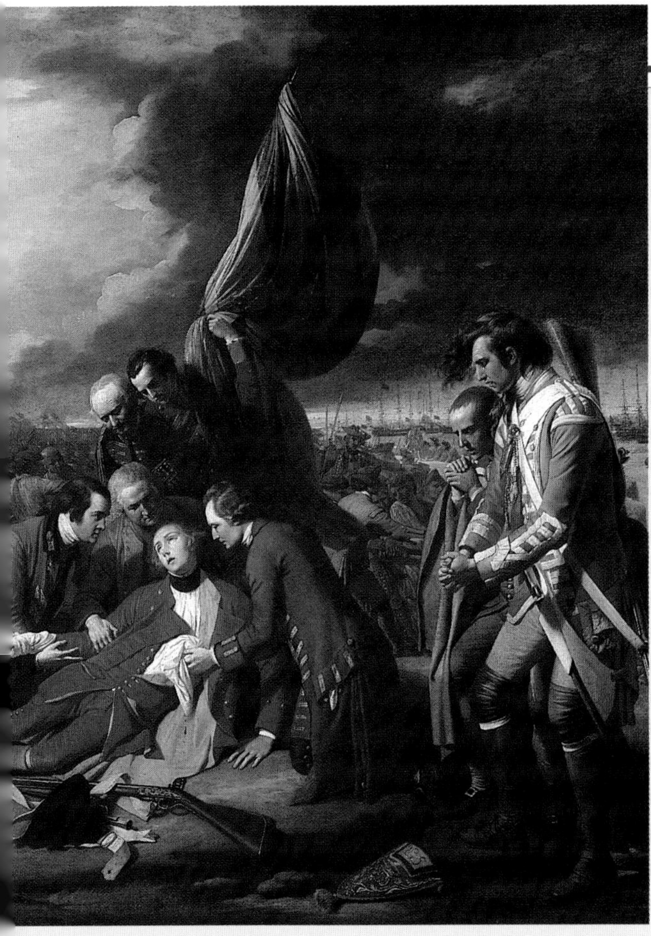

The Battle for Quebec

EVER SINCE the early 16th century, Britain and France had vied for possession of Canada. By the 1750s, both countries had well-established colonies there, which had been skirmishing for years. Matters finally came to a head in 1756, when Britain and France took opposing sides in the Seven Years War in Europe. Deciding to use the war as an opportunity to win sovereignty over Canada once and for all, Britain immediately sent troops across the Atlantic. After several engagements, however, neither side had gained the advantage.

The turning point came with the siege of Quebec, the heavily fortified French stronghold on the St Lawrence River. Both sides regarded possession of Quebec as vital, and in July 1759 the British commander, Brigadier-General James Wolfe, decided to attack the city. Wolfe apparently expected an easy victory, but the French, led by the Marquis de Montcalm, had Quebec's difficult terrain—in particular, its precipitous cliffs—in their favour, and after a six-week siege the city still seemed impregnable.

Wolfe eventually decided to make a risky surprise attack by scaling the cliffs on the night of September 12, 1759. The French were caught completely unawares and were quickly defeated in the ensuing battle, which claimed the lives of both Wolfe and Montcalm. In spite of Wolfe's death, Quebec was secured, and a year later the entire French colony capitulated to the British.

▲ In this celebrated painting by Benjamin West (1738–1820), Brigadier-General Wolfe lies dying at the battle for Quebec.

Stockaded houses of an early French-Canadian settlement, now carefully rebuilt for the benefit of modern visitors. ▶

▲ An 18th-century view of Quebec. On the left are the steep cliffs scaled by the British on the night of their bold attack.

CN

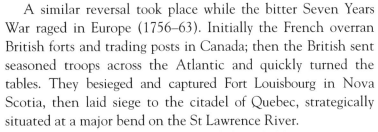

A similar reversal took place while the bitter Seven Years War raged in Europe (1756–63). Initially the French overran British forts and trading posts in Canada; then the British sent seasoned troops across the Atlantic and quickly turned the tables. They besieged and captured Fort Louisbourg in Nova Scotia, then laid siege to the citadel of Quebec, strategically situated at a major bend on the St Lawrence River.

Quebec was strongly fortified and defended by 6,000 troops under the Marquis de Montcalm; James Wolfe, who commanded the British, had only 4,000 troops. However, he had ships, which gave him control of the St Lawrence, and he also had the services of a brilliant young navigator—James Cook, who would later become famous as the greatest explorer of the Pacific.

Under Cook's guidance, Wolfe's army was moved secretly, at night, through rapids thought to be unnavigable; it then scaled cliffs thought to be impassable, and attacked the French from a completely unexpected direction. The battle that ensued was brief—it lasted only 15 minutes—but ferocious: Wolfe was killed and Montcalm mortally wounded. Still, the British won the day, and Quebec surrendered.

A few years later, the Peace of Paris (1763) formally handed all of Canada to Britain. It was the end of the dream of New France, and a bitter blow for French Canadians, who knew that they had lost their territory largely as a result of the apathy of their rulers in France. Whereas British statesmen like William Pitt referred to Canada as 'the fountain of our wealth', French intellectuals like Voltaire had seen no reason to defend 'a few miserable acres of snow'.

Building a Country

There have been formidable obstacles to the unification of Canada, and even today the dream of one united nation spanning the continent still has its problems.

The most pressing of these has been the legacy of New France. When Canada fell into British hands, Catholic farmers and fur traders along the St Lawrence refused point blank to become submissive Anglican subjects of an alien king. They demanded, and were wisely given, special rights. Under the Quebec Act of 1774 they retained their religion, civil laws, language and culture—clinging to them ever more tenaciously as they were progressively outnumbered by new British immigrants. In recent

◀ A goods train snakes its way through the Rockies. The Canadian Pacific Railway, built in the late 19th century, forged a vital link between the east and west coasts of this huge country.

decades, the threat of secession by Quebec Province has loomed large in Canadian politics, and only time will tell whether French Canadians do choose to separate from the rest of the country.

Another problem *could* have been the frontier with America. It is easy to forget that Canada and America have more than once been at war; indeed, the first act of the newly formed US Congress during the War of American Independence was to authorise not the severing of ties with England, but the invasion of Canada. However, on June 15, 1846, the Oregon Treaty fixed the 49th parallel as the boundary between the greater part of the two nations. It says much for the good sense of those on both sides of the border that for more than 100 years this has remained the longest undefended frontier in the world.

After the signing of the Oregon Treaty came the formation of a unified Dominion of Canada (1867), followed by the purchase of the vast territory controlled by the Hudson's Bay Company—a move that trebled the size of the emerging nation at a stroke. One other vital step took place on November 7, 1885, when at Craigellachie, British Columbia, the last spike was driven into the last sleeper of the Canadian Pacific Railway.

In 1870, the government in Ottawa had been asked to conduct a survey for a wagon road linking eastern and western Canada. Instead, it took the far-sighted view that a railway would be better and undertook to have one built in ten years. This marked the start of one of the 19th century's greatest feats of engineering, and there can be few better indicators of the wisdom of the project than the fact that the huge loans taken out to pay for it were repaid within a year of its completion.

The Lure of Gold

The extreme northwest of Canada is rich in natural resources such as timber, oil and salmon. But something more was needed to attract settlers to the beautiful yet remote regions of British Columbia and the Yukon. The magic ingredient turned up in 1856, when an Indian woman living near the Fraser River showed the local HBC agent a gold nugget, 'big as a pigeon's egg'.

It took two years for the news to leak out, and when it did Canada experienced its first bout of gold fever—the Cariboo Gold Rush had begun, and it soon had far-reaching consequences for the population of what is now British Columbia. In the early 1850s there were fewer than 1,000 people living west of the Rockies, most of them in the vicinity of Vancouver. A decade later, there were over 30,000, mainly Americans from the California gold fields, staked out in caves, dugouts and tents along the banks of the Fraser River and its tributaries.

▲ Barkerville, once a boom town that boasted 13 saloons and an opera house, is today a major tourist attraction.

A 19th-century depiction of prospectors at work during a gold rush. ▶

In this contemporary photograph of the Klondike Gold Rush, fortune-hunters camp in the snow of the Chilkoot Pass on the Alaska–Yukon border. ▼

Gold Rush!

One summer's day in 1856, an Indian woman living near the Fraser River in British Columbia appeared at Fort Kamloops with a gleaming yellow stone about the size of a pigeon's egg. The Hudson's Bay Company agent at the local trading post immediately recognised it as a gold nugget and casually exchanged it for some iron spoons. Two years later, when the nugget reached San Francisco for minting, news of its origins leaked out, provoking a stampede that became known as the Cariboo Gold Rush.

Within three years, over 30,000 prospectors had flooded into the Cariboo region, most of them Americans from the depleted Californian gold fields. Others came from as far afield as London, Hong Kong and Melbourne. All had high hopes, but only a few made any sizeable fortune in the wild, mountainous terrain they were trying to work. One of the lucky ones was Billy Barker, a 42-year-old Cornish sailor, who struck a giant seam just when most of his rivals were saying

▲ Two satisfied prospectors weigh up the fruits of a winter's hard work.

that the best of the gold had already been found. A collection of shacks and saloons soon sprang up around Billy's excavations, and when these grew into a town it was called Barkerville in his honour.

A few decades later, an even bigger stampede erupted when gold was found in the Klondike River on the Alaska–Yukon border. The area was staggeringly remote, yet summer and winter tens of thousands of men and women clambered through unforgiving mountain passes to try their luck. Many died on the way, not least because the authorities insisted that everyone entering the Yukon should have a year's supply of food and equipment—thereby forcing people to make the same journey up to 40 times.

Forty years later, in 1896, an altogether more rumbustious and spectacular gold rush drew prospectors in their tens of thousands into the Yukon. It started when Indian hunters found traces of gold in the gravel of a tributary of the Throndiuk (subsequently corrupted to Klondike) River on the Alaska–Yukon border—just about the most remote and inaccessible spot imaginable. Within a year, over 100,000 gold-seekers—'the roughest, toughest, most unkempt lot ever seen'—were heading for the squalid cluster of log cabins that would soon be known as Dawson City.

They endured a horrific journey through bleak terrain, dangerous rapids and snow-blocked passes: 16 weeks on the trail was considered good going. One mountain pass earned the name Dead Horse Trail, though horses were not its only victims. In winter, men froze to death; in spring, 60 were swept away by a single avalanche. Those who did get through to Dawson City found mainly cold, hunger and scurvy. Of course, some fortunes were made, but for the most part the Yukon proved that, like much of the Arctic, it can offer fabulous rewards for the strong while exacting terrible penalties from the weak.

▲ One of the immense dams that form part of the La Grande complex—the first phase of the controversial James Bay hydroelectric project in northern Quebec.

The Wilderness Today

Until recently, the Canadian north was one of the least developed areas on Earth. The small, mostly nomadic bands of Indian and Inuit hunters who roamed its vast forests and enormous expanses of tundra had, over thousands of years, evolved ways of life that were closely attuned to the land and caused only minimal damage to the environment. Their contact with the outside world was largely confined to a handful of fur traders, missionaries and explorers.

Since the Second World War, however, the wilderness has started to be dramatically transformed by large-scale economic development. Forestry has grown to become one of the country's major industries, and is for the most part very well managed. But in some areas, multinational companies have been allowed to destroy virgin forest by a controversial method known as 'clearcutting', whereby whole stands of trees are cut down. The process is quick and cheap, but it can also cause soil erosion, drive animals away and disrupt the lives of the people who depend on those animals for their livelihood. Environmentalists calculate that an acre of Canadian forest is clearcut every 12–14 seconds, leading some to suggest that the country is in danger of becoming 'the Brazil of the north'.

At the same time, wilderness areas are being opened up to many other kinds of development: mines, oilfields, nuclear-

Developing the Wilderness

LIKE ALL COUNTRIES with valuable natural resources, Canada is having to make critical ongoing decisions regarding economic development in, and of, its wilderness areas. For many people, the country's pristine wilderness should be preserved in its unspoilt state, safeguarded for future generations as a priceless national asset. For others, it is a vast storehouse of resources—such as oil, gas and timber—merely waiting to be capitalised for the benefit of the nation as a whole. Somewhere between these two views a balance needs to be found—in some cases with great urgency.

Nowhere is this more apparent than in northern Quebec, where rivers are being dammed on an enormous scale for one of the largest hydroelectric projects ever conceived. Towns, cities and industries throughout eastern Canada and the northeastern United States will benefit from the scheme; yet for the Cree and Inuit who have lived in the area for generations, and who even now make a living from hunting and trapping there, the project spells disaster. Not only have they seen valuable hunting grounds flooded and animals driven away, they have found fish poisoned by methyl mercury released from vegetation rotting beneath the reservoirs. The changes being wrought on the wilderness here are threatening to destroy forever an entire way of life. As a Cree Grand Chief recently explained, 'The destruction of our hunting land would put an end to the spiritual connection which my People have had with their land for at least 5,000 years.'

Standing in front of another massive dam, this Cree activist protests at the flooding of his people's hunting ground. ▶

▲ A natural gas plant in the midst of snowy peaks. Disposing of the plant's main by-product—5,000 tons of sulphur per week (inset)—is no easy matter.

A magnificent mountain scene marred by the unsightly aftermath of clearcut logging. ▼

Wilderness Havens

GIVEN THE SIZE of Canada's wilderness, it is hardly surprising that one of the world's largest national parks is situated here. Straddling the border between Alberta and the Northwest Territories, Wood Buffalo National Park covers 17,300 square miles—over twice the size of Wales. The park was established in 1922 to protect North America's few remaining wood bison, a larger relative of the animal that once roamed the Great Plains in its millions. Today the park is home to the world's largest herd of free-ranging bison, and is also a safe breeding ground for the five-foot-tall whooping crane, the rarest bird in North America.

In Dinosaur Provincial Park, the remains of animals long extinct are protected as if they were yet alive. Situated in the dramatic 'badlands' of Alberta, this park contains one of the most extensive deposits of dinosaur bones in the world—a site of immense value that has been plundered by both fossil-hunters and souvenir-hunters alike. To prevent further damage, visitors are kept strictly to specified hiking trails or bus tours, both of which allow them to view the remains of the giant beasts lying precisely where they fell millions of years ago.

Fragile, living environments receive no less attention—as is the case with the remarkable temperate rain forest on Vancouver Island, home to a rich variety of animals and plants, including the tallest and oldest trees in Canada—red cedars and Douglas firs, over 200 feet high and 800 years old.

▲ **Ferns and mosses adorn the trees in Vancouver Island's lush, dense rain forest.**

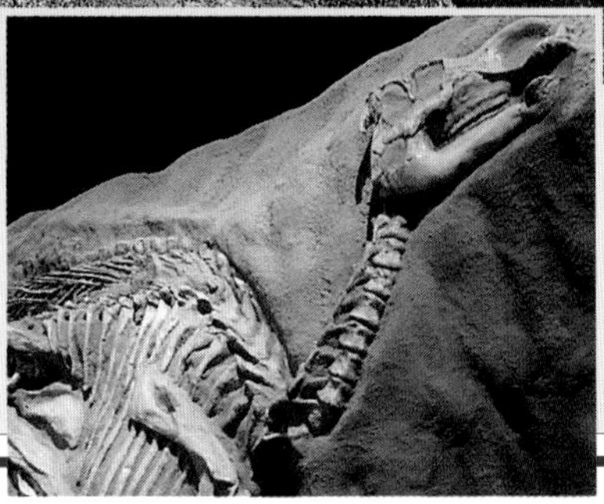

▲ **The land that time forgot: bizarre rock formations, known as hoodoos, in Alberta's so-called 'badlands', where entire dinosaur skeletons (inset) have been found intact.**

▲ A herd of wood bison roams undisturbed in the enormous national park established for their benefit.

In 1941, only 21 whooping cranes remained in the wild. Their numbers are now much higher, but these graceful birds are still extremely rare. ▼

waste disposal sites, and, perhaps most dramatic of all, hydro-electric schemes such as the James Bay project in Quebec.

James Bay is a U-shaped bight that stretches some 275 miles south from the bottom of Hudson Bay. The Cree and Inuit around its shores have always lived by hunting, fishing and trapping, but since 1975 they have lost more than 6,000 square miles of their territory to a string of 15 dams and nine generating stations that provide electricity for Quebec and Ontario.

For many Cree and Inuit, the effects have been disastrous. The habitats of lynx, wolverines, black bears and caribou have been destroyed over a huge expanse, while rotting vegetation in the flooded areas has released large quantities of methyl mercury—a toxic substance that poisons fish and anything or anyone who eats them. And yet, more dams have been planned. Those built so far represent only the first stage of a grand scheme to flood an area the size of Lake Erie, one of the four Great Lakes. If this were to happen, many people warn, it would mean the death of Cree culture and irreparable damage to the environment.

Towards the Future

Yet the wilderness has not been entirely abandoned. According to a recent report to their parliament, 'Canadians value nature and wilderness, and are committed to protecting areas of natural heritage.' To bear this out, protected areas in Canada have almost quadrupled over the last 30 years, and there are plans to conserve 12 per cent of each type of habitat in parks or reserves. The country already has 35 national parks and over 600 provincial parks, many of which are specifically dedicated to ensuring the survival of endangered species.

Introducing *Across the Wild Continent*

Nowadays, more than 20 million people venture briefly into the Canadian wilderness every year—some on hunting or fishing trips, some to admire the scenic splendour of the national parks. Few, however, could claim to know the area as intimately or love it as deeply as David Halsey did. His love of the wilderness was so strong it became almost an obsession, and he dreamed of crossing Canada from ocean to ocean, travelling only on foot, by canoe, or by dogsled. *Across the Wild Continent* is the story of how he made his dream come true: of the wonders he saw, the friendships he forged and the hardships he suffered in an epic two-year journey, with one companion and a half-wild coyote-dog, across the breadth of wilderness Canada.

PART 2 AN ADVENTURE

ACROSS THE WILD CONTINENT

by **David Halsey**
with Diana Landau

A condensation based on the book MAGNETIC NORTH

Prologue

On Wednesday, May 4, 1977, four young men shouldered backpacks in Vancouver, at the edge of the Pacific Ocean. Their goal was Tadoussac, a village on the St Lawrence River in Quebec—4,700 miles away. If successful, the modestly equipped quartet would be the first in modern times to traverse Canada coast to coast by a wilderness route, using only primitive means: hiking and snowshoeing, driving a dogsled, and canoeing.

Their leader, David Halsey, was only twenty. He had conceived and planned the journey while at college, scrutinising hundreds of maps and historical documents to create a route based on the historic paths of explorers, traders and trappers. Visionary and persuasive beyond his years, Dave had won the interest of the National Geographic Society, which provided advice, seed money and photographic equipment for his Trans-Canada Expedition.

A mere four days after it began, however, the expedition almost ended. On May 8, after hiking forty-five miles up the Fraser River to Fort Langley, Dave's three partners decided to abandon the journey.

'Quit trying to con us, Dave,' warned the photographer, Charlie Bratz. 'We're poorly equipped and on a ridiculous route. We'll never make it to Quebec, and you know it.'

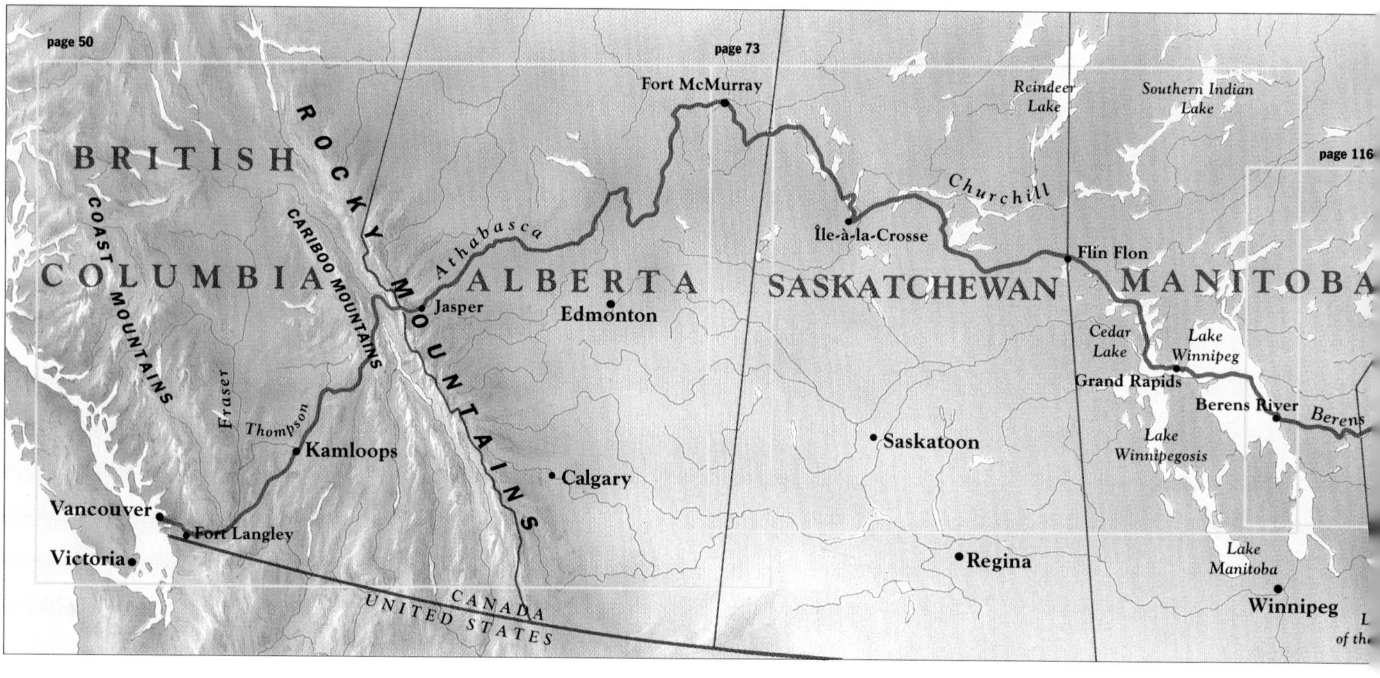

Pacing in circles, head lowered and arms flailing, Dave tried in vain to counter with reminders of the historic importance of their endeavour. The others just walked off, taking most of the equipment with them, including the tents.

Stunned by their desertion and personal attacks, Dave could not at first come to grips with the grim choice he faced: to continue on alone, ill-equipped for such a venture, or to acknowledge the wisdom of those who dismissed him as a dreamer.

When Dave phoned home that night for comfort and counsel, he found at least one person had no doubts about what he should do—his father. Maurice Halsey, a lobbyist for the natural gas industry and a dedicated fisherman, had whetted Dave's appetite for the Canadian backwoods by taking him on frequent fishing trips to the northern forests and lakes. On realising that his son's plan for dropping out of college to hike and paddle across Canada was no frivolous whim but a deeply rooted goal, he had done all he could to help. He and Dave's mother, Jean, had agreed to act as the expedition's supply coordinators, the basement of their home in McLean, Virginia, (a suburb of Washington DC) becoming the repository for hundreds of maps and charts; on these they would track his progress mile by mile across the continent.

Now, while commiserating angrily about the deserters, Maurice made his opinion plain: Dave ought to press on, at least for the present, and reconstitute the expedition later. There were hundreds of miles of backpacking through British Columbia that Dave could do alone before he would need a canoeing partner for the rivers of Alberta.

Dave's mother also supported his plan to continue solo, keeping private her fear of her son lying injured and alone in the middle of some roadless wilderness. Both parents knew how much he would regret abandoning the expedition, and had some insight, too, into Dave's amazing affinity—even hunger—for wilderness hardship. However, they left it to him to decide finally on his own course. ■

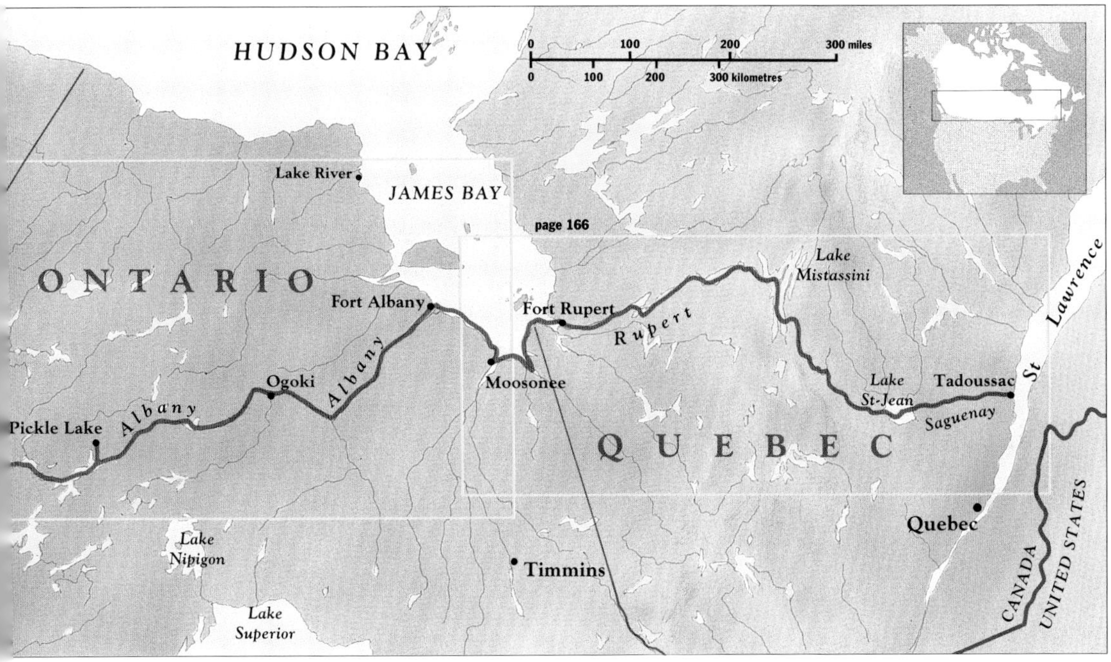

◀ A map of the 4,700-mile route taken by the Trans-Canada Expedition from Vancouver in the west of Canada to Tadoussac in the east.

CHAPTER 1

Making a Fresh Start

THE NIGHT AFTER MY PARTNERS split from the expedition, I was holding down a bar stool in a Fort Langley pub, staring into my beer glass and feeling pretty sorry for myself. So when the man on the next stool asked where I was headed—my monstrous pack would have been hard to miss—the dam broke. I obviously needed to complain to someone about the guys who had smashed my dreams, and Gary Richardson was just the right man at the right time.

Half an hour into the story, he was practically off his stool with excitement. 'Quit?' he protested. 'You can't quit. You sound like you know every lake, river and town from here to Quebec. You're going to have a great story to tell.' He shook his bearded head vehemently. 'To hell with those guys. Go for it alone.'

Gary's encouragement turned the tide for me, and I spent the next ten days resupplying, reorganising and replanning the route. When it was time for me to toss my pack on my back and start hiking towards Quebec, Gary left me with a book and the admonition to read it when I got discouraged. It was *The Venturesome Voyages of Captain Voss*, the harrowing tale of a man who sailed across three oceans, from Vancouver Island to London, in a dugout canoe. So who was I to worry about a few freshwater lakes?

A reconstruction of the interior of the Hudson's Bay Company store at Fort Langley, as it would have looked in the 19th century. In isolated communities, stores such as this still sell absolutely everything, including the kitchen sink. ▶

On May 20 I set out on the first leg of my journey—to Kamloops, 250 miles away. With four hours of daylight remaining, I began by walking past the campsite where my companions and I had parted ways, and took the ferry across the Fraser River.

▲ The author is dwarfed by the immense landscape of British Columbia. He alternated between following paths, roads, rivers and, as here, railway tracks.

Fort Langley is now a rural town of a few thousand, but in the nineteenth century it was, for a time, a major trading post of the Hudson's Bay Company. Back then, the Fraser River—one of North America's largest—could accommodate ocean-going vessels far upriver, and the big ships hauled imported goods to Fort Langley, from where they continued east into the interior by mule team. Making the return trip were wilderness riches, mainly smoked salmon and furs. Eventually, however, the river silted up and the fort became inaccessible to the larger vessels—at which point Fort Langley became yet another former boom town.

In the fading light I hiked along the gravel road parallel to the river. Ten miles down the road, I pitched a hasty camp in the dark and cooked coffee and oatmeal on the fire.

The next morning I hung around to watch the annual Fraser River Raft Race: twenty-odd miles of madness, with categories ranging from historic replicas to craft made entirely from beer kegs (sponsored by breweries, of course).

Fleeing the chaotic traffic jam in the aftermath of the race, I covered thirteen miles by walking alongside the river. Late in the afternoon I turned up a logging road into Douglas Provincial Forest: with trout on my mind, I was hoping for a campsite at a stream called Norrish Creek.

About three miles in, however, the trail was still climbing, and I was already 500 feet above where I was supposed to intersect the elusive Norrish Creek. I had just given up the logging road as a bad job when I came to a break in the thick brush—the path of an old avalanche. From the top I could see that the scree slide led straight down to the creek, so I decided to take the express route. Running steep scree (loose rocks and gravel) is not for novice hikers, but I had done it many times before. It is like a combination of snow skiing and surfing. I handled the slide all right, running in the traditional pedalling manner to keep from being buried in the wave of rock. I was thinking I ought to slow down a bit when I saw that the scree ended abruptly in a 100-foot sheer cliff. Instantly I was down on my back, letting my pack take the punishment while I aimed for something big enough to stop me.

My aim was good. I landed feet first on a solidly planted boulder not twenty feet from the verge. When my heart slowed I looked north and south for a route around the cliff, but in vain.

After bushwhacking about half a mile, I finally found a place where the cliff ended, in a steep slope solid with thistles and wild roses. I'd have to hang onto the rose stems for balance, but it looked like the only way down—so, pulling on spare socks for gloves and cursing my cut-off shorts, I stepped off. An hour later, scratched from head to foot, I reached the water.

Now for that trout. The creek was productive all right—but only of juvenile four-inch rainbows that hit my favourite flies with nearly every cast. Nothing more substantial obliged, and I eventually gave up.

Heavy clouds were now building in the west, and as I had no tent I was convinced a fairly miserable night lay ahead. Luck was with me, though: fifty yards upriver I found an ideal campsite—a beautiful natural cave arching into the rock, about twenty feet long, six feet deep and eight feet high. The ceiling, already black with soot, took on another coating with my blaze.

I spent the next day huddled in my sleeping-bag, waiting out the rain. By the following morning it had let up, so I set off downstream at a brisk pace, and by midmorning I was headed east on the Canadian Pacific Railway tracks.

For the next three days I alternated between railroad and highway, depending on the traffic. Walking along the sleepers was tiring: you can catch the scenery only in quick glances, as a poorly calculated step can easily result in a twisted ankle. So most of the time I took the easier route via the highway. I returned to the railroad tracks only when traffic on the highway became too heavy for me to enjoy the hike (about thirty cars per hour was my criterion).

On May 26, I reached the beautiful Lake of the Woods, two miles north of the town of Hope, and eighty miles and a week from Fort Langley. The lake is surrounded by inviting snow-covered ridges, and the atmosphere of the region holds a taste of homesteading and gold-rush days. There is a lively jade industry here, the legacy of Chinese railroad workers who were the first to recognise the local mineral. I spent three days there, logging many hours of successful trout fishing and cleaning myself and my clothes. The cool nights I spent catching up on my notes by candlelight and battling the slugs that seemed to find my ground sheet a dry haven. After a few nauseating encounters, I learned to sprinkle a fine film of salt on it every night in wet country.

I had planned to hike the remaining 170 miles to Kamloops via the Fraser Canyon highway, but five miles along I heard of an alternative route—a logging road up the Coquihalla River that would cut off nearly forty miles of hiking and also get me off the tourist route.

As I turned up the Coquihalla, I briefly regretted leaving the Fraser, which I had followed for 120 miles from Vancouver, but the grandeur of the Coquihalla Valley proved a worthwhile trade. The dirt-and-gravel road provided a nice change of pace from trains and traffic. In the first ten miles I counted no more than three cabins and half a dozen trucks.

At about the ten-mile point I stopped to observe one of those cabins: a horse was grazing in the adjacent clearing and smoke wisped from the chimney. Hoping for a cup of coffee and maybe some conversation, I rapped on the hand-hewn door. A rough-edged voice responded, 'Door's always open.'

Randy Davis and his girlfriend, Donna, welcomed me warmly and fed me an enormous meal of ham, potato and corn stew sopped up with bannock, the whole washed down with tea sweetened with syrup. After dinner we smoked and talked by the oil lamp. My host and hostess were both from Ontario. Randy was the son of a country-and-western singer and looked the part, with his Johnny Cash haircut and weather-beaten face. Donna's background was in high society, yet she too preferred the simple life of their Coquihalla cabin.

Randy was rightfully proud of the cabin—three soundly built rooms under a moss-covered roof, plus smokehouse and outhouse. There were two stoves, and running water was piped down directly from a nearby waterfall.

Climbing ever Higher

Two days and thirty miles later, I collapsed at the Coquihalla Lakes. (After hiking some 160 miles I still felt out of shape.) These lakes mark the boundary where an amazing climatic change occurs: here the coastal rain forest ends and the country changes to semi-arid over a one-day, fifteen-mile stretch. I was

The Arid Zone

THE WEST COAST of British Columbia is the lushest, most verdant area in Canada. Rain driven from the Pacific nurtures dense rain forests where mosses flourish on every surface and the trees grow taller than anywhere else in the country. Red cedars on Vancouver Island may be 200 feet tall, 14 feet in diameter and 1,200 years old.

However, a mere 100 miles inland (as the crow flies), the climate, vegetation and scenery undergo a dramatic change. Forests of cedar, Douglas fir and spruce give way to scrubby stands of pine and sprinklings of sagebrush and prickly pear. Erosion scars the dry hills, which are in places so bare that they have every appearance of belonging in a desert.

The cause of this remarkable metamorphosis in the environment is the Coast Mountains—the second-largest range in British Columbia after the Rockies. Stretching almost 1,000 miles from southern British Columbia to the Yukon, the Coast Mountains present an enormous barrier to the rainclouds that soak the forests on the coast. To the west of this range, rainfall may be as much as 200 inches per annum; to its east, a mere seven inches.

▲ An endless train winds through the Fraser River Canyon, which lies in the 'rain shadow' of the Coast Mountains. The river itself is fed by water from the Rockies.

looking forward to the dry country after weeks of daily showers and cool weather. But first I wanted to climb the beautiful snowy ridge 4,000 feet above the lakes.

From the logging road the climb looked simple enough, but the timber was heavier than I'd expected, and I first hit snow after about 500 vertical feet. The brush thickened and the islands of bare ground disappeared as I climbed higher, plunging into knee-deep snow with each step. Common sense suggested turning back, but I was committed and eventually emerged from the timber and rotten snow about two hours behind schedule.

Before me lay a glorious sight: a highway of hard-packed snow stretching unbroken for 2,000 feet up to the ridge. The ridgetop itself was hidden behind an awesome 500-foot crest of snow.

Reaching the ridge in another hour, I stopped to take in the view. I had planned to hike west along the ridgeline for about two miles as it gradually descended, but bad weather was coming and that argued for an earlier descent. A light breeze could develop into a fully fledged whiteout in a matter of minutes, and a snow-covered ridge is no place to camp.

The new route I chose—cutting a mile and a half off the ridge walk—did not look encouraging either. To reach the bowl below, I would have to traverse a steep slope for about 100 yards, directly under the crest, which was definitely avalanche

The Trans-Canada Expedition's route from Vancouver to Fort McMurray. The first leg of the journey was on foot, the second by canoe down the Athabasca River. ▼

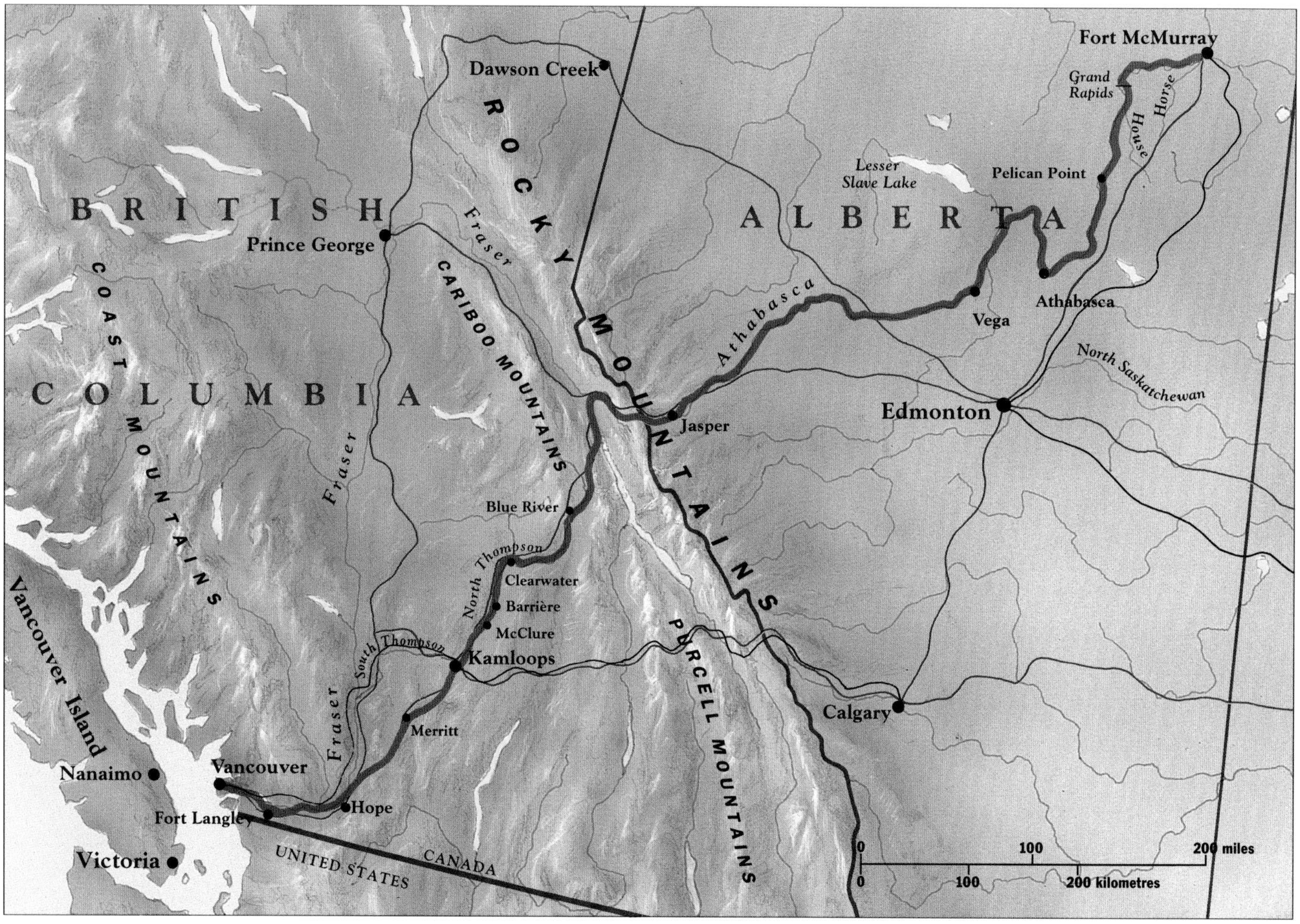

material. At least I would be out of the wind, sheltered by the crest from the southerly gale.

Lacking ice axe, rope or any other climbing gear, I held my camera tripod as a makeshift ice axe and started across the slope. Progress was painfully slow. Without crampons, each step kicked out with my boots had to be perfect.

Soon I was breathing more easily. The fledgling gale had turned out to be a false alarm. As I glissaded the remaining feet down to the bowl, a spectacular afternoon sun cracked the cloud cover. Enough sightseeing—with about three hours of light remaining, I would have to hustle to make the lakes by dark.

▲ **Canada's vertiginous mountain faces offer a considerable challenge to even the most experienced of climbers.**

A further glissade across the open bowl took me into the timber on the ridge. I had hoped for enough wind here to have kept the snow packed, but after thirty steps I plunged to my knees, and from then on the gap between plunges grew steadily less. With sixty pounds on my back, pulling out of deep snow was no fun at all. At that point I would have traded a six-month food supply for a pair of snowshoes.

Two hours after I had left the bowl I was only about halfway back to the logging road. With heavy cloud cover returning, I estimated that the sun had just set, or was about to, and that meant an hour of light left, at the outside.

Nervousness started to slide towards panic. To advance ten feet I had to walk thirty, zigzagging back and forth while hunting for packed snow. When I tried to move faster, I invariably ended up sprawled on my face. I knew that panic in the bush could bring the strongest men to their knees. I had never been close enough to know whether I would succumb to it, but now, perched on an island of firm crust, the realisation that I was close to panic washed over me like a freezing wave. The urge to dump my pack and run blindly was almost overwhelming, but I made myself sit still and consider my options.

If I gave up and bivouacked here overnight, I would probably be picked up by the local search-and-rescue team within forty-eight hours. On the other hand, this was supposed to be the easiest leg of the whole journey. For most of the 4,500 miles ahead there would be no search-and-rescue teams handy. If I gave in here, what could I expect when I had no choice?

A good self-thrashing calmed me down. It was time for another route. I was stuck with the valley, but a creek bisected it; I got up and headed towards it. The creek banks were impossibly steep and crusted, but the flowing water was only a foot deep. I had no idea what effect the near-freezing water would have on my bruised and abused shins. I didn't even worry about my feet; snow had been packed solidly between my socks and ankles for so many hours that I had long since stopped feeling them.

I made good time through the water, and sloshed along until eventually the terrain levelled out and the snow disappeared. The darkness was complete by now, though a half-moon shone through broken cloud cover to light my way.

The boggy muskeg (a swamp of sphagnum moss) I now stumbled through seemed to be continuing much too long. Could I have overshot the logging road? I didn't recognise my surroundings. It was certainly time to camp, but I wanted to fix my location first. I tried to compensate for a possible error by exaggerating a southwesterly course. It worked: I hit the logging road fifteen minutes later.

Collapsing on the road, I lit a candle and peeled off my socks to assess the damage. The skin on my feet was white, puffy and lifeless; the bruises on my ankles and lower shins had broken into open sores. Pain was returning to my feet—a good sign.

It must have been close to 11pm, and with six miles of downhill travel to the lakes, I might make it in two hours. Walking in a daze, I sang and talked to myself to keep moving, my heart set on reaching the lakes.

I never did, though. I must have missed the turnoff in the darkness. I dropped my pack, defeated, and crawled into my sleeping-bag with a cup of uncooked oatmeal. My legs cramped into a bent position, forcing me to sleep that way. Two days elapsed before I could walk normally again.

New Recruits

I left the Coquihalla River behind in early June, and with thawed feet and refreshed spirits bore north towards the town of Merritt. The first day, my still-healing legs held me to a mere five miles, but with the aid of a hard-packed road and improving weather, my daily mileage increased.

Despite its heat and dust, Merritt was a welcome sight, as it was one of my resupply points. Dad had wired a small amount of money ahead to the post office, just in time: for the last three days I had lived on oat flakes, rice and a bit of bouillon.

▲ A magnificent double rainbow set against slate-grey storm clouds. Note how the colours of the outer rainbow appear in reverse—red at the bottom, rather than the top.

After setting up camp in the town park I bathed in the river and luxuriated in the local laundromat with newspapers and junk food while my clothes ran through several wash cycles. I had some beers too, but not too many—my budget was never more than twenty dollars a week.

While in Merritt I also telephoned an old schoolfriend, C. W. Hughey—everyone called him CW. We decided that he would join me in Jasper at the end of July for the canoeing. I wished I could do it alone, but I knew I would only be fooling myself. I had learned a lot on that snow ridge, and I reckoned CW and I would get on.

By now the weather had turned really hot, with daytime temperatures of over 100°F, so I took it easy on the next stage—twenty miles to Lake Nicola—and then hoped to make the thirty-five miles to Kamloops in a night hike.

A short evening shower cooled the first five miles to Kamloops to a comfortable 60°. Then the clouds broke with perfect timing to reveal a double rainbow *and* a fiery sunset, brilliantly painting the sagebrush-covered hills. The rain-cooled road was good to my soles, and rather than slackening as the night wore on my pace actually picked up and my strides lengthened. This was a hiker's rare and magical moment: when muscles and mind are in balance, the body performing like a precision machine. With two miles to go and half an hour till sunrise I gazed down the valley of Kamloops to the town lights below.

Lying at the junction of the North and South Thompson rivers, Kamloops is a good-sized town of over fifty thousand inhabitants. Though it has the prestige of being British Columbia's largest inland city, I didn't appreciate its urban charms and felt eager to press on. Again low on funds, I wangled some 'handshake credit' from local merchants. Time and again throughout Canada, this tradition of trust saved me from having to abandon the trek.

Back on the road, as I hiked due north along the west bank of the North Thompson River between sage-dotted sandhills, the heat was staggering, and brought me nearly to the point of quitting. My progress plummeted, with hiking time restricted to early mornings and evenings. It wasn't until the McClure ferry, thirty miles north of Kamloops, that the desert-like terrain began to ease. Crossing to the east bank on the ferry, I made the remaining eleven miles to Barrière by midnight. Four more days of dust brought me to Clearwater, a growing town of about three thousand. Here my depression began to lift. The end of the heat I so detested could not be far away.

My high point in Clearwater was my meeting with a young photographer from Chicago called Pete Souchuk. A few weeks earlier Pete had read in *Quest*

The desert landscape around Kamloops belies the presence nearby of lakes renowned for their excellent trout. ▼

magazine that one David Halsey was hiking alone across Canada. (The *Quest* coverage was only one element in a modest media blitz that had surrounded the early part of the expedition.) The description of my adventure had struck a powerful note in Pete, who was restless in his job as a PR photographer. The opportunity to experience photographing in the Canadian wilderness and the possibility of breaking into *National Geographic* or other major publications were also strong incentives. Pete had contacted my parents and, after getting a reasonably good fix on my expected whereabouts, had loaded his car with camping and photographic gear and spent several days roaming round central British Columbia looking for me.

We spent an evening talking, and then we agreed to try a 'test hike' of about a week. It was incredibly hot and pretty boring hiking, mostly highway. I set a tough pace, but by the end of it I had a new partner. Pete had to return to the States to attend a course he was committed to, so we made plans to meet again in early September and continue with CW as a threesome.

And that wasn't all. One evening when Pete and I were cooking dinner, an exceptionally bold coyote strolled into camp looking for a handout. I figured that the scruffy-looking beast was probably a semi-domesticated husky-coyote cross. I wanted no part of it, but it continued to hang about for several days—I found out later that Pete was feeding it behind my back—and it soon became clear that, against my better judgment, I had acquired yet another team-mate. Still, the entirely unplanned company of both Pete and Ki (pronounced Kye) proved incredibly fortunate: they stuck with me through thick and thin, and I honestly believe I would never have completed the expedition without them.

▲ **Ki supervises last-minute packing of the new canoe, blissfully unaware of the dangers that lie ahead.**

About fifty miles past Clearwater, the snow-covered Cariboo Mountains rose above the central plateau, and the North Thompson River flexed its muscles, shedding its turbid southern cloak. Another couple of weeks at a conscientious pace took Ki and me seventy miles above Clearwater to Blue River, where at last I was truly free of the heat, sagebrush and sand, and then on to Jasper, 130 miles away across the Alberta border. There I met up with CW as planned. CW's future with the expedition was uncertain, though, as he had left a wife and young child back home.

In early August, after resting and reoutfitting in Jasper, CW, Ki and I set out in a new eighteen-foot aluminium freighter canoe on the next leg of the expedition: a 600-mile plunge down the Athabasca River, northeast through Alberta to the Saskatchewan border. The earliest stretch, however, was not yet remote wilderness—the gateway to the true bush was the town of Athabasca,

▲ Cotton-wool clouds hang in the chill air above the Athabasca River in Alberta. The river is fed by melted ice from glaciers high up in the Rockies.

about 400 miles downriver. Along this first part, settlements and farms dotted the riverbanks. Here we found open doors, hot meals and good company, guzzled apple cider with the farmers and talked of politics and crop failures while their wives plucked chickens for supper and set coffeepots on the stove.

On September 7, Pete Souchuk rejoined the Trans-Canada Expedition at Vega, and a week later CW left to return to his family in Virginia, where he was needed. Now the three of us, Pete, Ki and I, were poised to embark on the first truly hazardous portion of the journey: the last several hundred miles down the Athabasca River to Fort McMurray. This had some pretty treacherous rapids, and there wouldn't be any handy cabins to retreat to when things got tough. Yet, as I wrote in a letter home, I felt excited at the prospect:

> I wouldn't trade this trip for anything. After four-and-a-half months here I have noticed a dramatic change in myself. I now feel very accepting of whatever nature wants to dish out. You're constantly cold, constantly wet. Yet you learn to live with it. I guess what I am trying to say is that you get to the point where you want to say, 'To hell with it, Nature, gimme all you've got.'

A little further downriver, beyond the town of Athabasca, I was to find out just how much Nature still had in store!

▲ **A remnant of the ice age: the Athabasca Glacier flows down from the massive Columbia Icefield.**

▲ **The awesome grizzly bear finds refuge from its only enemy—man—in the remote fastness of the Rockies.**

The Magnificent Rockies

THE CANADIAN ROCKIES, which form the northern reaches of the great Rocky Mountains, are one of the world's most breathtakingly beautiful ranges. Hundreds of glaciers crowd into steep, rocky canyons; alpine flowers bloom prolifically in broad meadows surrounded by coniferous forests; and magnificent lakes of crystal-clear meltwater lie placidly beneath fearsome, ragged peaks. No visitor can fail to appreciate the vast scale of Nature's architectural achievement here: man can but admire it with awe.

Like other major natural features in Canada—such as the Canadian Shield and the Great Lakes—the Rockies owe much of their present shape and appearance to the effects of the last great ice age, when most of the country was covered by vast sheets of ice. Drawn by gravity, these ice sheets bulldozed their way through the landscape, carving hills into crags, valleys into canyons, and flat basins into lakes. Smaller glaciers continue the process even today—especially in the Columbia Icefield, where ice up to 1,000 feet deep covers an area of 125 square miles.

Four enormous national parks—Banff, Jasper, Kootenay and Yoho—protect almost 8,000 square miles of this spectacular wilderness and the many wild creatures that have their refuge here. One of these is the mountain goat, a relative of the European Alpine chamois and, like that animal, a conqueror of the dizziest precipices. Mountain lions may prey on them in the valleys, but not among the heights, where their greatest natural enemies are avalanches.

The Rockies are also one of the last homes of the brown or grizzly bear—an animal that once roamed over half the North American continent, and is elsewhere often shot on sight as a threat to people and livestock.

A cunning mountain lion uses a fallen log to move quietly through woodland grasses. ▶

▲ The crystalline waters of Maligne Lake, 5,400 feet up in the Rockies. The lake, which is over 17 miles long, was formed by the passage of a glacier some 11,000 years ago.

▲ Cheerful blooms, such as these Easter daisies, enliven the slopes of the Rockies throughout the spring and summer.

◀ Mountain goats clamber about on the steepest of precipices as if they were on level ground. This one takes a regal view of its domain.

CHAPTER 2

The River Strikes

On Saturday, September 24, we returned to the river late in the evening, thanks to a send-off party at Athabasca. Normally we wouldn't touch alcohol while on the river, but we knew of no fast water just ahead. We left Athabasca at 8pm with Ki proudly atop his perch on the food pack, and by ten that night a three-quarter moon with a glorious halo had risen to illuminate our path. The river experienced a total metamorphosis by moonlight: the current became serene and conversation rarely broke the silence.

Wildlife, highlighted by the moon's glow, was much easier to approach. We passed within twenty feet of a shoal crowded with geese and cranes, and with thoughts of a royal dinner I raised the shotgun. But almost in the same motion I returned it to its place, ashamed to disturb the humbling silence. For nearly twenty miles we drifted, even dozing now and then, and after several hours cradled in comfort we made shore to sleep at about 3am as the morning mist was gathering.

Three days of uneventful paddling put seventy miles between us and Athabasca. September's chill had finished off the last of the mosquitoes, but this advantage was offset by the heaviest river traffic we had yet encountered. The

A scene of breathtaking serenity, the perfect stillness broken only by gentle ripples as the canoe glides across the silken water. ▶

big-game season had opened, and rarely did an hour pass without sight of a jet boat laden with moose hunters bullying its way upriver.

Our first experience of Canada's hunting season left us dismayed. Most of these people were stereotypical city-bred hunters: loud and obnoxious. At the confluence with the Calling River, we interrupted a father–son shooting lesson, the boy of fourteen awkwardly peppering a tree-stump target not 100 feet from us. The pair, dressed in eye-grabbing scarlet, eyed our grimy flannels with disapproval.

'Better get out of here if you're not wearing red,' the father warned. 'Lots of inexperienced hunters around.'

Despite the mobs of hunters, game was thick, and tender young grouse accompanied nearly every dinner those first few days. Ki had made a science of the grouse hunt, rooting through the leaves in an ever-widening circle around camp as Pete and I sat by the fire sipping tea and discussing the day's events. Eventually we'd hear the unmistakable whirr of grouse wings, and I would grab the shotgun. While the birds sizzled on roasting sticks, Ki savoured his reward of grouse giblets.

Late on day four out of Athabasca, at about the 100-mile point, we spotted the bright glow of torches through the rain-laden dusk. This had to be Dick Naumann's place in Upper Wells—a well-known haven for weary canoeists and a welcome sight to us after paddling through cold rain all day. Dick greeted us at the door, and announced in a heavy German accent that we would be staying the night. 'You are just in time to have dinner. The weather is too bad for you to go on tonight.' We didn't argue.

▲ **Tomatoes and cabbages thrive in Dick Naumann's extraordinary garden even in late autumn, protected from the cold by his remarkable natural-gas torches.**

The gas torches scattered throughout Dick's vegetable garden were fuelled by a natural gas well that had once powered a sawmill (and given rise to the name Upper Wells). Dick had moved to the abandoned site a decade earlier and tapped into the shallow reservoir for all his energy needs. The gas heated his cabins, powered his stove and lights, even ran an old washing machine. Most amazing of all, it fuelled dozens of torches in the huge garden so that here, less than 300 miles from the Northwest Territories, Dick was serving us fresh tomatoes with dinner, though the first frost had been more than a month ago. He sometimes harvested cantaloupe melons on Halloween!

While we silently consumed many bowls of moose stew with gravy-sopped bread still warm from the oven, followed by nut cake and tea, Dick told us his history. Immigrating from Germany just after the war, before moving to his present location he had homesteaded half a dozen miles downriver, where he and his Cree Indian wife had raised two children. For a while he had made a good living in furs but, as trapping deteriorated, all the other settlers moved on and they were left alone. When his wife died, Dick packed his threadbare furnishings onto a flat-bottomed boat called a scow and moved to Upper Wells.

After a food-drugged sleep, we spent most of the next day touring the homestead and hearing Dick's tales of river life. When we finally pushed off late in the afternoon, we carried his parting gift of fresh bread and tomatoes, and some badly needed ammunition.

Several miles downriver we stopped for dinner at Dick's old home, the now deserted settlement at Pelican Point. Outside one cabin, near a cache of oil drums maintained by hunting guides, lay the rotting skeleton of a thirty-foot scow. I imagined a youthful Dick Naumann navigating that scow upriver through the swift current. A movement nearby caught my eye, and I looked up towards a rusty Model T Ford mired in the bog. A ghostly glow shimmered behind the steering wheel, causing my pulse to race. When we crept closer, hearts pounding, we found the ghost not in the car but behind it: natural gas bubbling from the pond had ignited, the eerie flames flickering through the wreck.

Beneath a rising full moon we reloaded the canoe and headed off into our first white water. This was Pelican Rapid, an easy stretch that the canoe rode well, and we had grown so accustomed to night travel that we decided to run the next as well. It, too, proved easily navigable by moonlight, and as we rounded the point below we were rewarded by the welcoming beacon of a hunter's campfire a few miles ahead.

Within half an hour we were greeted by a dozen moose hunters on vacation from the USA with their three guides from Edmonton. This group had hunted together for more than a decade, and their well-organised camp was a pleasure to visit compared with the slapdash, shoot-'em-up style of other hunters we had

▲ **The will-o'-the-wisp is shrouded in superstition. In this fanciful portrayal, the phenomenon is shown as an impish creature with a torch luring an unfortunate gentleman from his homeward path into a deadly bog.**

The Ghostly Will-o'-the-wisp

One of Nature's most eerie phenomena has to be the will-o'-the-wisp, also known as the jack-o'-lantern. Best seen in the dark of night, it appears as a pale flame hovering a few feet above shallow waters, boggy marshland or dank graveyards. According to popular legend, a will-o'-the-wisp is the soul of a person who has been rejected by hell and condemned to wander the earth carrying his glowing 'hell-coals'. Certainly, this mysterious, flickering light, having no obvious cause, could easily appear to be some weird supernatural occurrence.

Scientists, however, have an explanation that is much more down to earth—literally. They explain that damp, decomposing organic matter in the ground produces gases such as methane and diphosphane, which can ignite to create a spooky, fluttering flame.

Such a prosaic explanation nevertheless fails to convince the superstitious, for whom the will-o'-the-wisp remains a harbinger of bad luck: too many people have followed its light only to stumble to a watery death in a dark bog.

seen. We had barely beached the canoe before cold beers were passed to us and extra moose steaks thrown on the fire.

The festivities ran late; it seemed I had barely closed my eyes when the moose-call alarm sounded at 5am. After cups of potent coffee, Pete and I packed and prepared to set off—probably our earliest start of the entire expedition. Then Gerry, one of the guides, pulled us aside for a parting word. 'Take care downriver, boys. Those rapids you'll be running have caused too many obituaries. I want to hear from you, not read about you.'

We had been hearing such warnings for the last 200 miles. In fact, the white water of the many rapids lying ahead had claimed at least one canoeist from Athabasca each year, and autumn's low water now added to the danger.

Running the Rapids

Thick fog shrouded our departure, but it began to clear as we approached the last minor rapid before the big sets. The Rapides du Joli Fou (Merry Fool Rapids) was a bucking thrill ride rather than a serious threat and dispelled much of the ominous feeling Gerry had left us with.

Our lunch stop was at the mouth of the House River, the point of no return, since past it the current would be too fast for us to turn round. Sitting on the north bank of the House in the afternoon sun, we were practically giddy with excitement. On the point stands a cluster of Indian graves, but even that sight failed to dampen our adventurous mood.

We heard the low roar of Grand Rapids a full three miles before reaching it late in the afternoon. The growing thunder is the only warning of this two-mile-long series of rapids and falls, which are nearly invisible until it is too late. As we approached, however, we could discern the halo of spray thrown up by the staircase-steep falls. The vertical drop was a full sixty feet over three-quarters of a mile.

▲ Portaging—carrying a canoe along the riverbank when the water becomes too treacherous—can be a dangerous and lengthy business. In this 19th-century painting by Sir George Back, a small group is about to negotiate a difficult portage over a rockface.

Grand Rapids is split down the middle by Grand Island, a half-mile-long and very narrow slice of land, but landing on the island was too hazardous at the present low-water stage, so we decided to bypass Grand Rapids completely and carry the canoe via the mile-and-a-half-long Free Traders Portage, which winds up and along the east bank. The half-mile of water before the portage was treacherous. We careened off one unseen rock, narrowly avoided a dump (being swamped), and then made for shore to search for the trail entrance.

After walking nearly half a mile up and down the shoreline without finding the trail, Pete and I split up and searched through the last hour of light. But we never did find the trail that night and we searched for another hour the next morning before finally spotting it. We walked its length without the canoe first, to fix the landmarks. The first stretch was a steep gradient of mud and rock. At

▲ **Pete Souchuk, the author's companion, reading by the light of a blazing campfire.**

the top it blurred into a grassy plateau, then dropped again into a boot-sucking muskeg. We began the portage in late afternoon, Pete hauling the first pack load and I the canoe. Of hundreds of portage trails I've hiked before and since, Grand Rapids topped the list of dehumanisers; it was an exhausting battle with mud and canoe and brush and with rubber boots that stayed behind as we lurched forward. In the end we left the canoe halfway along the trail while we camped for the night at the far end, leaving the last part of the slog till morning.

That night's camp was on a scenic gravel bar below the main rapids. Across the river, a wall of white plumes and spray boiled up in a deafening roar. We were exhilarated to have crossed the forbidding barrier of Grand Rapids, even if on foot. The night was calm and clear, so we vetoed the tent and, in honour of our safe passage, built a monstrous blaze with driftwood. Pete spent roll after roll of film on the moonlit cascade, and we retired full and content. I woke around 3am to see a cow moose coaxing her calf across the river in the light of our fire.

In the morning, after completing the portage and reloading gear, we set off on our first big day of rapids. Ten stretches of white water lay between us and Fort McMurray, the first of which was less than a mile downstream.

Twenty feet from the lip of the chute, I saw that we weren't going to make it. The first wave hit nearly broadside as I jammed hard to turn the bow into the assault. It seemed to me that we took the first two waves well; Pete's body in the bow acted as a break against the main volume of water rushing in. But as we entered the third wave straight on, I watched in amazement as the front six feet of canoe were buried. The water we had shipped with the impact of the first two waves acted like a sloshing lead weight, and the heavy canoe dived into rather than over the third, sinking the gunwales to the water line. Then we were through the rapid, sitting silently in water up to our waists. After a stunned moment we came to life, Ki light-footing it to the highest pack while Pete and I lunged for sleeping-bags, maps, anything that might float away.

By the time we had dragged what we could to shore, we began to realise the true dimensions of the adventure we had so eagerly anticipated beside the House River. We hadn't reached the really bad rapids yet and already we'd had a serious dunking. Pete shook his 300mm lens and listened to the water sloshing within. I started to shiver.

When we finally tallied the damages from the spill, actual losses amounted to no more than one sleeping-bag, one tripod, one glove and one map—but the last happened to be the topographic map covering the entire series of rapids ahead. We would now have to run them entirely from memory. On the other hand, the pot of beans I had set to soak underneath the stern seat the day before had come through unscathed, every silly bean still in the pot.

When we returned to the river that afternoon, Pete didn't speak of his apprehensions. Neither did I.

Three miles along, the current quietened and we enjoyed a few hours of peace amid wildness. This area was untouched by hunters; the yearling moose and deer had probably never seen humans. We counted half a dozen mule deer and as many moose by evening. A family of four whitetails watched us from a sandy point as we made camp, curious and unafraid. A flight of geese, one of the last we would see, passed overhead. We had made twenty-two miles, and we decided to save the next set of rapids, Brule, until morning. Running white water in the evening was an invitation to careless decision-making, not to mention hypothermia.

▲ **This mature bull moose has just lifted his head from under the water, where he has been feasting on water lilies and weeds.**

That night the weather turned foul, and though we bagged a young duck and a grouse for dinner, they couldn't roast properly in the falling sleet. Ki, at least, didn't seem to mind. Pete and I slept poorly, scrunched together under the one sleeping-bag.

By morning the rain had matured to a steady drizzle. Facing nine rapids we packed in weary silence and set out, hoping to pass the first three—Brule, Boiler and Middle—by nightfall. Lowered visibility would heighten the risk of these already formidable waters, and ideally we should have waited for better weather. But time was running short, and our craving for a warm, dry bedroll in Fort McMurray may have influenced our decision to push on. Lack of sleep undoubtedly slowed our actions and clouded our thinking as well. We scouted Brule, then discussed it for half an hour: should we portage or go for it? We chose to go for it, and I fought to keep the canoe in the only semblance of a channel as Pete shouted, 'Left, left, *left!*'

We ended that battle as victors and broke for a rest, talking strategy for the upcoming rapid over a healing fire and leftover barley porridge. Originally called 'Joe's Rapid', Boiler Rapid was renamed nearly 100 years ago when a scow upturned in it, depositing in the river a steamboat boiler destined for Fort McMurray. Several lives were lost in that accident.

▲ **Split-second decisions and perfect judgment can mean the difference between life and death in rapids such as these.**

Three times during the approach we ran what we thought was Boiler Rapid, but all guessing ceased when Pete spotted the unbroken white line of the real thing a full mile ahead. Our lost notes had indicated that Boiler could be run only along the left bank, but our faulty memories chose the right instead. We realised our error 200 yards from the main cascade—much too late for a change of plan. 'Dig, dig, dig, *hard right!*' I screamed, while the canoe surged towards a wall of white. As the shoreline loomed, I jammed the bow upstream to avoid a collision. We grounded safely and, after securing the canoe, walked down for a look at the cascade.

Disaster

'No way in an open canoe,' Pete announced with finality, after scouting the crisscross of froth spilling over a series of limestone ledges. Nor was there any portage trail; wet, round, slippery boulders sloped into the foaming water. Lining (walking along the shore and guiding the canoe down on ropes fore and aft) was our only resource. The craft responded well as Pete and I jumped from rock to rock, alternately paying out and taking in the steering ropes. But at one point the bow slipped too far to the left, and the current took advantage of the opportunity. Water began to pile up heavily on the stern and, in one awesomely smooth gesture, sucked it under.

I immediately released the rope, knowing we had no chance against the thousands of pounds of pull created by a foundering canoe. Pete, though, didn't let go in time and was hurled into the river. Recovering quickly, he floundered out of the shallow water and we both sprinted downstream after the tumbling vessel. I slipped on a rock and fell behind; when I caught up with Pete a quarter of a mile further down, he was back in the water. With an amazing effort he had managed, in chest-deep water midstream, to reach the canoe and pin it against a rock in the swift current. Now he strained at one of the ropes, trying to keep the craft from pivoting off its perch.

I inched towards him, an ill-placed step tossing my legs behind me as I fought to stay upright in the surge. Finally I reached him, and for the next half-hour we struggled to get the canoe back to shore. Eventually we managed to manhandle it off the rock and angle it through the current to a landing downstream.

Shivering, not speaking, we stood on shore amid the remains of our gear. Both the rifle and the shotgun now lay on the river bottom, along with all our food, maps and cooking equipment. Pete had been in the water longer than me and his body was shaking uncontrollably with the cold. Though he needed immediate attention, the only wood in the area was cottonwood, useless for a fire.

Once the tent was erected and some water wrung from the sleeping-bag, I installed Pete inside. Then I nursed and cursed a single gasping flame for an hour before giving up on the idea of a fire. During my vain search for dry wood, I discovered one jar of food that had washed up onto the sand, and we shared its contents for dinner: a bowl of uncooked cornmeal and water. We slept tangled in one mass to optimise shared body heat, using Ki for a pillow.

Morning brought the first sun we had seen in two days, but also a thick blanket of frost. We walked around camp prising frozen pieces of clothing and gear from where we had dropped them the night before. We were too weak to load the canoe properly, or to care. Dripping, half-thawed clothing and various odds and ends were tossed in haphazardly.

Exposure and lack of food had taken their toll and I was haunted by self-doubt. It was Pete who had saved the canoe from the rapids, and I had even failed at my task of providing a life-giving flame. Yet it was Pete's faith that now kept me from breaking down, and I suppose the idea of my leadership, however much an illusion, gave him strength. Still, it was time to face facts. Before shoving off, I made a kind of speech to Pete.

◀ **The aftermath of the team's disastrous encounter with Boiler Rapid. The scarred underside of the canoe speaks volumes about the rough boulders against which it was hurled.**

'We won't survive another dump. We get up each morning with half the strength of the day before. We're already too weak to lift a full pack, much less portage it. There's hardly any food, and with no gun we're not going to get any more. We're going to have to keep our movements to a minimum by drifting with the current when we can and running every rapid on blind faith.'

Ki watched me as I spoke. He hadn't eaten in two days, yet he never left us to search for game. He chose companionship over a full belly.

If we flipped in another rapid, we would be done for. But somehow the act of stating our chances baldly seemed to brighten the dreary outlook. Two major rapids down, seven to go before reaching the safety of Fort McMurray.

The first 200 yards of Middle Rapids were a constant zigzag between rocks, and we slammed hard into one with an agonising grate of aluminium on stone. We spent several minutes helplessly stuck there before easing ourselves free and paddling on.

The current now eased to a lethargic pace, and the miles dragged on to the monotonous dip of the canoe paddle. Then, as we rounded the point just before Long Rapids, the familiar dull roar returned, seeming to come from all directions. We went through the procedure like robots: stopping, scouting, discussing the channel in forced-casual tones. We spoke of last-ditch emergency measures and survival tactics. But we didn't have to use them. We passed Long Rapids, tearing through the standing waves with apparently divine luck.

There was a two-mile breather before the next test, Crooked Rapids. A point of rock prevented us from studying these rapids; we would have to run them blind. We were riding the waves well as we arced round the blind hairpin turn between the limestone cliffs. But the hidden stretch that now lay before us was crisscrossed by four-foot walls of water separated by narrow, deep troughs. Worst of all, the channel angled to midstream, eliminating any chance of a quick beaching should we dump. We were doomed.

There was no dramatic canoe-flip; we simply sank beneath the battering of the waves. Our canoe turned keel-up, and we clung to the hull. After a few minutes of this, Ki left the canoe, gained the left bank, then ran along the shore trying to keep us in sight. We were tempted to follow him, but it would be suicide to lose the canoe now. Neither of us spoke as we kicked in a futile effort to swim the canoe to shore. We had both lost our boots, the current literally sucking them off our feet, and each time we neared the riverbank a crosscurrent swept us back to the middle.

Eventually Crooked Rapids spat us out and deposited us without pause into the new onslaught of Rock Rapids. True to its name, boulders beneath the surface battered our legs. There was no pain on impact, just the sensation of a leg being shoved unnaturally aside. About twenty minutes had passed since we first grasped the upturned canoe; violent cramps gripped my legs and arms. I could hear Pete's voice clearly, saying we had to leave the canoe and make for shore, and my last clear picture is of the canoe slipping from beneath my unfeeling hands. Then I remember a fleeting glimpse of a stone ledge, and something in my hands as I climbed the embankment—a rock, a tree root? I fell forward headfirst onto level ground above the ledge. My last sensation for a while was of damp earth on my cheek. An object was crouching over me. Then suddenly it rose up and began moving away. Its touch against my skin had felt good. I wanted it to stay...

Fight for Survival

I must have lost consciousness again, but not for long. It was only now becoming full dark, and for the first time I realised that the object hovering above me had been Pete. It seemed like days ago that we had been in the water. I looked around through swirling wet snow that melted upon everything it struck. I was on a ledge twenty feet above the river, covered with dirt and leaves. Bare footprints in the sand led away from me, and a vague memory returned of Pete shouting something to me. We were a full thirty miles from Fort McMurray, but he must be trying to walk there.

I grew conscious of having difficulty breathing and thought: My God, my lungs are stopping. I began choking and snorting, unable to get enough air. Was this the final stage of hypothermia—the lungs contracting? Finally the spasms slowed to a steady, hard breathing; I wanted to burst my lungs with the beautiful air.

It was dark now and from across the river I could hear Ki howling. Get out of the wind, I thought. I had to get out of the wind if I was to survive the night. I'd been wearing my poncho when we dumped; now I drew my knees to my chin and wadded the poncho hood into the head hole to block any heat loss. To my surprise, I stayed relatively warm. My thoughts turned to Pete. I wondered if he was fighting the same battle.

It wasn't my imagination: it *was* getting light. I continued my vigil under the poncho, though the temptation to throw it off was nearly overwhelming. Finally, when I believed there was more light and heat than the wind could overcome, I raised the poncho from my head and groped my way down the limestone face to the river. For the rest of the morning I sat unmoving in a small cave. I was loath

Late autumn ice encroaches on a crystalline Canadian river. As the ice spreads and thickens, so the animals living in and around the river will be forced to adapt to the new harsh conditions. ▶

to leave its protection, but the thought that Pete might still be alive somewhere downriver finally drove me back out into the wind. My idea was born of simple desperation: if I could find the canoe, I would simply shove off into the river. With three rapids ahead and no paddle, my chances of drifting the thirty miles to town were nearly nonexistent. Yet I was sure I wouldn't last another night.

I found the canoe some time that afternoon, lying on its side half out of the water. The packs were still strapped in place, but much of their contents had spilled. Too weak to carry the packs, I yanked the sleeping-bag and tent free, along with a jar of rice and a few bouillon cubes. But when the time came to invert the canoe to drain it, I couldn't even lift the bow. So much for getting back on the river.

At least I could now make a semblance of a camp. The tent wobbled, threatening to collapse; inside I piled everything that might be of some use to me. Then, crawling under the still-soaking sleeping-bag, I propped up on an elbow, chewed a handful of raw rice and washed a bouillon cube down with icy river water.

Depression set in immediately as I lay there, nearly warm, thinking of Pete's cold corpse resting on some shore. Gazing at the tent ceiling and listening to the rainfly flap in the wind, I felt a powerful desire to trade places with him.

A little while later I awoke to the sound of an engine growling somewhere in the distance. I dismissed it. The flight pattern to Fort McMurray paralleled the river, and I'd already heard three planes. They obviously couldn't see me.

But the sound was getting louder, not fading away. Finally, I tore open the tent flap. Not 200 yards downriver was a powerboat headed towards me. I don't recall the mad screaming and arm-waving I must have performed, or the tears that streamed down my face. The boat's occupants (Mike and Rita Jones) looked shaken as they disembarked and cautiously approached me. Rita led me down to the boat as Mike began storing my gear under the canoe for salvage later.

Both were strangely silent as they went about their tasks. Not until I was safely bundled into the boat did they begin to answer my babbled questions. The first was about Pete. I dreaded the answer, but Mike replied calmly that he was fine and probably at the hospital by now. 'Pete said you were dead. That's why we were so surprised when we found you.'

Then I remembered Ki and tried to insist that we go back and look for him. Though I hadn't heard his barking since the night before, I believed that he was still patiently waiting on the other side of the river. But Mike and Rita gently refused, assuring me that we could search for Ki later. During the remaining half-hour or so of the trip to Fort McMurray, they filled me in on what they knew of Pete's ordeal. But I hardly heard them, or noticed the town as it grew from behind the river bend. Part of me was still back with Ki, on the limestone cliffs of the Athabasca River.

▲ A peaceful, early-morning spring scene in Quebec—one that could be replicated beside tens of thousands of lakes throughout the country.

Flashes of orange lichen cling to the ancient, glacier-smoothed rock of the Canadian Shield—filigreed here with branches of dwarf willow. ▶

During the Canadian autumn, deciduous trees display an infinity of subtly varied reds, oranges and yellows. ▼

▲ The autumn homecoming of sockeye salmon, struggling back to their spawning grounds in the rivers of British Columbia.

The Changing Colours of Canada

THE CANADIAN COUNTRYSIDE is famously varied, with its towering mountain peaks, deep pine forests and endless prairies. Yet the landscape owes its dramatic diversity not just to the changing terrain, but also to the changing seasons.

Over most of the country, a short but sun-soaked spring and summer give way to a serene autumn and then a long, harsh winter; and with each shift, Nature adjusts the palette with which it paints its multifarious features. In spring, for instance, as the last of the snows recede, fiery orange lichens are revealed on the grey rocks of the Canadian Shield, and vibrant green leaves return to birch and oak woods. With summer approaching, the Rockies light up with a brilliant blaze of alpine flowers.

In autumn, vast tracts of woodland seem to catch fire as the leaves turn to vibrant red and orange, the shades proliferating and intensifying as each day passes. No wonder that the symbol of the scarlet maple leaf dominates the design of Canada's national flag. The theme of autumn scarlet extends to the waterways of British Columbia too, where the rivers run red with sockeye salmon swarming back to their spawning grounds.

If summer and autumn seem daubed in exuberant oil paints, winter suggests subdued watercolours. The heavy snows occasionally lend a monochrome look to the countryside, but on a fine crisp day you can watch a brilliant blue sky decline into a splendid array of sumptuous pinks and purples at sunset.

◄ Alpine wildflowers make the most of their brief lives by putting on a dazzling summer carnival.

Far in the frozen north, another winter day—tinged, it seems, with a sad beauty—draws to an early close. ▼

CHAPTER 3

Walking into Winter

▲ **The pale, gold light of a winter dawn reveals a fresh fall of snow on a frozen lake.**

THE FIRST FEW DAYS in Fort McMurray are still rather blurred, but I know Pete and I talked most of the night after the nurse escorted me into our double room. Neither of us could relax until reunited, even though we'd been told repeatedly that the other was safe. We spoke in excited spurts, then grew weak and slept for short stretches, waking to begin again. We passionately wanted to re-create the accident before sleep fogged our memories. Nurses came in and out to push more vitamins and fluid into us, and to scold us for talking instead of resting.

Pete told me that after half an hour in the freezing water he had, like me, collapsed in the shallows, but had somehow lunged forward to retrieve the escaping canoe, and dragged it onto the shore. He had then stumbled upriver to find me half-consciously digging a nest in which to bury myself. Recognising signs of hypothermic shock, he had decided to set out in search of help.

The snow had not bothered him too much, but the clouds that blocked the light of the moon did. He remembered groping his way along the riverbank, crashing into trees and falling off rock ledges. Glancing upriver, he had noticed smears of blood on the rocks he had just crossed. He had not been able to feel his feet and it occurred to him that they might not last the night. So he had torn his rainproof trousers in half and wrapped one trouser leg around each foot.

Around noon the following day the jet boat of a river research team had churned up the Athabasca. He screamed and threw stones but the boat had raced by without its occupants seeing him. As he sank to his knees in despair he heard a second boat. He waved, and this time the boat had slowed and turned.

The second day we felt stronger but still disorientated. I phoned my parents again, not remembering I had already done so. An added misery for me was anxiety over the future. All that day I waited for Pete to announce that he was leaving the expedition.

Finally he rolled over in bed and introduced the subject himself. 'You know, Dave, it's a damn shame we don't have our maps with us. We could be planning our winter travel right now.' This was a man whose shredded feet could barely carry him from bed to the toilet, much less across a continent.

Now my only remaining worry was Ki. I couldn't stop thinking that he might starve waiting on the riverbank for us to come back. Or that he had been injured and couldn't hunt, maybe falling prey to wolves. I truly thought we wouldn't find him, and I was somehow almost resigned to it.

That same afternoon, a hearty, cigar-puffing man burst into our room with a furious nurse on his heels. After grinding out his cigar with an apologetic 'Jeez,

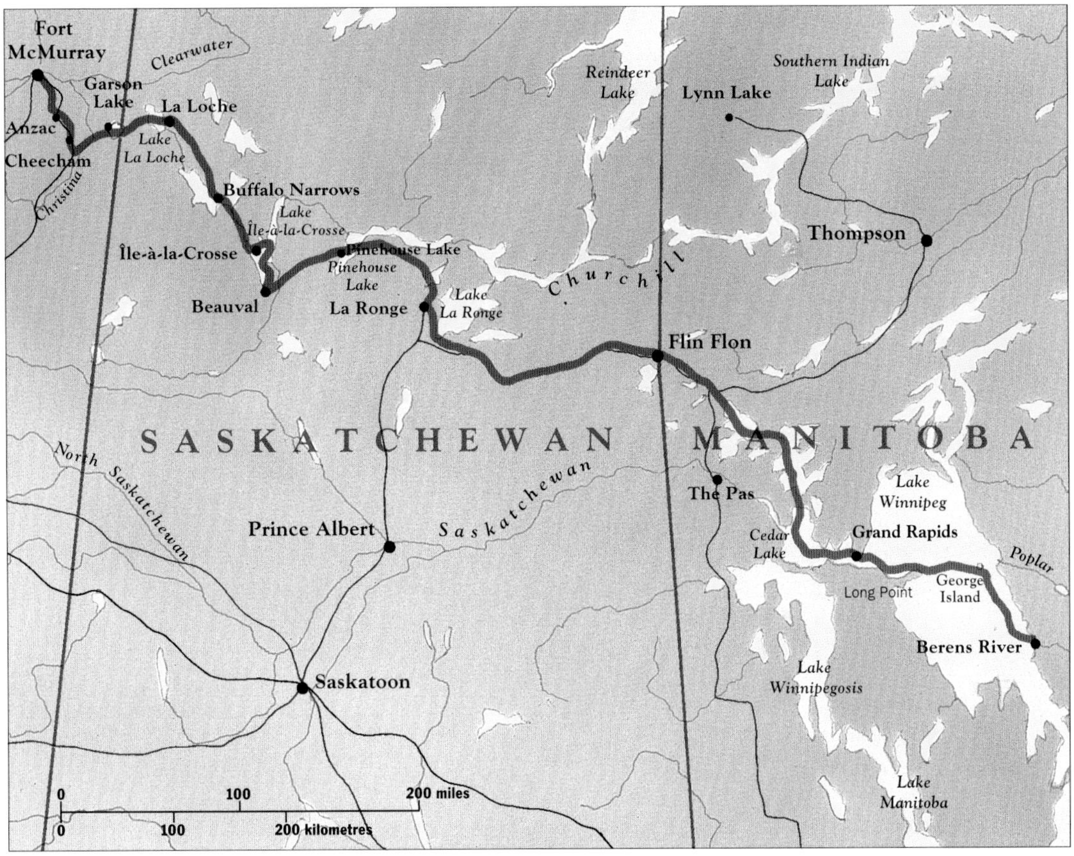

◀ **The winter route of the Trans-Canada Expedition from Fort McMurray to the eastern shore of Lake Winnipeg.**

sorry!' he introduced himself as Joe Camp, vice-president of Great Canadian Oil Sands Company, the local boom industry. Through his work as an energy lobbyist, my father knew of the Fort McMurray operation. A few phone calls led him to Joe Camp, who took it on himself to become our saviour.

He took me home from the hospital on day three, with a stop on the way to replace my hopelessly filthy and mangled clothing and footwear. Pete's damaged feet required a few more days of hospitalisation, after which he joined me. And thus began two weeks of unlimited hospitality.

Carolina Camp's Italian heritage translated into fussy mothering. She was not content unless certain that the pillow behind my head was perfectly positioned, and for the first two days after Pete arrived she didn't allow him to walk without her supporting arm. Her culinary speciality was pasta, and she'd plop heap after steaming heap of lasagne on our plates. She was apparently convinced that our frail bodies needed mounds of it. When our shrunken stomachs could hold no more, she would scold: 'How are you going to go back to your expedition if you don't eat more? Come to think of it, I don't know why I'm trying to help you get better. You'll just go and freeze yourselves again. Your mothers must be grey with worry!'

Joe, meanwhile, made it his mission to educate us about Fort McMurray. As our strength increased we explored more of the town. Like other parts of Alberta, it had been transformed by new-found energy wealth, its population leaping from five thousand to nearly thirty thousand in less than a decade. Joe Camp's company had pioneered a process to extract oil from the sticky, foul-smelling deposits of tar sands lining the Athabasca. Twenty-storey buildings stand not far from the spot where, in 1790, a fur-trading post was established at the junction of the Clearwater and Athabasca rivers.

The vâlley of the Mackenzie River, to the north, was a fur trader's paradise, and the Hudson's Bay Company and its chief agent, William McMurray, had little use for the extensive deposits of tar, or oil, sands found throughout the region. A few used them to waterproof their cabin roofs or seal the seams of birchbark canoes, but most considered them merely a further inconvenience of living at a wilderness outpost. Today there is no longer a market for birchbark seam sealer, but two-ton shovels scoop the goo onto conveyor belts bound for refineries, which produce in excess of 150,000 barrels of oil daily.

Joe was a good storyteller and really warmed up when describing his hunting and fishing adventures. His tales of fish too heavy to lift had me squinting with scepticism, until he produced his photo albums to back them up.

The Camps, originally from Texas, had three daughters. The two eldest, in their twenties, were living back in their home state. That left seven-year-old Valeri Jo, for whom Pete and I represented new Monopoly victims. The Camp clan was rounded out by a German shepherd named Sunshine. Every time she wagged her tail, my thoughts returned to Ki.

Fort McMurray's Black Sands

Visitors to Fort McMurray on the Athabasca River may be excused for thinking they have stumbled on the most appalling ecological disaster: for, in the middle of a pristine wilderness, lie some 9,000 square miles of sand soaked in sticky, black, bituminous oil.

But this is a natural oil spill, rather than a man-made one—the result of naturally occurring crude oil that has seeped to the surface from deep below the ground. These tar sands, as they are called, mark the site of the largest oil reserves ever discovered. Experts calculate that some 300 billion barrels of oil may eventually be recovered—twice as much as the deserts of Saudi Arabia will yield, and enough to supply the needs of Canada and the USA well into the next century.

Commercial exploitation of the tar sands began in the 1960s with the digging of massive open-pit mines. As a result, Fort McMurray became a boom town. Yet local Indians had found a use for the oil centuries earlier—not as fuel, but as waterproofing for their canoes.

▲ **A gargantuan piece of machinery scoops up oil-drenched sand at the site of the world's largest known oil reserve, on the Athabasca River.**

Ten days had now elapsed since we had swum to the right bank of the Athabasca and Ki to the left. Fort McMurray's newspapers had repeatedly described him in the hope he might be spotted by a passing moose hunter, but there had been no sign. At one point I planned to backpack the thirty miles back, on the chance he might be somewhere along the way. But that plan died early; I couldn't even lift the pack to my shoulder without stumbling.

Return of a Faithful Friend

When the knock on the Camps' door came on October 15, we were completely unprepared. Mike Jones and Derek Tripp (Pete's rescuers) smiled through the window; between them stood an emaciated animal in a serious state of shock. Its eyes divulged no recognition or emotion, and it chose its steps with great care, as if it might fall at any moment.

Ki had apparently watched and waited near my campsite for the last nine days, refusing to believe that we had deserted him. Hunters passed by, but Ki was waiting for the humans he knew and did not reveal himself. Then two moose hunters spotted our canoe and gear and recognised it as the fateful camp they'd heard about on the radio. They loaded our canoe and tied it behind their boat, planning to tow it back to Fort McMurray. Intending to protect our gear from intruders, Ki leaped into the river and swam towards their departing boat. When the astonished hunters pulled him from the river, they were surprised at how weak he was. It was obvious he had chosen not to leave his sentry post, even to search for food, in case we might return during his absence.

Ki seemed close to death. I was afraid to touch him for fear the slightest pressure would cause him to collapse. In two more days I doubt he would have had the strength to whine, much less swim toward his rescuers. Yet I was sure he would have continued to wait. Pete and I cried that night.

Thanks mainly to Carolina, Ki made an amazingly fast recovery, but nearly three weeks later Pete and I still could not walk more than a mile through Fort McMurray without sitting down to rest. Pete walked with a pronounced limp, which wasn't surprising, but our lingering weakness was. Meanwhile, I noted with growing alarm the changes in the river and countryside as winter closed in at the end of October. Instead of a slight skim of ice, the Athabasca's eddies were trapped under a thin but solid sheet. The locals' predictions of an early, hard winter seemed alarmingly accurate.

We had hoped to push into Saskatchewan by canoe before freeze-up gripped the rivers, but now winter's ice would force us onto a land route from Fort McMurray. It was difficult for me to accept. I had judged the first 1,200 miles to be the easiest of the journey, yet those 'easy' miles had nearly killed my two companions and me. What would we encounter during the 3,500 'tough' miles that lay ahead?

Though I questioned my judgment, there was no questioning my desire—or Pete's—to continue. However, the change in route necessitated an equipment switch, and fortunately National Geographic now came through with a grant that would help offset re-equipment expenses.

Meanwhile, the thirty-mile boat ride from the accident site to Fort McMurray had represented a break in my official record-breaking journey. I had some ground to make up. Though I couldn't travel on foot the exact route we would have canoed, I felt that a thirty-mile round trip along the nearby Horse River would symbolically balance the books. Pete had already paid his mileage dues and more with his all-night walk.

▲ **This tubby red squirrel is well protected by his thick coat and extra fat reserves against the ravages of the cold. Red squirrels do not hibernate, but take refuge in their lairs during particularly chilly spells.**

I set out with Ki and a light pack, following a trail in the muffled stillness of the winter woods; Ki bounded ahead in search of squirrels. There was no wind, and it was all a winter walk should be.

At dusk I came upon a sheltering stand of spruce—a good campsite. Relying on a weather forecast for continuing moderate temperatures, I'd left the tent behind and I laid my sleeping-bag on a snow-free bed of spruce needles under a sheltering canopy of boughs. After a simple supper I lay in the gathering dark, Ki curled into a ball at my feet. It was a good way to begin the winter.

Next morning, our return route led us through a picturesque valley. Trudging back through unbroken snow soon left me a sweating, dripping mess, but Ki loved it. At each rabbit den he buried his head, sniffing for occupants, then a sneeze to clear his nostrils, and he was ready for the next hunt. As we topped the last hill above Fort McMurray, there was Pete, the ever-present camera dangling from his neck, waving at us from the street.

On Our Way Again

It was 1.30pm on departure day (December 2) before we finished shaking hands with local friends and posing for newspaper photos by the railroad tracks. Then Pete and I headed east along the Northern Alberta Railway towards the small community of Anzac, twenty-seven miles away. The snow wasn't deep enough to call for our five-foot-long Alaskan-type snowshoes, chosen for fast travel through open country, and our progress was far from swift. Alberta's railroads were no more comfortable to walk along than British Columbia's: the sleepers were set too close together for us to step on each one, yet too far apart to take two in a stride.

The temperature—in the minus twenties—was not impossibly cold nor particularly comfortable, just cold enough to keep us moving. Our route snaked through stands of spruce along a meandering river. Occasionally we flushed grouse from the trees, though always just out of range of my .22 rifle. We spoke little during that first day's hike, each experiencing his own blend of exhilaration and apprehension, neither wanting to intrude on the other's thoughts.

That night we camped no more than seven miles from Fort McMurray. We were tired, sore and out of shape. The temperature soon hit –30°F, and our only source of heat was a single-burner gas stove. (In our ignorance of winter camping, we didn't yet know how easy it is to maintain a bonfire against a reflective snowbank.) We munched half-grilled cheese sandwiches and jogged around camp to stay warm. The next morning we awoke inside an ice castle of hoarfrost from our own condensed breath.

The second day, our progress was even more disappointing, advancing us a mere six miles. Hiking with a full pack through unbroken snow was vastly different from carrying a light load over a well-packed trail. It became painfully obvious that we were simply packing too much weight to make adequate progress in these conditions. At least we didn't have to pitch a camp that night, luckily stumbling on the small cabin of a trapper called Julian Powder. Julian welcomed the diversion; we swapped tales around his tin stove, on which a peppery pork stew bubbled and a bannock toasted. He suggested several tricks to speed our adjustment to winter travel, and shook his head over our boots. 'No wonder you're so damn tired. Those things'll kill you.' When we protested that everyone in the city had recommended them he retorted, 'Forget all that bull

Dazzling winter sunshine highlights every snow-laden branch in this forest clearing. ▼

▲ The author, with his beard, moustache and eyebrows frosted up by daytime temperatures in the minus thirties. Frostbite, which destroys tissue in the body's extremities, is a constant threat in such conditions.

you heard in the city. Caribou moccasins—that's what you need. You should be able to have some made for you in the next Indian town.'

He was similarly critical of our heavy packs. 'You should travel light the first few weeks. Make short trips between settlements until you've gotten rid of your city-softness; then you can pack heavier loads.' When Julian said that some friends of his were travelling to Fort McMurray in the morning, we had an idea. Could they take our packs with them? That would let us hike bareback to Anzac, and our packs could be shipped there by rail.

Julian agreed, and the next morning after a pancake breakfast we left him our packs and a box of .22 cartridges that he needed, then returned to the cursed railroad tracks. We carried only our standard lunch: a fist-sized piece of bannock, four inches of garlic sausage and a candy bar apiece, along with a quart of orange drink.

Fourteen miles without packs hardly constitutes a strenuous day, but two more inches of snow had fallen, increasing the ground cover to fourteen inches. We walked through a strong head wind all afternoon. It intensified the cold and by the time the sun set at a quarter past three my right nostril was solidly plugged with ice and felt as hard as wood. Pete was limping, and Ki's trail was dappled with blood.

Despite our exhaustion, we began to develop a pattern of travel. Preferring a quick pace, I would barge ahead in a two-mile spurt, then rest while waiting for Pete to catch up. His steady pace drove me mad; besides, I needed a short break every hour. Pete, on the other hand, could walk for hours without resting at his deliberate, energy-saving pace. This tortoise-and-hare combination worked just fine: throughout the day I pushed him to move faster, and by day's end I was the first to begin spotting promising campsites. But the tortoise was never ready to camp and always managed to drag me two miles further down the trail.

By full dark we still hadn't reached Anzac. Only the sleepers beneath our feet told us we were heading in the right direction. Just as we'd begun to wonder if we could somehow have missed it, its lights flashed ahead and a forestry bunkhouse appeared through the gloom. After gulping hot tea we managed to swallow a few bites of food. I remember climbing into a bed—but nothing more.

During the night the temperature dropped to –58°, and we awoke to find Anzac obscured by a shroud of ice fog. It would not rise above –35° that day. We were stiff and sore, and our faces burned at the slightest exposure to the cold; it was a good day to heed Julian's suggestion that we ease into life in the winter bush. We spent it visiting some local residents, trapper Jim Mulawka and his Chipewyan wife, Lenora. Their trapping cabin was twenty-five miles southeast, along our route, and Jim offered it to us if it was too cold to camp when we got there.

After loading our packs onto the train bound for Cheecham, the next stop on the line, we left Anzac around noon the next day with only a camera, a rifle and lunch. The temperature was –44°. By four, just after dark, we had refrozen our faces and felt the waves of shaking exhaustion. Poor Ki was now carefully balancing his every step along one of the iron rails to avoid the burning snow that packed between his pads.

By six I was unashamedly afraid. I feared that we had walked further than we realised, passed Cheecham, and were now following the tracks away from the settlement. We found a railroad switchman's hut, maybe four by six feet, and huddled there, having our first argument of the winter. I argued that we should spend the night in the hut; Pete thought we should keep moving. This was an odd reversal of roles: normally I was the risk-taker and Pete the cautious one.

Finally I agreed to keep going, and we shuffled onwards—towards Cheecham or away from it. At 7.30pm, four hours after sunset, we rounded a bend and spotted the lights of a cabin. Baxter Gillingham flung open the door and introduced himself. He had to repeat his name much later, since we were then oblivious to words. I saw only a scruffy salt-and-pepper beard below water-blue eyes as he escorted us into the cabin and helped us into chairs. Ki followed and dropped beneath the table.

▲ A typical trapper's cabin and its smokehouse (left) in the remote wilds of Canada. The plastic sheeting over the main building helps keep out the worst of the wind.

A Gift of Bushcraft

Baxter had been expecting us. When the twice-weekly train had stopped near his cabin that afternoon, the baggage man had tossed out our packs and snowshoes, along with the news that we were hoofing it down from Anzac. Baxter, who had spent most of his sixty-odd years in the bush, had planned to trap that day, but decided to straighten up his cabin instead when he saw the temperature nudging –50°. He knew that two unseasoned Americans would be in trouble after walking twenty-one miles on such a day, and considered going out to look for us. But he remembered his younger days, when in similar circumstances he would rather have dropped in his tracks than be rescued. 'I'll give 'em a few more hours,' he had decided.

Having thawed out himself countless times, Baxter wasn't surprised that we couldn't talk or so much as acknowledge his presence when we first arrived. He kept our mugs full of heavily sweetened tea but refrained from asking questions for the first half-hour or so, knowing he could expect only garbled replies. This thawing period, a return to normality, would become standard evening procedure for Pete and me. Our minds had been operating in a trancelike state from the energy drain of moving all day in extreme cold. It is a form of shock, the mind gearing down for self-preservation. Were the mind to continue functioning at normal capacity, the sensations of pain, hunger and cold would overrule the need to maintain forward motion. So consciousness narrows to the primary drive: to keep walking.

Slowly our voices and appetites returned. We ate some bannock and got acquainted with our host and his young Chipewyan bride. Both had much to offer us in the way of bush lore, and we talked long into the night.

Baxter frowned at our cumbersome boots but smiled in approval at our scabbed faces, assuring us that moderate frostbite would eventually toughen the skin and prevent further discomfort. We'd already discovered what all trappers know: face masks are impractical, becoming hopelessly encrusted with ice from breath condensation within minutes in extreme conditions.

Our most priceless lesson from Baxter came the next morning, when he showed us his string of rabbit snares in a nearby willow thicket where the creatures congregated to feed on the bark. ('Rabbit' in this part of the world always means the large white snowshoe hare.) Baxter described how to make a snare. A rabbit trail is selected and its sides blocked with small fences made of sticks. When the rabbit is funnelled onto the trail it usually doesn't see the snare hanging in the middle of the path and pulls the wire loop tight trying to free itself.

▲ **The snowshoe hare gets its name from its large, furry hind feet, which enable it to run across fresh snow at up to 30 miles per hour.**

In productive country, setting out a dozen such snares can yield three to four rabbits by morning, and Baxter's gift of bushcraft would provide us with literally hundreds of meals over the next 3,500 miles.

Baxter's cabin was overcrowded with the addition of us and our gear, but Jim Mulawka's trapping cabin was located four miles down the trail towards the Saskatchewan border, now just fifty miles east; so we decided Jim's cabin was the logical place to wait out the cold spell. Following the directions Jim had given us back in Anzac, we had no trouble finding it.

It was more luxurious than we had anticipated: two large, well-furnished rooms lit by double-glazed windows. Opposite a wall lined with bookshelves was a huge cast-iron stove. An array of rifles and shotguns hung from pegs above the door, and a radio sat on the kitchen table. To our surprise and delight, the reception was excellent: Jim had strung an entire spool of snare wire through the trees and thence into the cabin. We tuned in to a central Alberta station and caught up with world news while doing our evening chores. Pete serviced the camera equipment while I excitedly twisted length after length of snare wire—Baxter's farewell gift.

Taking a flashlight outside, I set eight snares along rabbit runs in the woods behind the cabin. The temperature was about –30°, and the damaged skin on my face stung in the frozen air, but I was in a fine mood and cheered by the warm glow that radiated from the cabin.

Baxter's tutoring and my efforts were rewarded the next morning by three fat white hares. After skinning and cleaning them, we dropped them whole into boiling water and cooked them for an hour. Removing them from the pot, I took the meat off the bones in small chunks and returned it to the cooking broth, adding split peas, potatoes, onions, powdered soup mix, tomato sauce and seasonings. This boiled slowly for several more hours, until the meat fell apart in tender shreds. Thus was born our version of rabbit stew, which became our staple winter meal. At the time we found it superb. Months later, after eating it day after day, we had to force the stuff into our mouths, and I cursed the day I'd invented the recipe. Five years later I still find it hard to enter a kitchen where rabbits are cooking.

Our fourth night in the cabin was the end of our 'vacation'. I had caught a total of fourteen rabbits to supplement our food supply. The pain in Pete's feet, a remnant of his ordeal on the Athabasca River, had vanished, and Ki's paws were rapidly healing. The damaged skin on our faces was greatly reduced, though the right side of my nose was still hidden beneath a shell of scabs. The weather, though, was our chief motivation to resume travel: on December 10 the temperature climbed to a remarkably comfortable –5°.

Jim Mulawka showed up that night, a fortunate piece of timing. He had a small overnight cabin we could stay in seven miles east on Hay Creek, he told us, and without his directions we probably wouldn't have found it. That was the good news. The bad news, he said, was that as yet this season no one had traversed the *next* ten miles between Hay Creek and trapper Jean-Marie Janvier's cabin on the Christina River. We would have to break our own trail through two feet of snow.

The seven-mile hike to Jim's mini-cabin was quick and uneventful. The pleasant temperature of +10°F didn't bother our healing faces, and the trail was well packed and easy to follow. Even Ki's paws were not a problem, though they weren't quite ready for steady travel. I imitated some leather dog moccasins I'd seen by fashioning bootees out of a large woollen sock and snare wire. When I put them on, Ki pranced around in distaste, shook his feet and tried to chew off the strange objects, but eventually he quit complaining and joined us on the trail. He lost three of the four by the day's end, but they stayed in place long enough to prevent his wounds from reopening.

▲ **The art of snowshoeing is not quickly mastered, as Pete soon finds out!**

At sunrise on Hay Creek, Pete and I eyed our snowshoes warily before donning them for the first time. Neither of us had ever used snowshoes. Perched innocently in a storefront window at Fort McMurray, they had symbolised to me all the romantic wildness of northern Canada. Now they were simply tools to aid our advance to the next destination.

We fell frequently until we began to master the simple snowshoer's stride. But there were plenty of other hazards. Branches hidden beneath the snow took particular pleasure in tripping us. Once I turned just in time to see Pete dive headlong into the snow, one snowshoe impaled on a buried branch. A step further on, another branch lay in wait for me. Pete zipped past as I rolled over and tried to regain my footing.

Jean-Marie's trapping cabin was more typical of the species. It had one small, soot-streaked window, and the secondhand stove was rusted nearly through. Strips of smoked, dried moose meat hung from the rafters. We unrolled our sleeping-bags on the cleanest section of floor, where the brown snuff-spit stains and frozen rabbit blood and entrails seemed thinnest.

We spent the entire next day searching for the trail to Saskatchewan. A day later we finally found it, then managed to advance thirteen miles before stopping to camp—not more than twelve miles from the border.

This was our first pleasant outdoor camp of the winter, as the temperature was quite moderate. No longer would we make the mistake of using our tent in wintertime; since Fort McMurray it had been dead weight in our packs. Instead we snowshoed back and forth to level a sleeping platform, then gathered armloads of spruce boughs to make a thick, insulating mattress for our sleeping-bags. The arrangement was far more comfortable than the cramped, frosty tent. We fell asleep with the comforting knowledge that one more day's travel would bring us to a small Chipewyan village in Saskatchewan called Garson Lake. There, we'd been told, we could purchase supplies from the resident fur trader.

A Chipewyan Settlement

Our last day in Alberta began windy and overcast. We huddled by the fire, trying to dodge the wind, and ate the last of our rice and bannock for breakfast. I'd hoped that my snares would provide lunch, but they yielded only one rabbit, which we'd promised to Ki. We hadn't been able to feed him for two days, and he knew this rabbit was his. He watched in dignified anticipation as I skinned it.

It should have been possible to bag a grouse or two during our morning hike—I counted four easy shots in a parklike stand of spruce and tamarack (a type of larch) just west of the provincial border—but I had dropped the .22 and broken its front sight, rendering the gun worthless. In any case chronic hunger was the best motivation to hike a few more miles each day, aiming for that hot meal at the next supply point.

Shortly after noon we reached the west shore of Garson Lake, which straddles the two provinces, and an hour later, the Saskatchewan border. We didn't stop to celebrate, as we were in the middle of snowshoeing across the ten-mile-long lake and the wind had increased substantially. At each point of land extending into the lake, we encountered eight-foot-tall pressure ridges—chaotic hummocks of upheaved ice. They weren't difficult to cross but they broke our trancelike state and reminded us of our growing cold, hunger and exhaustion. Darkness fell quickly, and we squinted towards the horizon trying to spot a welcoming flicker of light from the Garson Lake settlement. Finally, it appeared, and we adjusted our course to head straight for it.

Soon we could hear skidoos, or snowmobiles, and children laughing. Headlights darted up and down a hill in front of the settlement as they raced one another down the slope. We were spotted while still half a mile away, and the headlights raced towards us. Four boys aged about twelve to sixteen pulled up and stared at us with bewildered expressions. 'You're white!' the oldest announced. 'Where did you crash?' They weren't accustomed to anyone but Chipewyan trappers arriving from the west, and the only explanation that made sense to them was that we'd walked out from a plane crash.

Garson Lake consisted of about a dozen cabins, occupied by six Chipewyan families, clustered around a wide skidoo trail. By the time we topped the hill and entered the village our entourage had grown to ten Chipewyan kids, giggling

◀ **Through the Canadian wilderness: a scene that epitomises the challenges faced by the Trans-Canada Expedition.**

and pushing each other out of the way for the privilege of being our closest escort. Ki was not so warmly welcomed, as he challenged every Indian dog he met in the process of establishing 'his' territory.

The trading post turned out to be an unlit cabin with a cold, smokeless stovepipe. The trader had packed up and left the week before, and the nearest stores were in La Loche, thirty miles northeast across Lake La Loche. This was devastating news, since we were totally out of food, and detouring through La Loche would add unnecessary miles to our route.

For the moment we would have to depend on handouts, and we set up camp in the trader's cabin before beginning our hunt for food. By now the villagers knew we had no food, and although none could spare enough to take us as far as La Loche, everyone brought a small contribution to our evening meal. Even Ki wasn't forgotten: a shy eight-year-old boy stole a large moose bone from his father's dogs and appeared in our doorway with his gift.

Quite a crowd gathered in the trader's cabin, and the adults, through their bilingual children, plied us with questions about life in the United States. Some had never heard of our country. They knew of cities to the south, but weren't aware of another nation 'down there'. In fact, the whole concept of separate countries was foreign to them. When I drew pictures of skyscrapers, one boy shouted, 'New York! Rod Stewart!' Rock'n'roll: the universal language.

After our hosts dispersed, Pete and I studied the map and debated our dilemma. The thirty-mile trail to La Loche was evidently well packed and frequently travelled, but this didn't solve our food shortage.

The next day a solution appeared out of the sky with the arrival of one of the rare flights from La Loche. The pilot of the single-engine Beaver was to fly a family to La Loche, with a return planned for the same afternoon. I could hitch a ride and bring back the food we needed for the hike, while Pete stayed behind to take advantage of Garson Lake's photo opportunities.

La Loche was a good-sized village of about 1,200 Chipewyans and a dozen or so white teachers, nurses, government employees and Hudson's Bay Company staff. On landing at the terminal—a mobile home next to a bulldozed runway—I didn't stop to sightsee but rushed to purchase enough food for a two-day hike. I was back at the terminal in an hour, only to learn that ice fog had cancelled any further flights that day. 'Come back tomorrow,' the pilot advised, 'and we'll see if we can't get in the air.'

With nothing else to do, I ambled over to George LaPrize's café, which serves the best (and only) burgers in town. The buns drip with grease and the french

A typical modern Indian settlement in northern Canada, where for several months of the year skidoos replace cars as the best means of transport. ▶

fries likewise are limp and translucent. But fat is what the body craves in temperatures of –30° or less; a normal fast-food burger would taste as dry as sawdust. As I happily scoffed down the food, a barrel-chested man introduced himself as Ron McCormick, the local parole officer. On hearing of my plight, he invited me to spend the night in his trailer.

Skidoo by Moonlight

▲ **Riding off into the sunset on a skidoo... The modern way may be less romantic than the old, but it involves much less hard work.**

Next morning there was still too much ice fog to risk flying, so Ron suggested an alternative plan. A trapper from Garson Lake was in La Loche picking up a fifty-gallon drum of gasoline for the settlement. The drum was already lashed to a toboggan, hitched to his skidoo. All was ready for departure—except the trapper, who Ron suspected was by now too drunk to drive back to Garson Lake.

Ron directed me to a tarpaper-covered two-room cabin in the centre of town. Frozen laundry hung on a clothes line above two ancient dog kennels. Inside, an obese Chipewyan woman stopped skinning rabbits long enough to point out the trapper, who was indeed past the point of navigating a skidoo anywhere. He was delighted to have me finish his errand so he could proceed with his binge.

I had never driven a skidoo before, and had only a vague idea of the trail back to Garson Lake. Since I'd planned to fly back, I was without map or compass. It was past 3pm, so I would make most of the thirty-mile trip—twelve miles across the lake and eighteen through the bush—in the dark. But I was anxious about Pete, so I bade Ron farewell and yanked the starter cord. Ron pulled off his finely crafted caribou mittens and offered them to me, saying, 'They're Eskimo. I got them when I was in the Northwest Territories. Take them. How are you gonna write to me if you freeze your hands off?'

My problems began on the far shore of the lake, near a three-cabin mini-settlement called La Loche West. The lake bank was so steep I couldn't top it with my load. Six times I raced towards it from different directions, getting three-quarters of the way up only to stall and slide back down. Finally an elderly Indian, hearing the commotion, walked to the bank from his cabin and wordlessly pointed downshore. A few hundred yards further on was another trail, where I topped the crest on the first attempt.

Four miles down this narrow, crooked trail, the toboggan swung wide on a tight turn and rolled. Fortunately the drum didn't break its lashings and tumble down the embankment, but there was no way I could right the load alone. Angry and embarrassed, I unhitched the snowmobile and went for help. Back at La Loche West I met Narsis Janvier, whose father, Joe, had directed me earlier. The father and son quickly agreed to follow me to the stranded toboggan, which we soon righted.

The three of us stood there in the moonlight, awkwardly smiling at each other. I wanted to compensate them for the gas their skidoo had burned, but thought they might be offended by an offer of money. The white man's giving cash as thanks is often resented in the northern bush. If I'd had my pack, I could have offered a handful of ammunition, a standard expression of thanks.

Finally I remembered the chocolate bars in my grocery bag and passed two to each of them. Narsis broke the ice: 'Chocolate is the best!' he pronounced while munching the frozen bar.

We shook hands and parted friends. Before going on I filled the gas tank by siphoning fuel from the drum. My hands were drenched with gas and burned in the night air; once I fumbled and dropped the funnel in the snow. Retrieving it, I finished the siphoning, started up and continued down the trail.

Ten miles short of Garson Lake the engine died. The sudden silence was profound, broken only by my unprintable cursing. Scared to delay, I grabbed the groceries and jog-trotted on down the trail. After what I guessed was five miles, I became certain I'd taken the wrong turn somewhere. 'I'll just top this hill, then turn around and try another trail,' I thought aloud.

At the foot of the hill, a magnificent white tablecloth stretched to the horizon beneath the moon: Garson Lake. I ran down the slope towards a single faint light about a mile away. It came from the trader's cabin, and some time after 2am I flung open the door. Pete, lying in bed in his long underwear reading a novel, looked shocked to see me.

'Don't even come looking for me; that's OK,' I chided.

'Dave! I thought you were in La Loche having a good time!' In fairness to Pete, he had hardly been enjoying himself. He had eaten nothing but rice and bannock during my thirty-six-hour absence.

The residents were understanding about my problems with the skidoo when I explained things in the morning. Two young trappers offered to haul our packs as far as La Loche West while we hiked there on foot. On the way there they would stop to repair the skidoo, which one of them could drive back to Garson Lake.

When we met them on the trail at noon, they had fixed the machine and had a roaring fire waiting. Over mugs of heavily sweetened tea they explained the mechanical problem: water had got into the fuel line and frozen. I remembered dropping the funnel in the snow while siphoning and not bothering to dry it afterwards. I was too embarrassed to admit my mistake.

We caught up with our packs at Narsis and Joe's cabin around suppertime. I had no more chocolate to give them, so we tried to repay their hospitality by helping them decipher some paperwork: government documents, bank statements and so on. It turned out that Narsis was behind on his skidoo payments because he didn't understand interest. Try explaining that to a man who prides himself on his honesty.

The hike next morning across Lake La Loche was not difficult, and a quarter of a mile from town we spotted Ron McCormick waving to us from the road. As we approached he shouted, 'You boys sure take your time! I've been waiting for ya to join me for burgers since yesterday!' We proceeded directly to George

▲ The edge of the great boreal forest, where a land of plenty gives way to a 'land of little sticks'.

LaPrize's café for another round of oozing burgers and vinegar-soaked fries. Nor was Ki forgotten, enjoying a feast of bones and table scraps that the waitress sneaked to him outside.

Christmas in the Land of Little Sticks

Our plans to stop only overnight in La Loche soon changed. Christmas was only a week away, and neither of us particularly wanted to spend it on the trail. Our brief layover turned into nine days, with plenty of opportunities to witness the good and bad of life in a Chipewyan town.

The Chipewyans live in settlements throughout northwestern Saskatchewan and northeastern Alberta. They are a small, subarctic tribe, whom the Inuit, or Eskimo, have pushed south out of the bountiful tundra into the 'land of little sticks'—a thinly forested belt of muskeg where game and timber are poor.

La Loche is the northernmost town in Saskatchewan that can be reached by road. As in most Indian bush towns some people still make a living by traditional means—trapping, trading, ice fishing—but most live on welfare. Although selling liquor in this part of the country is illegal, alcoholism is a way of life. Children begin by drinking mouthwash, aftershave or vanilla extract; later they advance to sniffing gasoline. The really far-gone consume antifreeze and shoe polish; one old-timer told me that the best high was achieved by drinking melted record albums. (He used only old 78rpm records as 'the new ones don't work.')

John, a senior member of the Chipewyan council, honoured Pete and me with an invitation to their Christmas party. The atmosphere was festive, and apparently the liquor ordinance was being ignored in honour of the holiday. As I sat playing cards and sharing a bottle of rye with John and some other older Indians, I grew bold enough to ask how a strong, proud people could destroy itself with alcohol.

It was probably foolish to expect an in-depth answer under the circumstances, but John did his best. He related his people's history of being kicked around by stronger tribes and told how plagues of smallpox and tuberculosis had devastated his father's generation. 'The government builds us houses and gives us money because they say we can't make enough from a trapline to feed a family. We survived the wars and the disease, and now they say that we can't support ourselves. What else is there to do but drink?'

Such unhappiness, however, was not our dominant impression of La Loche—quite the opposite. People went out of their way for us, and we were the beneficiaries of all sorts of bush wisdom. Through Ron McCormick we met Jim Perry and George Frederick, schoolteachers who spent much of their spare time training sled dogs and gill-netting through the four-foot lake ice. Pete and I sometimes helped them with their daily net checks. It was some of the coldest, most miserable work I'd ever experienced.

▲ A Canadian Indian trapper, his complexion ruddied by exposure to the extreme cold in which he works all winter.

To reach the net lines, you had to chop through the foot of ice that formed overnight in established holes. Someone then had the unfortunate job of reaching into the water, perhaps to his shoulder, to catch the line with a hooked stick. He began to pull, walking backwards across the ice to haul net and fish out.

As the net spread out on the ice, two other people stood on either side to remove the thrashing fish, working quickly yet carefully so as not to tear the fragile netting. The most difficult part of the job was untangling, with frozen fingers, the sections of net snarled by fish flailing around in it. The prize was usually worth the effort, though. George and Jim often netted over a hundred pounds of fish daily, saving the whitefish and walleye for their own dinners and feeding the pike and other rough fish whole to their dogs.

Our friendship with Jim and George, and their passion for training sled dogs, led to a major change in our expedition. When we first toured their kennels Jim remarked, 'You know, you two are crazy to haul those packs when a team of dogs could do the work for you.' We talked about the possibility of acquiring a dog team, but the whole thing seemed so complicated. We would need a sled, harnesses, dog food—and purebred racing Siberian huskies cost a minimum of 500 dollars each.

Siberians are bred to pull light loads at high speed, but Jim convinced us that what we needed were freight dogs: wolf-husky crosses, thick-skulled, 100-pound brutes that could pull tremendous weight over long distances. Indians had been using such dogs for generations, but current economic reality had replaced freight teams with noxious skidoos. The working dog team was becoming a thing of the past.

Jim knew one old trapper, however, who refused to abandon tradition. Just now he was up north somewhere with his dogs, but he was expected back shortly. 'I'll bet,' Jim speculated, 'that if you catch him in a good mood, that cranky old fool would sell you some dogs.' The idea of having a dogsledding outfit ourselves was beginning to seem more feasible.

By the time the trapper did return, we only needed two more animals, for in the meantime we had been given a couple of year-old pups. They had never worked in harness, and their legs sometimes got tangled when they walked. But they were adventurous and, weighing in at 100 pounds already, they showed potential for great strength. We named the caramel-coloured pup Scotch, and the brown and white one Wheels.

Pete then managed to purchase two more dogs from the old trapper for a bargain price of thirty-five dollars, including chains and harnesses. These dogs were half the size of the pups, about fifty pounds each, with more mongrel and less husky blood. Their personalities were even more strikingly different. These were seasoned trail dogs, survivors who would fight their team-mates to the death for scraps of food. They had lived by the whip, never knowing affection.

Silver was the most foul-tempered mongrel we had ever seen. Whiskey was a one-eyed lead dog who walked a little crookedly in harness. Unlike Silver, who only became meaner with each lashing, Whiskey's spirit had been broken and he cowered when he saw the whip. Given a chance, though, his urge to kill was equal to Silver's.

Scotch and Wheels, in contrast, acted as if they were still teething; had it been spring, they would have passed the time chasing butterflies. Putting these two Bambis together with seasoned killers seemed a terrible mismatch. Then there was Ki: how would he view this infringement on his territory?

The Catholic priest of La Loche donated a whip. We weren't sure we wanted it, but the priest had travelled thousands of miles by dogsled in his younger days and assured us we would need it. The braided moosehide was long, thin and greasy-black, a veteran of many freight teams, and I wondered if I'd ever be able to use it to lash the back of a dog.

We scrounged the remaining harnesses and chains here and there. Though chains may sound sinister, they were used merely to confine the dogs when they were unharnessed, so they wouldn't run off or attack each other.

Jim provided an old handmade six-foot birchwood toboggan, and with his help we spent an afternoon sanding its bottom and rerigging its sides with fresh hemp. Like the ribs of a canoe, its rope framework was the supporting structure for the elongated open canvas sack that would hold our food and gear. Jim added a touch of new technology to this venerable vehicle, gluing strips of Teflon to the underside to decrease its drag against the snow.

Our last evening in town was frantic with packing, preparation and nervous apprehension. Pete organised 250 pounds of food and equipment—half the weight being frozen fish for dog food—while I sewed canvas bags and cut strips of untanned moosehide for snowshoe and harness repairs and general lashing-down.

Our personal gear, too, had evolved from modern to traditional materials. The boots were gone, and our feet were cradled in moosehide moccasins, made to order by a Chipewyan woman from heavy hides she had tanned herself and stitched together in the traditional wraparound design, bound with moosehide thongs. The upper had a canvas top that reached to midcalf and acted like a gaiter to prevent snow from packing beneath the trouser legs. The moccasins were extremely light and conformed to the shape of our feet; insulated with felt insoles and liners, duffle socks and three pairs of woollen socks, they were much more comfortable than the bulky boots. Also our mitts were now of caribou skin, moosehide and beaver. I had even trimmed my parka hood with strips of black bear fur. We were properly equipped, we thought, for breaking in our green team of dogs, and we were eager to resume our journey.

◀ **This team of sled dogs has just polished off a well-earned meal after hauling a trapper's belongings to his remote cabin.**

▲ **While Wheels looks on enviously, Silver finds that one of the author's new moccasins makes a wonderful pillow.**

▲ **The magnificent snowy owl, with its heavily feathered talons, here showing its camouflage to best advantage in the middle of winter.**

◀ **In common with many other small animals, the ermine knows that snow is a remarkable insulator. This animal has spent the night in a cosy snow hole.**

Adapting to Winter

By the time that the bitter cold of the Canadian winter has taken hold in earnest, many animals will have chosen the simplest response—retreat. Migratory birds will have flown far south; bighorn sheep will have descended from mountain heights into valleys where they can find grass; and bears, both brown and black, will have retreated to comfortable dens where they can sleep through the worst of the weather.

But there are also many animals that do not flee the winter, and have adapted to cope with it in a number of remarkable ways. The snowshoe hare, for example, has exceptionally broad and furry hind feet, which act like snowshoes, allowing it to run at high speed across newly fallen snow. This hare, in common with several other northern creatures, also has the ability to change its colour. In summer, it hides from its enemies by adopting a coat of mottled brown; in winter, it turns pure white to match its surroundings.

Predators, however, have learned the very same trick. The Arctic fox and the small but ferocious ermine both become snowy white, the better to pursue their prey in a monochrome landscape. By contrast, the snowy owl and the polar bear—the largest predator in the Americas—don't bother changing their wintry attire. Both spend so much of their time in the far north that they remain white all year round.

▲ Winter has arrived, but only one of these Arctic foxes has made the transition from summer grey to winter white. Its unfortunate companion, probably a juvenile, will need to work much harder to catch its food.

◀ This bighorn sheep, having passed the summer leaping about the mountain peaks, will spend its winter in the valleys below.

Not dead, but cooling off! Polar bears have such warm coats that they sometimes have difficulty staying cool in the summer. ▼

▲ Preparing for winter: a brown bear scrapes armfuls of dry leaves into its den, where they will provide insulation and bedding.

◀ An adroit sideways bound on its large hind feet takes this snowshoe hare just out of reach of a hungry mountain lion's outstretched paws.

CHAPTER 4

Strong Medicine

DECEMBER 29 WAS OUR FIRST DAY as dogsled masters. The toboggan was loaded and the dogs were in harness. A small crowd had gathered to witness our departure. Since we hadn't found reliable directions through the hills, we'd decided to take the more direct route, 100 miles south by road to Île-à-la-Crosse.

With Pete out ahead of the team and me behind, I slapped the whip and yelled '*Marsh!*' (from the French *marcher*—'to walk', and sometimes corrupted to 'mush!'). Ki yawned. Our mismatched team lurched forward, barely missing the skidoo ahead of us. Within the first twenty yards it was apparent that the dogs would not respond to our feeble commands of '*Gee!*' (right) and '*Haw!*' (left), though we'd been told Whiskey knew them. Over the next half-mile through town we managed to create three dogfights, overturn the toboggan twice, collide with another toboggan, get stuck in a snowdrift, and probably cause more than one terrified child to wet his pants.

The Chipewyans obviously found the show great fun. We, on the other hand, were never more eager to get out of town. The dogs fought far more than they pulled, and we tried everything we could think of to stop them. Finally—and it didn't take long—we resorted to the whip.

We had them harnessed in what seemed like the logical pulling order, but it caused problems from the start. One-eyed Whiskey was in the lead, the position he was supposedly trained to, with Scotch second, Silver third and Wheels in the 'wheel' spot, closest to the toboggan. By alternating the veterans and pups, we had hoped to minimise fighting between the old dogs and goofing-off by the youngsters. Most important, we hoped that if the pups had nothing to do but watch a master sledder just ahead, they might get the hang of their job.

It was a good idea in theory, a disaster in practice. Since Wheels hadn't yet caught on to pulling, every time the toboggan lurched forward he got smacked on the rump. This prompted him to run forward, thereby butting Silver squarely in the backside. When this happened, Silver dived for Wheels's throat; poor Wheels would scream and try to climb onto the toboggan, naturally jerking the two foremost dogs back in their harnesses.

To Scotch, this signal meant playtime or rest time, but the lead dog, Whiskey, was having none of it and proceeded to give Scotch a harsh lesson in sledding etiquette. Eventually they would collapse, not from defeat in battle but simply from exhaustion and pain from us beating them, and another fight was over. Pete and I would stare at each other in shock, horrified at the violence we had just witnessed and inflicted. Neither of us had ever struck an animal with anything but a folded newspaper; now, if we had not intervened, ignoring our pet-loving past, we would sooner or later have had dead dogs. Yet the experience always left us with sour mouths and nagging guilt.

Ki wasn't crazy about the new situation, either. He sometimes tried to butt into the lead, huffing and snorting like a make-believe sled dog, but the real workers ignored him. Between brawls we did manage to advance a few miles, though our progress wasn't impressive: twelve miles the first day, fifteen the second. Rather than following a pristine trapper's trail or an expanse of lake ice, we were travelling on the unromantic shoulder of a road, the gravel-strewn snow dragging like sandpaper against the bottom of the toboggan. But this was the only practical route at present. The part of north-central Saskatchewan we were traversing on the way to the Manitoba border is lowland, often marshy, and heavily laced with lakes and rivers. So we were stuck with the road as far south as Île-à-la-Crosse, where we would pick up a network of trails east to Pinehouse Lake and thence to La Ronge.

We spent our first night out of La Loche in an empty cabin at Post Creek, home to half a dozen families who make fence posts for a company in Saskatoon. Both Pete and I felt ill, maybe in reaction to too much celebrating prior to our departure—or maybe it was just the year-end blues. The dogs acted up nearly as badly the second day, but we made it as far as Bear Creek settlement, where we

A brief rest on the trail for a hot cup of tea. Pete—alias Father Christmas, with his red coat and frosted beard—gives the dogs a quick snack too. ▼

spent a couple of hours with two old Chipewyan men. The one who spoke a little English told us an amazing tale, which went something like this:

> Be careful crossing ice. Giant green frog monsters live in some lakes. They make traps by thawing the ice and covering the hole with snow. If you fall through, they eat you.

▲ **This Indian trapper has every reason to look pleased with himself as his head pokes out from a mountain of valuable fox and lynx pelts.**

Though we were still feverish the next day, we decided to travel on, but managed only nine miles. Both of us felt sick enough to rest on New Year's Day and we woke refreshed on the 2nd. At last we had a better day: with the dogs performing well, we covered twenty miles, reaching Buffalo Narrows by late afternoon. This was the largest settlement in the area, so we stocked up on supplies at the Hudson's Bay Company post and reloaded the toboggan with sixty pounds of fish for the dogs.

We made minimal progress the two days after leaving Buffalo Narrows, as the dogs went on strike, probably from overfeeding. Eventually, however, we set a hard pace, making twenty-one miles—our record to date—and pulling into Île-à-la-Crosse around 10pm. After setting us up for the night at the Canada Manpower trailer (the ubiquitous social-service agency), a trapper named George Malbuth dragged us off to his house for a party, which ended in the traditional gift exchange.

George had had great luck that winter and was in a generous mood; he offered us lynx and wolverine pelts (which we refused) and insisted we take a bearhide, two lynx traps, a 12-gauge shotgun and ten pounds of moose meat for the dogs. All we had given him was my .22 rifle with the broken sight; I added 400 rounds of ammunition to even things up a bit.

George, like most of the locals, was mostly Cree; we had passed out of Chipewyan country on leaving La Loche. The Cree hold fast to many old customs, and George flattered me by choosing to share one. At the end of the trading session, he placed in my hand a tiny caribou-skin pouch no bigger than a man's thumb: an Indian lynx lure. It would bring good fortune to his *kiskwa kistimugiman tutum* (crazy American friends), he explained.

Like most Indian medicines, the lynx lure is supposed to be forbidden to white men. I didn't know what was inside the tiny bag (George said its powers would be lost if it were opened), but from its smell and feel I guessed some kind of roots. Its faint odour of decaying plants and soil took me deep into the boreal forest, as if I were sleeping on the ground with my face buried in rich humus. That smell is the source of its practical magic: you simply rub it on some sticks near a trap and the sticks act as a lure. George's recent success seemed proof of its effectiveness.

A Hard Trail to Follow

We spent two days repairing gear, baking bannock, making snares, reading, writing and photographing—the usual stopover chores. We looked forward to starting out for Pinehouse the next day; some trappers had just told us about a short cut that trimmed the distance to sixty miles, almost due east. We planned to make it a three-day run: eighteen miles the first day to a couple of Cree cabins on the Pine River, twenty-one miles the next to Senyk Lake, and another twenty-one miles by winter road to Pinehouse Lake on the third.

The first day went well, though we didn't quite make it to the cabins. The dogs pulled like champions early in the day, even with our heaviest load yet (280 pounds). Around four in the afternoon they got baulky, but we pushed on. Around 10.30pm we hit a large lake; it was clear the dogs could go no further, even though Pete had found the cabins by scouting a mile or so ahead.

We spent a comfortable night on a bed of pine boughs. By now our winter camping routine was pretty well set, each of us seeing to our preferred chores. We'd travel until 7 or 8pm, perhaps as late as ten if the dogs were running well.

◀ **Cree Indians building their base camp for the winter trapping season. Canvas will later be draped over the wooden framework, and spruce boughs will be laid on the ground to provide a dry, fragrant floor.**

After we had both unhitched and fed the dogs, Pete did most of the wood-collecting—about two hours' work, whether we camped or stayed in a cabin—while I cut the wood, tended the fire and cooked (about another two hours in all). I then set the snares and we retired, with perhaps a few minutes to read or chat. Breaking camp in the morning was time-consuming, too, with game to clean (if we were lucky) and breakfast to cook. Generally we didn't get on the trail until around 11am, but we were constantly learning new tricks to speed our pace.

On the second day, our progress dropped to about ten miles, and on the next day even less, for by then it was snowing heavily and the trail was hard to follow. Late that day we crossed an unnamed lake and when we found a trapper's tent at the edge of the wind-blown muskeg, our frozen moccasins persuaded us to camp there. On the morning of Friday the thirteenth, we found that the trail ended half a mile south of the tent, but we decided to push on south to search for the winter road to Pinehouse—about ten miles away, we'd been told. But after

▲ **In this modern Cree painting, a wetigo gorges itself on whole beavers.**

The Wetigo—Monster of the Forest

According to several subarctic Indian tribes, a ferocious monster stalks the wilds in the depths of winter. It stands over 20 feet tall, has a heart made of ice and eyes that are set in pools of blood. It leaves a trail of blood wherever it goes and, worst of all, it has terrible, jagged teeth with which it feeds on living flesh—especially human flesh. Different tribes have slightly different names for this monster—windigo, wetigo, or witiko—but all agree that it inspires terror wherever it lurks.

The wetigo, so the story goes, was once a hunter—a perfectly normal man—who one day lost his way in winter and, in order to avoid starving to death, was forced to eat human flesh. This act of cannibalism turned him into a monster that has remained in the wilderness ever since, preying on other human beings.

Since then, whenever people fail to return from the wilderness, they are said to have been eaten by the wetigo. Furthermore, the Indians say that anyone who eats human flesh—and in the ferocious subarctic winter the scarcity of food has sometimes forced people to contemplate this horrendous act—will himself turn into a wetigo.

progressing only three, we hit heavy bush and had to retreat to the tent. We would have to backtrack thirty miles to the winter road from Île-à-la-Crosse.

Now the dogs were out of food. Snow fell overnight and on the next morning we got a late start. The temperature dropped fifty degrees in the late afternoon to almost –40°F.

The dogs were already weak with hunger. At half past five, Whiskey collapsed in convulsions. For the next hour I carried him while Pete harnessed himself in the lead spot and helped to pull. By half past six, Whiskey was so bad that we shot him. At least we were spared the task of feeding him to his fellow dogs, as we feared he might be diseased.

Around 10pm, halfway across another unnamed lake, the dogs gave up. We unharnessed them and dragged the toboggan to shore ourselves, leaving it and the dogs there while we walked to the town of Beauval and gorged on a hot dinner at Rose's Café. We left some rabbits we'd snared earlier for the dogs—they were the first game we'd got in days.

Leonard, the café owner, helped us to retrieve the dogs and toboggan the following day with his truck and skidoo. We stayed in Beauval three more days, both of us recovering from flu and Pete getting treated for blood poisoning from a cut hand as well. We worked a bit in the café for our keep, bought supplies, and gave the dogs a well-deserved rest.

A Run of Bad Luck

One night in the café I was brooding about our run of bad luck since Île-à-la-Crosse. My medicine bag didn't seem to be working. I glanced up in surprise to see Vic, an old white trader from La Loche, and over coffee I quizzed him. 'Say, Vic,' I began, 'you've been living with these people most of your life, eh?'

'Hell, yes,' he replied.

'Well, then, tell me.' I set the lure before him. 'Ever seen one of these?'

'Goddamn! How the hell'd a kid like you get ahold of that? That stuff's powerful; don't go ...' Vic's warning was cut off as a Cree woman yanked me from my seat and hustled me into the back room. Her eyes burned into mine as she whispered, 'Fool! Stupid white fool. That medicine was made for you alone. You show your medicine to that man like it was a joke. You have made the Maker angry. Wetigo [a forest monster] will not leave your camp now'.

She told me that the only way to make peace with the Maker was to take the medicine deep into the bush and bury it in a safe place, along with a gift. 'Tell him you are sorry. Tell the Maker that you are white and do not know about these things. This is the only way to drive Wetigo from your camp.'

The encounter impressed me, but I wasn't ready to be scared. We set off for Pinehouse on the twentieth. We rested for three days in a cabin at Pinehouse Lake, Bing Crosby's old fishing haunt, and then travelled on again to La Ronge.

The dogs were finally looking like a team, with Silver at least adequate in his new role as leader. The pups had lost most of their baby fat and were amazingly strong. They no longer fought, and now that they were used to us and their roles we could at last show them affection.

Outside La Ronge, a modestly booming resort town of five thousand, the dogs were so excited by the new scents that I had to ride the last three miles to keep them down to a reasonable pace.

Our ill-luck continued. We spent February 1, the halfway mark of our winter travel, flying in a Cessna to check our proposed route to Flin Flon via Wapawekka Lake, only to find that the trail ended after forty miles. Most winters this route is as hard-packed as a highway, but it hadn't been used that year. So now we were condemned to the drudgery of 170 miles to Flin Flon by road.

After checking around in vain for some fresh sled dogs, we left La Ronge on February 4, looking forward to a few days of easy travel. Instead, we got winds from a southern Saskatchewan blizzard. And the dirt road had just been scraped by snowploughs, leaving mostly bare gravel to drag the toboggan over.

We covered a scant twenty-five miles in two days, and then decided that Pete would have to hitchhike back to La Ronge to buy wheels for the toboggan. The dogs simply wouldn't be able

Pete and Ki offer moral support out front, but have a harder time keeping ahead of the team now that the toboggan has been fitted with wheels. ▼

to drag it over gravel for hundreds of miles. When Pete got back that night, I tentatively raised the question of our miserable luck since receiving the lynx lure in Île-à-la-Crosse. He and I agreed that a person makes his own luck—but I was beginning to wonder.

On February 8 my snares were still empty, and at last I knew I had to bury that damn lure, but I had no suitable gift that I could bury with it. Then, as I turned from the last empty snare, I saw a flash of white in the moonlight and heard the thrashing of a rabbit in the snare. Immediately I realised what it was: this was the gift.

Ki sat at the edge of the ravine as I dug through the snow and moss with my bare hands. Carefully removing the braided wire from its neck, I placed the still-warm rabbit in the hole, curled as if asleep. I sniffed the lure for the last time, placed it between the rabbit's forelegs, then covered the grave with moss and snow.

That rabbit, the first I had snared in many days, marked a turning point. Within the next couple of days I caught four more rabbits and, though there were some rough spots to come, our fortunes certainly changed dramatically for the better.

To the Shores of Lake Winnipeg

The last two months of winter 1978, February 4 to April 4, were a relatively uneventful slog—330 miles in all, from La Ronge to the western shore of frozen Lake Winnipeg in Manitoba—with a three-week break in Flin Flon, taking in such north-country diversions as snow carnivals, dog races, ice-hockey games and an annual trappers' festival. Mainly, though, we just ground out the miles along snow-covered roads and lakes.

Game was scarce in the scrubby spruce forests of western Manitoba. Sometimes the only food for the dogs was meagre scraps of fish scavenged from abandoned commercial fishing sites. Whenever we spotted circling ravens, Ki would race ahead to chase the birds away and guard the pile of fish entrails from their diving raids until the rest of us caught up.

Children enjoying a spontaneous game of ice hockey in Flin Flon. This highly popular sport probably originated among British soldiers stationed in Canada in the 1860s. ▼

March's climbing temperatures made travel increasingly miserable. The added friction of pulling over wet snow often exhausted the dogs after just a few miles. Our feet in waterlogged moccasins strained to lift snowshoes weighted with soggy snow. All winter we had complained of the bitter cold—now we moaned that it was too hot!

But a final daunting stretch of winter travel loomed just ahead: a 120-mile crossing of Lake Winnipeg, which promised some of the journey's most spectacular sledding. Lake Winnipeg is among Canada's largest. A major resort area in summer, in winter it represented a formidable obstacle, with fierce winds, huge pressure ridges to negotiate and few means of resupplying.

These 120 miles would be the last covered by dogsled; on Lake Winnipeg's eastern shore, at the mouth of the Berens River, the expedition would make the transition back to canoe travel. There, too, we would celebrate reaching Mile 2,400—just past the halfway point of the entire journey. There could be no further dawdling now, however; we had to make it across the lake before the spring thaw began in earnest—which could be any time after mid-April.

Last stop before the crossing was the village of Grand Rapids, where we reorganised our supplies for speed, gave a talk to high-school students and were entertained by Royal Canadian Mounted Police Sergeant Dominic French and his Inuit wife, Alice. These two were local celebrities: Alice had published a book about her childhood in the Arctic, and Dom had twice been chosen by the RCMP as royal escort to the Queen.

Ice Sledding

On April 7, as Dom and Alice French stood on the shore of Lake Winnipeg and waved goodbye, I glanced over my shoulder for a last look at Grand Rapids, then turned to survey an expanse of ice stretching across the horizon and the dogs strung out ahead of the toboggan. Before us lay the last leg of our 1,200-mile winter trek. Any day now the temperature could rise above freezing and leave us stranded in a sea of slush. Though the ice was still six feet thick, it's nearly impossible to drive a team over wet snow.

I doubted we'd make many miles that first day. Pete and I had just recovered from flu and were quite weak. The dogs were also questionable. Wheels had sprained a leg two weeks earlier and had had to be replaced. We traded him for an expressionless Indian dog, whose strength and uncomplaining nature won him the workhorse wheel position. He didn't have a name and for weeks we simply referred to him as 'the new guy'—so, naturally, New Guy became his permanent name. Silver also became worn out a few days before Grand Rapids. To run him further in harness would have killed him, so we reluctantly retired him.

That left only Scotch from our original team. We'd promoted him to lead dog, which suited his ego just fine. For a third, we borrowed a bony Irish setter-cross called Jack, who looked more at home in front of a fireplace than on a freight team. Yet he turned out to work surprisingly well in harness, and the others accepted him immediately, which is uncommon. Usually a new dog must endure a week of fighting and harassment while a new pecking order is established. Ki remained the loafer of the bunch, usually running out in front with Pete, sometimes dropping in line ahead of Scotch to make believe *he* was lead dog.

Conditions were good that day, and we covered a respectable twenty-two miles before stopping to camp at half past seven on Long Point, a huge dagger of land jutting a third of the way out into Lake Winnipeg. Pete began setting up camp in a clump of scrub willows, while I unharnessed and chained the dogs, tossing each a frozen fish. Scotch held the frozen fish in his front paws and ate it from head to tail. Rooting around in the snow for a last crumb and finding nothing more, he looked up at me with a hint of betrayal in his chocolate-brown eyes.

Pete and I splurged on our own supper with grilled cheese sandwiches, enjoying the rare luxury of store-bought bread. The temperature hung around zero and our goosedown bags on spruce-bough beds were warm and comfortable.

Next morning, after a leisurely breakfast of pancakes, tea and moose sausage, we set off in the hope of reaching the tip of Long Point, twenty-four miles east, by the end of the day. That afternoon, though, we were pinned down by a whiteout blizzard after covering twenty-one miles and had to set up a hasty camp. As night fell, the temperature rose and the snow changed to rain, which continued all night. I slept little, rolling from one puddle to another and dodging the stream of ice water that trickled through the breathing hole in my sleeping-bag. That morning we were too cold, wet and depressed to bother with breakfast.

▲ A tumbledown shack—a valuable haven for travellers caught out in winter storms.

We'd heard a rumour back in Grand Rapids about a few old cabins near the end of Long Point, about four miles from our present camp. This sounded like the most attractive immediate prospect, so we stumbled along the shoreline, squinting through the steady drizzle for a sign of them, until finally Pete shouted, *'Cabin!'*

Three structures stood (more or less) in an overgrown clearing among the pines. Two had no roofs at all; the best one had three walls and half a roof, which, if braced, could make it a passable shelter. Poking around, we found miscellaneous pieces of burnt-out wood stoves, which we jury-rigged into a functioning stove. Set up near the sagging entryway, it sent smoke drifting out where the caved-in roof had been. Firewood came from the walls of an adjoining cabin.

We spent two days huddled in this makeshift lean-to. Our dripping sleeping-bags hung near the stove by day but, alas, absorbed more smoke than heat. At

▲ **Lead-dog Scotch needs to be coaxed by the author through a jumbled landscape of crevasses and massive pressure ridges on Lake Winnipeg.**

night we bedded down on the floor where there had been a pile of rotting fishnets. Our town treats were gone, and we fell back on standard fare: two meals a day of split pea, potato and salt-pork stew. Our only hope of finding more food lay in a lighthouse forty miles out on the lake. The Royal Canadian Mounted Police had given us permission to raid it, but we couldn't always rely on their advice. They had also said there would be fish caches on Long Point for our dogs, and we'd arranged with them for a 100-pound airdrop of fish. But we'd found no caches and heard no planes.

Dense fog held us on Long Point. Our route angled southeast from the point, and between us and the Berens River settlement lay seventy-five miles of open ice. There were islands, the Sandy Islands chain, at twenty, thirty and forty miles out; the first would be our next camp.

Under ideal conditions, visibility over the ice was ten miles, but for several days it had been almost nil. Proceeding by compass alone left too much risk of missing the islands altogether. We even considered turning back to Grand Rapids, waiting for breakup and canoeing across the lake, but I'd heard horrifying tales of canoe travel on this windswept expanse.

The next morning brought temperatures in the twenties and a blessed cloudless sky. After a final check of the compass, I tapped a whip on the toboggan and shouted, *'Marsh!'*

The pressure ridges were fantastic. The lake looked like a mountain range. Stark blue-white towers rose over giant slabs of ice. From valleys of glaring, eye-searing snow, sheltered from the wind by ice walls, heat rose in shimmering waves. There was no noise here, not even a whistling wind. We meandered between the ridges, inching along and feeling for hidden holes and crevasses that crisscrossed the surface. The dogs baulked in fear of the cracks, jerking back in their harnesses; Scotch refused to lead unless I walked ahead and yanked him along. While the rest of us struggled, Ki played pathfinder, leaping from ridge to ridge as if mocking the harnessed dogs.

Eventually we broke free of the pressure ice and gazed to the horizon across a vast tabletop of snow. Somewhere out there, eighteen miles or so further, was our island. As the day wore on, I began to doubt we would ever find it. It seemed as if we had been shuffling across this featureless desert for weeks. Hours went by with no sign of land, and I fell into the dangerous habit of questioning the compass. But we were still cutting across the wind-carved fishscale pattern in the snow at the same angle. The island *had* to be ahead.

Pete and I both falsely spotted land several times. Each time it turned out to be a low-lying cloud or discoloured pressure ridge. Towards mid-afternoon, though, we sighted three points that refused to dissolve.

Sledding towards a distant speck of land is agony: miles go by beneath your feet and still the island appears no closer. You want to stop and ease your leaden feet, but each step takes you a yard further, and conscience urges you on.

The low-pitched hum of the toboggan sliding over crusted snow, combined with the rhythm of moccasined feet, had a hypnotic effect. If I lagged, the brake

Conifers of the boreal forest dramatically silhouetted against a ravishing winter sunset of pinks and mauves. ▶

rope jerked me forward, an insistent reminder to keep the pace. Occasionally I would glance ahead to see Pete plodding in front of the team, or behind, to make sure that we were keeping a straight course. But most of the time my eyes were lowered, watching the snow slide by underfoot.

Travelling long distances by dogsled requires a certain mindlessness that takes months to learn. You must remain alert for any of a hundred mishaps that can cripple humans or dogs, yet the monotony can only be endured by shutting off thought. Thus eight miles become two, hours become minutes, and torturous days become tolerable—even pleasurable.

The sun was now low in the sky, turning our back-trail into a silver ribbon that unrolled to the horizon. The setting sun painted the snow and the sky exactly the same salmon-pink colour, producing the weird sensation that there was no up or down, left or right.

Three miles from land, just as we could begin to discern individual trees, the dusk faded to darkness. To our surprise, a beacon began to flash, presumably on one of the Sandy Islands chain. Hoping to find an occupied cabin there, we drove the dogs on, but the island was deserted, its only structure a fifty-foot steel tower topped with the beacon, which guided summer boaters round the shoals.

Soon a roaring campfire blaze illuminated the surrounding trees. We gratefully hugged its warmth, letting it saturate to the very core of our bodies: the temperature had dropped well below zero and our sweat-soaked clothes had done little to keep out the cold.

Saved by a Dream

We retired early, ate a dinner of watery moose stew in bed and slept fully clothed, right down to our moccasins. But, even dressed, I slept poorly, as my sleeping-bag was still fairly wet. I spent the night in a shivering ball, my knees drawn up to my chin, and woke to find Pete gone. Bewildered, I got up and followed his tracks through the snow to a small bay on the far side of the island. Six dilapidated cabins dotted a clearing; smoke rose from the one Pete's tracks led to. I found him in front of a massive iron cooking stove. Its fire compartment had rusted away, so he had built his fire in the main oven space, after knocking a hole in the back wall.

This appeared to be an abandoned fishing camp. The cabins looked as though they hadn't been occupied for twenty years or more. As I browsed around his discovery, Pete explained what had led him there. 'I've never been so cold as I was last night. A few hours before sunrise I got up to build a fire, but it was too cold to hold the match. I went back to bed and began to really worry about how cold I was. I dozed for a minute and had a dream: two men dressed like fishermen walked up to my sleeping-bag and one, who called himself Isaac, spoke to me, saying that if I didn't go to the cabins I'd freeze. When they walked away, I woke up and started walking in the same direction they had gone. The dream led me straight to these cabins.'

Then he pointed to a spot on the plank wall above the stove where a name and date were carved. The date was 1846 and the name was Isaac.

While Pete brewed up a welcome pot of tea, I sat down by the stove and began making rabbit snares. I had fashioned so many of them over the winter that I'd got an assembly-line method of production. I fed sections of brass wire across the floor with my right hand while the axe in my left rose and fell in matching rhythm, severing wire at two-foot intervals. Suddenly I heard an odd-sounding 'chop' and looked down at the wire. The end of my thumb, nail and all, lay on the floor. The axe had grazed the corner of the thumb, exposing the bone.

I paced in circles, gripping my hand high in the air and nodding my head up and down, trying to block out the pain. Like other 'nonessentials', the first-aid kit had been left behind to save weight. I pulled my snotty, soot-streaked bandanna from my pocket and threw it into the brewing tea; then, after packing the wound with salt, I wrapped the bandanna tightly round the thumb. I hoped that the salt and the tannic acid from the tea would be enough to overcome any germs.

An hour later we were back on the ice, heading south towards another speck of land on the horizon. This was George Island where, the RCMP had assured us, there was a lighthouse well stocked with emergency supplies. I held my hand above my head and staggered along behind the dogs, grateful for the numbing cold. It was 2am and we were twenty-two miles from the morning's camp when we rounded the point of George Island. Silhouetted against the sky, a line of cabins fronted a lighthouse that cast its cheery beacon in all directions.

We stayed on George Island for two days, resting the dogs and our own weary bodies. In the lighthouse keeper's home we found the food that the mounted police had promised. It was just macaroni, flour, potatoes and rice, but it would be enough to get us to the Hudson's Bay Company trading post at Berens River. We found no first-aid kit, but my thumb survived the hot-tea-and-salt treatment.

A simmering pot of moose-à-la-wilderness. After a day in the icy cold, even this stark fare seems appetising. ▼

It was only another twelve miles to Lake Winnipeg's eastern shore, and then another thirty-five miles south to Berens River. The prospect of mild daytime temperatures prompted us to travel at night, taking advantage of the refrozen surface.

Knowing the dogs were well rested, I allowed myself the luxury of hitching rides now and then. As they marched eastwards with Pete trotting ahead, dodging a few crevasses and checking the compass by flashlight, it was a delight to lie gazing skywards at the pale wash of northern lights; to be lulled to sleep by the soft sound of crunching snow and the gentle sway of the toboggan.

Long past midnight a skidoo headlight appeared in the distance. We met near shore; the driver and his partner, two young Salteaux Indians, were surprised to see us but were friendly. They were from Poplar River, a few miles from our landfall on the eastern shore, and were heading south to buy bootleg for illegal sale on the 'dry' reserves to the north. Assuring us that we were just where our calculations should have brought us, they wished us well on our journey.

The next day we decided to try for Berens River in one push, even though thirty-five miles was twice our daily average. Their bellies full of potatoes, the

◀ The author catches up on the latest news with the occupants of this tank-like winter vehicle.

dogs pulled relentlessly. We met the young smugglers again early in the day, their toboggan sagging under a load of bottles. A little later we met a family of Salteaux driving a huge, heated and enclosed two-track snow machine. After a pleasant chat, they left us with a dozen freshly baked cinnamon rolls. In the warmth of the afternoon sun I lay back on the toboggan, nursing a cup of rye and a cinnamon roll and leafing through an old *Playboy*.

Our winter was over. Behind us lay 2,400 miles of Canada, half our journey. As I lazed in the hot tub that night at Jack Clarkson's boarding house on Berens River, I thought about our faithful sled dogs, whom we would now leave behind. They had pulled us all those miles, often going without food for days, because it was their nature to pull and to please us. Some were already gone, of course: I thought of Whiskey, lying beside a trail in Beauval; Wheels, probably recovering from his sprained leg and now part of a sled team on a Manitoba reserve; Silver, worn out by age and miles, being nursed back to health by an Indian boy in Grand Rapids.

Scotch, who had grown from a goofy pup into a strong and loyal lead dog, would be shipped back to Grand Rapids to become part of an Indian team destined for the traplines, along with New Guy and Jack. Pete and I would fly back to the States for a month or two, to await the breakup of ice on the river and gather the equipment to continue by canoe. Ki was to stay in Berens River while we were gone, looked after by Brother Leach at the Roman Catholic mission. We were sad to leave him, but thought of him as our representative—our link to the trail. It was like leaving part of ourselves in the bush.

▲ **A trapper and his dogs—some people in remote areas still prefer the ancient partnership of man and beast to the modern alternatives.**

The Stalwart Husky—Man's Best Friend

Were it not for one remarkable creature—the sled dog—many pioneering expeditions into the Arctic and Antarctic might never have been possible. Capable of withstanding extremes of cold, strong enough to pull a massive load, and loyal to the death, dogs accompanied many of the greatest polar explorers—notably Roald Amundsen, who in 1911 became the first man to reach the South Pole, and Sir Ernest Shackleton, who set out to cross Antarctica three years later.

In Alaska, Greenland and Canada, sled dogs were the longstanding servants of the Inuit, who used them as a vital means of transport. The Inuit employed various breeds—principally the true Siberian husky, the Alaskan Malamute and the Samoyed, all of them probably descended in part from wolves and often collectively referred to by the general name 'husky'.

The Inuit continued to use huskies widely until the advent of the skidoo, or snowmobile. Nowadays, the dogs are used more for sport than anything else. At the annual Iditarod race in Alaska, for example, teams of up to 18 huskies sprint over 1,100 miles, aiming to complete their arduous journey in only 11 days.

Some people still choose to work with dogs, however; for, as one explorer explains: 'No one could deny that huskies inspired more love and entertainment in isolated groups of men than could be matched by machines.'

◀ **Striking pale blue eyes and distinctive markings identify this dog as a Siberian husky.**

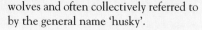

▲ Not exactly a lap dog! This huge Canadian sled dog was one of 69 that Sir Ernest Shackleton took with him on his Trans-Antarctic Expedition of 1914.

Shackleton's dogs watch in bewilderment as their ship, the *Endurance*, is crushed by ice. ▶

Competitors in Alaska's hotly contested Iditarod race gallop towards a first prize of over $30,000—and several huge bowls of dog food! ▼

With each dog able to haul twice its own weight, this team of 12 huskies can pull their Inuit master and all his belongings across hundreds of miles of ice and snow. ▼

CHAPTER 5

Back on the Water

On Saturday, June 3, as the Perimeter Airways Twin Otter taxied down the dirt airstrip to the Hudson's Bay Company post at Berens River, I spotted Pete and Ki waiting by the terminal—a converted motor home. They were a grand sight: Pete in a new Gore-Tex waterproof suit that still smelt of its packing, and Ki sporting newly sun-bleached fur and his usual smug expression.

We set off immediately to see our new gear, most of it donated by a Winnipeg outfitter. Everything was crisp and clean and shiny; anticipation lay in every smooth surface and sharp crease. The final 2,300 miles of our journey would be entirely on water, and our eighteen-foot aluminium canoe lay keel-up, its hull brilliantly unblemished, the canvas spray cover stiff with factory starch. Freshly varnished canoe paddles reflected the sun, fairly begging for the punishment of river rocks.

The next three days were occupied with modifying our canoe for the challenging river travel just ahead: heading upstream from the mouth of the Berens River to its source, 350 miles away in Ontario. At that point we would cross a watershed and go back to downriver running, following the Albany River system all the way to James Bay.

The most important modification to the canoe was the addition of a sailing rig: a ten-foot collapsible aluminium mast, its steel ring bolted to the centre ribs and thwart, and a T-bar atop the mast. The sail itself was fifty-eight inches wide by ninety inches tall, with horizontal poles at the top and bottom to retain its shape and prevent wind spillage.

With ropes running through rings on the mast to the tie-off point in the stern, I could quickly raise and lower the sail, while Pete in the bow controlled the degree of tack. For steering, I threaded a cable through a hole in the stern, to which my paddle could be attached with a quick-release ring.

Our home on the river was further customised with spray-cover hooks bolted to the gunwales, and the bow was painted flat black to reduce the sun's glare. So that our paddle blades might survive their inevitable bashing against rocky river bottoms, we bolted thin sheets of aluminium round the tips.

At last we were ready, our supplies purchased and packed, all the gear strewn before us on the beach in front of the Roman Catholic mission. We had no way of knowing if our modifications would actually work, but with no further excuses to delay us we swung the bow out into the river's current.

The Berens River was first explored in 1767 and later named after Joseph Berens Jr, Governor of the Hudson's Bay Company from 1812 to 1822. Today, canoe groups regularly make the run down the river, but we would be among the first to paddle *up* its length since aeroplanes replaced the old freight brigades in the 1930s. Back then, two Salteaux Indians could ferry more than 1,000 pounds of freight 120 miles upriver to Little Grand Rapids, our next destination, in forty-eight hours. I calculated that it would take Pete and me a week to cover the same distance.

For the first 250 miles from its mouth, the Berens is a relatively fast and powerful river, with rocky, forested banks sometimes steepening into canyons, and many rapids. It flows in and out of lakes all along its course. Then it gradually slows as the country changes, creeping up towards its source through a maze of marshy waterways.

The first few days' travel were joyous, sweeping away our anxious expectations. The sail billowed magnificently before steady tail winds. My view from the stern obstructed by the sail, I did little except steer, while Pete relayed descriptions of river bends and eddies and Ki dozed peacefully on the spray cover. A few minutes' fishing yielded more walleye and pike than we could consume in a day; ducks and geese rose at nearly every bend, promising that we'd never go hungry even if the fish disappeared.

Campsites, too, were luxurious. Granite slabs of Canadian Shield bedrock—some of the oldest rock in the world—ran cleanly to the river's edge, cushioned with sweet-scented beds of pine needles. Most of our camps were long-abandoned Indian camps, marked by Salteaux symbols blazed on trees, and we

◀ **A river splashes over granite slabs of the Canadian Shield—a massive geological formation composed of rocks created when the Earth was in its infancy.**

found rotting dogsleds and tent poles that crumbled at a touch. Some of these surely dated back to freight teams at the turn of the century.

We navigated the rapids and falls we encountered in various ways. Portages round falls were quite simple. Since canoeists coming downriver also had to portage round these barriers, the trails were well trodden. But rapids that could be run by downstream canoeists were another matter. These had long since lost their trails, forcing us to cut our own through the bush.

In spots where the current was too swift to paddle against, yet still navigable, we often managed to ascend by poling. The poles were stout eight-to-ten-foot lengths of spruce. Green wood was essential; a dead, dry pole, though lighter and easier to wield, is not flexible enough. At the end of each rapid we

The author prepares to portage on the Berens River. Canoeing upstream meant that many rapids were simply too difficult to negotiate. ▶

would discard the poles, cutting fresh ones next time. Poling is a dying art. I know of no other canoe skill as difficult to master, and we never became really adept at it.

Where the riverbank terrain permitted, we preferred to line the canoe from shore; the firm granite banks of the Berens were ideal for this technique. We used a 150-foot hemp rope: hemp is much more comfortable in the hands than synthetic rope and holds knots better. Pete would walk ahead to scout the rapid and relay the location of optimum channels. I played out the bow line while holding taut the stern line, allowing the canoe to angle out slightly into midstream. (Reversing this process brings the canoe back to shore.)

▲ The clearly carved inscription left by agent Angus McKay in 1897. Agents worked for the government, liaising with Indians over treaties by which the government could purchase their land.

Our favourite way to ascend rapids, though, was to cheat by sailing up them. Under a strong enough wind our modest square rig allowed us to inch up rapids that were far too swift and deep to pole against. Of course, we could not sail through large standing waves and deep troughs, but we often claimed victory over swift, narrow chutes. In many such cases, portaging would have been more logical, but not nearly as much fun.

The river spoke to us through the names of its rapids and falls. Some were historical: English Rapids, where years back an Englishman had drowned; Conjuring Falls, where Salteaux medicine men beat their drums to conjure spirits; Old Fort Rapids and Old Fort Falls, where the Hudson's Bay Company had built a short-lived fort in 1816. Other names described geographic features: Crooked Falls, Canyon Rapids, Smoothrock Falls, Sharpstone Falls and Pine Island Rapids.

A few miles before reaching Old Fort Falls, where we were to camp, we stopped at Flag Portage. Here, carved into a granite face, as precisely as a tombstone epitaph, was the legend, 'A MKay 1897'. We later learned that the region's first Indian agent, Angus McKay, had camped there with his men on their way upriver to pay treaty money to the Salteaux at Little Grand Rapids. It was June 20, 1897, the day of Queen Victoria's Diamond Jubilee, and in honour of his monarch's sixty-year reign Mr McKay gave his men a holiday and hoisted a Union Jack. Hence, of course, Flag Portage.

The Berens never seemed to rest for long, and our city-softened muscles tired easily, reducing our daily average to just under ten miles. Occasionally the river widened, as if to pause before its next onslaught of white water; then we took advantage of the slackened pace to stretch knotted muscles and reach for a quick handful of raisins. Yet even in the slower current a one-minute break gave the river a chance to regain ground, and we paid for our rest by paddling the same stretch over again.

The forty-five river miles between our camp at Old Fort Falls and the Salteaux village of Little Grand Rapids challenged us with thirty-four major falls and rapids. At many of these the only portage trail was that of the old freight brigades, now lost under fifty years' growth. We spent more time hacking a path with axe and saw than actually portaging.

On Tuesday, June 13, we set camp half a mile above Big Moose Falls. Six hundred yards downriver, a prehistoric red ochre pictograph dominated the lichen-shrouded granite face of the north bank like the sentry of this stretch of river. The country we were entering contained many such cliff paintings, the brooding record of a vanished Indian culture.

In the River's Grip

A few miles before Little Grand Rapids we ran out of supplies. We made the last portage of the day around Night Owl Falls with empty stomachs and aching muscles, but decided to press on. At this moment, thinking a change would be distracting, I agreed to switch positions.

Above a set of rapids, dangerous crosscurrents often lie hidden beneath a deceptively placid surface. Without strong compensating paddle strokes from the sternman, such swirling currents under the surface can easily drag a canoe back into the white water. Pete hadn't paddled from the stern in such a situation before, and as we set off after the falls I realised in horror that I had forgotten to

▲ **Messages, spiritual symbols or just doodles? Some figures are easy to identify, but the radiant circles here may represent the sun or a spirit being.**

Indian Rock Art

THROUGHOUT NORTH AMERICA there are sites where Indians have painted, chipped or carved pictures, symbols and signs on rock faces. Some images are easy to recognise—animals, people fishing or hunting—while others are more abstract and obscure: a four-legged, bird-like figure surrounded by stars might represent a deity, a spirit, or a mysterious combination of ideas. Many of these pictures are very ancient, while others—showing, for example, Spanish conquistadors on horseback—are clearly more recent.

Such pictographs, as they are called, are an intriguing record of a bygone age, but in many cases no one can say with certainty what they mean. Some rock faces are so crammed with images that experts suggest they may have been primitive bulletin boards, used by people leaving messages for each other—about where they were hunting that year, or whether they had encountered any enemies recently.

Certain pictographs, however, defy such explanations and may have been created for spiritual purposes: to invoke a god or the spirit of an animal that was to be hunted; or perhaps to compensate an animal after it had been killed.

warn him about crosscurrents. But it was already too late: we had been sucked into a chute and were being driven backwards towards the lip of the falls.

We paddled like madmen, occasionally glancing at the falls like convicted men at a gallows. For the first minute we managed to hold our position, 200 feet above the falls. During the second minute, as arrows of pain shot through our biceps and backs, we lost two or three canoe lengths. We recovered during the third minute and held the canoe 150 feet from the lip of the falls. Few words were spoken. Every cell in our bodies begged to be free of the river's grip.

At four minutes we lost momentum and were quickly less than 100 feet from the black line where the river ended at the falls with empty space beyond. I started to shout to Pete to leap out before we went over and try to ride down the falls feet first, but halted at the sight of a humped white boulder in midstream. Pete veered the canoe broadside, and in three strokes we crashed up against our stone life raft.

After a few minutes of hugging the rock for dear life, we prepared to make a desperate dash to shore. We would have only seconds before our paddles grabbed open air over the falls. Pete crouched in the bow holding the coiled rope, ready to jump for the nearest tree. From the stern, I released my hold on our rock and leaned hard on my paddle. The bow struck the riverbank with a concussion that nearly threw me from the canoe; Pete leaped for a spruce, then held us fast with the bow rope. For the next half an hour we just sat, exhausted, on the bank and watched water cascade over the lip of the falls, no more than forty feet away.

The day after our close call with Night Owl Falls we pulled the canoe up to the last portage before Little Grand Rapids. While skipping along the portage trail in anticipation of hot baths and store-bought food, I braked in midstride at the sound of shrill laughter, causing the canoe to sway on my shoulders. We rounded a bend and came face to face with two women who appeared to have just left a picnic in a city park. We exchanged brief stares, then one of them—dressed in polyester slacks, short-sleeved blouse, floppy hat and sandals—shrieked and turned to flee, and it occurred to us belatedly how we must look, and smell, to anyone not used to bush travel.

Their husbands approached cautiously, armed with fishing rods. I advanced with my right hand extended, which they ignored, tightening their grips on their fishing rods and standing their ground. Were we going to rush their women? Pete by now was struggling to keep a straight face.

Five minutes later all six of us were downing cold beers and laughing over the episode. Winnipeg suburbanites, they explained that this was their first experience with the wilderness. After expressing our appreciation for the beers, Pete and I left.

Just before Little Grand Rapids, the Berens River enters windswept Family Lake—the last obstacle between us and hot baths. A fierce tail wind bowed our sail as we headed across, leaving Pete mostly awash in the bow. This was a real road test; never before had we tried our sail design on such a large body of water. The mast could snap, the sail could tear, or the canoe could flip under the stress of a sharp turn.

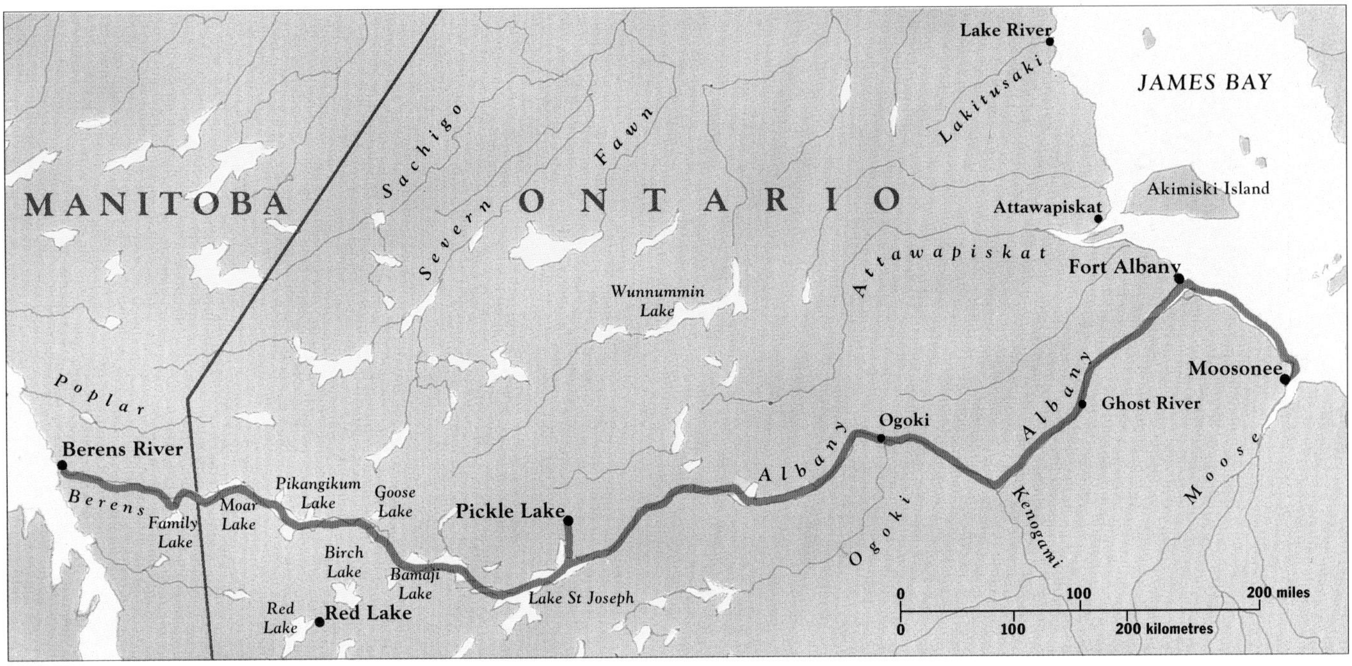

▲ **The Trans-Canada Expedition's canoeing route from Lake Winnipeg to Moosonee, on James Bay.**

Pete shouted over the spray that we should drop sail, but that would be too risky in such a high wind. The weight shift needed to lower sail would be more apt to roll the canoe over than the thrust of continuing under full sail. A hundred yards to our port side, two gnarled pines grasped footholds in the cracks of a ten-yard-long island of granite. Landing there seemed the best bet just then, so I yelled, 'Take in six inches on the right!' Pete whirled to trim the sail while I heaved against the rudder shaft to make a sharp left-hand turn towards the tiny island.

A four-foot whitecapped wave slammed Pete in the chest. Entirely awash, the canoe lurched indecisively. For a panicky second it seemed to succumb to a trough between waves; then it shook itself free of foam and charged towards the island. Pete shouted his surprise and I yelled back in exhilaration, 'She's got it, Pete! She's really got it!'

Our little canoe and sail had outperformed any expectations. Jubilant, I turned wide of the island and swung the bow back towards Little Grand Rapids on the far shore. Another five miles of heavy sailing and the white frame buildings of the Hudson's Bay Company post appeared on the horizon—the same sight that had greeted fur and freight brigades for a hundred years.

It's an isolated life for the 800 Salteaux and few dozen whites of Little Grand Rapids. Other than the regular supply plane from Winnipeg, outside contact is scanty. Weather permitting, the few residents who own televisions can receive one station; radio reception is equally subject to weather.

We spent our first night in the settlement with a couple of guys from the HBC post, and the next day we did our usual stopover chores: writing, cleaning gear and ourselves, buying supplies. The HBC stocks seemed odd to us: there was no garlic sausage, which we'd been able to buy everywhere since Vancouver, but we found shelves upon shelves of white beans. The Indians buy them by the case, not to eat but to ferment into their famously potent 'bean juice'. A few days upriver from Little Grand Rapids we would pass a depressing pair of ruined cabins perched above a spongy point of muskeg. These were the 'cursed cabins', where two Indians killed each other over a last cup of bean juice. No Salteaux has since stepped upon this land.

The Sacred Tepee

The next day, Saturday, June 17, was stormy and windy, so we stayed on. I was lucky to meet a seventy-year-old Salteaux trapper named Walter Moar, who was willing to talk about traditional Salteaux customs like the ancient 'Shaking Tent'. Apparently the only remaining Salteaux shaman in the region, a man named David Eaglestick, still practised the ceremony. He and an elder of the tribe would enter a sacred tepee-like pole-and-canvas tent as a crowd gathered outside. Soon wild howls, shrieks and grunts would erupt from the tent; these were said to be the voices of animal spirits, explaining the secrets of the bush to the shaman. The ritual culminated in a violent shaking of the tent, as a mosquito whispered news of the future into the shaman's ear: who would die, who would have a bountiful trapline that season and other vital matters.

Nonbelievers scoffed at the custom, claiming that Eaglestick made the noises and shook the tent himself. Since it was strictly forbidden for anyone outside the tribe to witness the ceremony, the 'truth' will probably remain in doubt—but does it matter? It was a belief that went with a way of life, and that way is rapidly disappearing among the Salteaux and most of the northern tribes.

In 1978, there were no telephones in Little Grand Rapids, but it can now be reached by a seven-digit telephone number, as I learned when I tried several years later to call the village via the Hudson's Bay Company radio. Someone found Walter Moar and put him on the line. We talked about the changes. David Eaglestick doesn't do the Shaking Tent any more, 'because nobody will come to listen to him,' Walter told me. 'Everybody believes in Jesus. That's OK, though. We still gotta cook our food, get our water and put wood in the stove when it's cold. It doesn't matter who the god is.

▲ Ancient Indian ways are juxtaposed with more recent ideas as a Canadian Indian sews moosehide gloves beneath an image of Christ.

'I'm old now. I can't trap any more. Watching TV is better than watching your stove. I still like watching my stove sometimes, though.'

The mention of stove-watching made me smile. The glow from a trapper's wood stove had often been our evening's entertainment during the first winter of the expedition. You don't really focus on the stove itself. It's just a screen, like a

▲ **Archaeologist Vic Pelshea is seen here making detailed traces of pictographs onto rice paper. Note the numerous black flies, the scourge of summer in this region, crawling all over Vic's hand, arm and face.**

TV set, which serves as a backdrop for a flow of images from memory and visions of the future. We had discovered this bush practice as everyone does: through prolonged solitude.

Pictographs and Mennonites

On Friday, June 23, we crossed the border from Manitoba into Ontario, passing the provincial boundary marker—a sun-bleached skull nailed to a tree—on the north shore of Moar Lake. This followed a frustrating episode of trying to navigate the lake, with its hundreds of islands—our first taste of the bewildering lake country ahead. It turned out that we had passed our exit channel several times, thinking it a blind bay.

We had heard that there were archaeologists documenting an Indian pictograph site on Sharpstone Lake, just east of the Ontario border, and we found them with little trouble. To be truthful, their camp held more attractions than the survey work alone. Supplied by floatplane, it possessed every backwoods luxury imaginable, from outboard motors to cabin-size tents to tables and chairs. Not to mention the archaeologist Vic Pelshea's assistant, Sheryl, who had the distracting habit of walking around camp casually topless. The fact that I bashed our bow into a prominent rock upon landing at the camp was pure coincidence, of course.

The work was fascinating. Once the site's dimensions were recorded, along with latitude, longitude and compass orientation, the pictographs were sponged with water. Ultra-thin sheets of rice paper were then spread across the vertical surface; the paper becomes semi-transparent when wet, allowing the pictograph to show through in perfect detail. For hours at a time, Vic would painstakingly trace the images onto the rice paper, Sheryl acting something like a surgeon's nurse, exchanging pens as needed, remoistening the paper to prolong its adherence, sketching general site illustrations, and hosing down Vic's back when the flies became intolerable. The completed rice-paper murals were spread on the granite shore to dry. In this way, an entire site could be documented in the most minute detail, to exact scale and without damage to the paintings.

Two days' travel from Vic's camp found us battling torrential rains and high winds in the middle of another large lake. As we neared land, though, the wind abruptly dropped. The sky hung so low it seemed we could touch the sooty clouds; the waves subsided from vicious whitecaps to syrupy swells.

Rounding a point, we dropped our paddles and stared at a bizarre sight. Spread peacefully on the hillside before us was a Midwestern farm straight off a Norman Rockwell canvas: freshly painted barns, neatly tended gardens, fenced pastures. Even stranger than coming on this pastoral scene in the remote wilderness was that it wasn't marked on our recent maps.

An eerie screaming, as if from thousands of birds, led us towards a big barn, and when we opened the door we walked smack into a basketball game! We stood there open-mouthed, our waterproof gear dripping on the court, while kids darted by in uniforms, referees blew whistles, and an audience of adults in sober black and white garb cheered on their teams.

This was our introduction to the Northern Lights Gospel Mission, a Mennonite retreat and Christian boarding school for native children. A classic island of self-sufficiency, its facilities included a gymnasium and baseball diamond, a wood shop, dormitories and a working farm. Some of the mission's income came from artfully crafted cedar-strip canoes hand-built by thirteen-year-olds and exported. Older teenagers milled wood from the surrounding forest and built comfortable frame houses for their teachers. Some food was flown in but most was grown on the farm or harvested from the bush. Dozens of moose and bear quarters, along with pike, walleye and whitefish, lay packed in slabs of winter-cut lake ice.

◀ Mennonites—followers of a branch of Protestantism—reject many of the trappings of the modern world, such as cars or fashionable clothing, in favour of a simple, austere lifestyle, as this picture shows.

Deliberately isolated to avoid outside corruption, the mission nevertheless made us cautiously welcome. We could photograph anything and stay as long as we liked on condition that we followed a few rules: we mustn't talk to the kids about life on the 'outside' or consume any of the 'drugs' in our packs (coffee, tea and tobacco) on the premises. We honoured their wishes.

The first day we were given a tour. One person explained the farm operation; another led us through the construction projects; still others showed off the school, the kitchen and the laundry facilities. The place seemed nervously repressed. If an unmarried girl, dressed in the standard black skirt and bonnet, approached us to ask a question, her mother would briskly hustle her away.

Apparently we won some kind of approval, though, as things opened up on the second day. Women gave our grimy clothes their best laundering since Winnipeg. Kids demanded piggyback rides, and their elders behaved in a more relaxed way, some inviting us to look in on their lives.

To walk into a home here was to step back into the 1920s. A bearded man in black hat and overalls would greet you at the door, while his wife interrupted her quilting to set an extra place at the table beside the wood stove. The only distraction during dinner might be the ring of a hand-cranked phone, which connected the settlement's buildings. Afterwards, the husband would escort you to the parlour for 'man talk': perhaps a description of his mare's new foal or of the chipmunk that was eluding his traps. The evening ended early.

Our third and last day at the mission included a festival featuring volleyball, races, songs, huge vats of potato salad and hundreds of hot dogs. We were part of the entertainment, too, contributing a short talk about our travels.

As we paddled onwards the next day, I had conflicting thoughts about the work of the mission. I did not like the idea that native children were being given no choice about their religion and cultural heritage—every Bible lesson was a step away from the beliefs illustrated by the pictographs. On the other hand, these children were spared the terrible ills that beset so many Indians: alcoholism and its related violence, and the lost pride that caused them to desert the traplines for the welfare handouts.

Moose and Muskeg

July 1 found us on giant Lake Pikangikum trying to buy supplies in the Ojibway Indian settlement where there is a store and nursing station. Pete was led around town with an interpreter and met people like Maggie Black, who still makes birch baskets the old way, with spruce roots as lashings, and Helgie Suggashie, who does beadwork on moosehide moccasins. All in all, we were very impressed with this clean, proud settlement.

▲ **Helgie Suggashie sewing an intricate bead design onto a pair of moosehide mittens.**

As we continued to climb the Berens, we grew ever more concerned about our slow pace. A recent lack of tail winds had cut our daily mileage, but the crushing blow was the heat, with the temperature in the eighties as July began. It shimmered off the water and sapped our energy: I caught myself falling asleep while paddling. Pete and I found short-lived relief by rolling off the canoe into the icy river, but Ki never swam unless it was a survival issue. He would lie on the spray cover with eyes closed and tongue lolling, his head swaying with the gentle current swells.

The main reason for worries over our schedule was that we had an appointment to keep. My father, an avid fisherman and the expedition's ground control, had arranged to fly north and join us for a week during his vacation. We were due to meet at Pickle Lake, about 350 river miles from Pikangikum, in ten days' time. The figures didn't work out: at best we had averaged no more than twenty-one miles of upriver paddling per day. And what would happen to our progress when the river narrowed to a mere creek? Casting round for an

◀ Dinner being caught at a fly-in fishing camp in the last rays of the evening sun.

alternative rendezvous, I thought of a fishing camp on Birch Lake, a more reasonable 150 miles away. The only problem was how to communicate the change in plans to my father.

On July 4 the now sluggish Berens River suddenly unfolded into a glistening oasis of open water—Goose Lake. Here we enjoyed a much-needed break at the fishing camp of Bill and Louise Coppen. The Coppens, in their first year as resort operators, typified the hardy breed who manage to wrest a home and a living from the bush. We felt a strong kinship with such folk, who had spent years chipping a niche in this land. They knew both the dangers and pleasures of the country in a way that their clients never could, and this seemed to give them a special appreciation of our adventures.

As we paddled in, we came upon Louise and her Ojibway helper sinking a log structure to support a pier. She brushed the hair out of her face and marched us up to the main cabin for freshly baked chocolate-chip cookies. When Bill Coppen returned, we explained our urgent need to contact my father. Bill promptly led us to his two-way radio, and we spent the next hour trying to raise the operator at Red Lake. But the static was worse than usual, and we never got through. We left the next morning with Bill's assurance that the next passing aircraft would carry our message upriver.

The mighty Berens River was rapidly decaying to a syrupy trickle. For a while, the channel remained about twelve feet wide—just enough to pass through without having to part the overhanging branches from the banks. A few miles further on it narrowed to eight feet, then six. The first twenty miles of the

Wild rice, which flourishes in the waterlogged lowlands of Canada, is here laboriously harvested by an Ojibway Indian using sticks to beat the grain from the stem. ▶

river—the last twenty, for us—squeezed through a channel no more than four feet wide and three feet deep.

Our progress now barely qualified as river travel. The scrub willows lining the banks joined at midstream. Pete rarely paddled any more; his hands groped forward, parting the branches, while he tucked his scratched face beneath an armpit to avoid further punishment. I poled from the stern, standing or kneeling and scanning the terrain for signs of suitable campsites in the soggy lowland.

Where we couldn't make any progress poling, we portaged—sometimes through the spongy muskeg but here and there over outcrops of high, rocky ground. The most interesting feature of this region was its huge moose population; we saw more of them here than anywhere else in Canada. The only human signs were old Ojibway wild-rice harvesting camps.

Exactly one month after we began our 350-mile ascent of the Berens, on July 8, we entered a small, shallow, unnamed lake—the river's source. Only a half-mile portage lay between us and Shabumeni Lake, and the start of some 800 miles of *downriver* travel on the Albany River system. But this portage proved to be among the Berens's worst. The trail hadn't been used in many years and was so overgrown that we often had to backtrack to look for an axe cut, a paint scrape, any clue that might keep us on track. Poles laid by the Indians to support footsteps through the muskeg had long since rotted away. The blackflies were terrible.

On a hill partway across the portage we came upon the grave of James Cat Lake, an Ojibway who died in 1943 at the age of twenty-three. Scattered round the grave were rusty trinkets, the gifts of family mourners. The sight stayed in my mind as we finished the portage and took shelter from a drizzle inside the crumbling remains of a trapper's cabin. Munching a raw-potato lunch, I gazed out across the waves slapping the shore of Shabumeni Lake.

Those waves were destined to travel northeast to Hudson Bay. A year later, the rain now drumming on our canoe might be part of an ice floe off Baffin Island, trod by a polar bear stalking dozing seals. Half a mile away, on the other side of the watershed, the rain feeding the current with which we had contended for a month would find its way west to Lake Winnipeg, where sailboats cut the water. A little boy on a beach outside the city of Winnipeg might cry when his sandcastle was washed away by water that had fallen on James Cat Lake's grave.

Vacation Time

I had to look twice to recognise my father, the dignified Washington lobbyist, beneath a ridiculous canary-yellow fishing cap and several days' growth of beard. Over celebratory beers, we learned how Bill Coppen had managed to get our message through and Dad had been rerouted from Pickle Lake to Birch Lake, and we filled him in on our last few days.

▲ Canoeists paddle across a lake, its surface sculpted by the wind into ever-changing patterns.

We had jumped from lake to lake in the watershed, relying heavily on the compass and portaging when that seemed the quickest route. We were late already and didn't want to add undue worry to my father's undoubted bewilderment, but young streams trying to find their way will investigate every hillside pockmark, eating away at the point of least resistance until they find a passage through which they can tumble into the next lowland. The result is a tangle of bays and waterways that can confuse even experienced boaters.

We now planned to take Dad on board with us and paddle sixty-five miles to a camp on Bamaji Lake, where he'd instructed his pilot to pick him up in a week's time. We could have covered the distance more quickly, but this was his vacation from the office—and our vacation from the expedition. Pete and I had been together for more than a year and badly needed a break from each other's sole company. The prospect of a third party gave us both an emotional lift.

Dad had shared his flight in with Karl Koeszur, a seventy-year-old prospector with a homestead on Birch Lake. Before leaving, we paid a visit to Karl and his wife, Polly, an archaeologist. Their homestead was remarkable. Sipping glasses of Polly's homemade wine, we toured the assorted cabins, one filled with sophisticated prospecting equipment, another with Polly's 1,700-volume library. With stamina and zest to rival those of people half their age, Karl and Polly had even transported a cast-iron stove over the lake ice for their main cabin. Their lifestyle might be considered eccentric, but to me it was enviable.

After a hurried breakfast, Pete and I took our usual places in the bow and stern. Dad made space among the packs amidships, and Ki stalked back and forth, irritated at having to relinquish his spot in the canoe to this intruder. We rode low in the water. With an extra man as well as extra gear and food, our total weight jumped from an average of 550 pounds to 780 pounds—uncomfortably close to the canoe's listed maximum capacity of 845.

But for the first few days it didn't really matter. We enjoyed a leisurely paddle, taking our time to fish and explore. We encountered only minor rapids, as well as a more difficult one that Pete and I ran while Dad photographed from shore. Evenings around the campfire were spent gorging on fried fish and tales. For a short time the Trans-Canada Expedition did not exist. We were just three guys on a canoe adventure. Dad's excitement over the country and activities that had become routine to us breathed new life into the trip. And for me there was another reward: I felt I was repaying all the lessons he had taught me through life.

One highlight of Dad's visit was a near catastrophe on the third day, when our passage to the next lake was blocked by a set of deep rapids. Standing waves approached five feet, but the rapids still looked runnable and even fun with a two-man crew. We portaged most of our gear and Pete remained on shore with Ki and Dad's camera while the other two of us made the run.

Dad whooped with delight as one wave after another slammed into the bow, burying him nearly to his neck. A dead tree hanging over the water was coming up fast, and I leaned into my paddle to avoid it. We missed it, but the correction put our bow at the wrong angle; we hit the next wave and rolled.

When my head broke the surface I looked around for Dad, but he wasn't up yet. Seconds ticked by before he finally surfaced on the other side of the canoe. He had spent those seconds wondering if his head would be crushed against a rock as we were swept along. Later, though, while we dried our clothes by the fire and drank hot coffee, it seemed as if he had actually appreciated the experience. Pete and I had had similar reactions after a near miss; once the terror is past, the knowledge of having survived the challenge more than offsets any grim memory.

At Slate Falls, a tiny Ojibway settlement on Bamaji Lake, we repacked while waiting for the plane that would bring us supplies from Red Lake and fly Dad out. All too soon the floatplane taxied to the dock. The pilot held the pontoon as the three of us shook hands. Dad patted Ki's head and stepped onto the pontoon. I would see his smiling face through the window long after the plane slipped over the horizon.

Land of the Ojibway

Soon after Dad's plane departed, an Ontario Provincial Police aircraft banked over the cabins. The police were returning to Slate Falls to bury the body of an Ojibway man, Johnny Loon, who had fallen off a speedboat and drowned. Within hours, overloaded boats of Ojibway families began arriving from outlying camps for the funeral. The visitors milled about, setting up housekeeping camps and chattering with friends. Plump women in calico dresses hefted blankets and pots from the boats; the men seemed content to stand around puffing on pipes and discussing the weather.

Slate Falls was rapidly filling up with guests, but Pete and I found lodging for the night with John Reed, a retired railroad man from Pennsylvania who had spent the last thirty summers prospecting for gold in country to the north. (The Red Lake region is a magnet for prospectors.) He was waiting in a rented cabin in Slate Falls for an available boat and guide to transport him and his supplies. As none of the Ojibway wanted to leave the settlement until after the funeral, John had to wait and was glad of our company. The conversation flowed freely until I touched on the subject of his prospecting success. At this point he clammed up and gave the prospector's typically evasive answer: 'Oh, a bit here and a bit there.'

We left Slate Falls and two days later, paddling down Lake St Joseph, paused for a handful of raisins. I swallowed the first mouthful, then glanced down and gagged. 'Augghl! Pete, the raisins are full of maggots!' The raisins had been in one of several airtight packages that hadn't been opened since they were packed in Red Lake. I tore open the package of garlic sausage; little white commas crawled through the rancid meat. We had been swindled. For Ki it was manna from heaven; for us it was back to fish.

▲ **An Ojibway woman lays out fish to smoke over a wood fire in the time-honoured manner. Smoking preserves the fish so that they can be eaten right through the winter, when fresh food is harder to come by.**

A day's poling up the Doghole River brought us to the village of Doghole Bay, where Ojibway women were smoking fish in preparation for the autumn trapping season. We had reached the halfway mark of our 1,100-mile paddle from Lake Winnipeg to James Bay and were about to embark on the rough-and-tumble waters of the upper Albany River. Our canoeing outfit was showing the wear and tear of six weeks in the bush, so we decided to transport it and us to Pickle Lake, the nearest town where we were likely to find hardware for repairs.

An Ontario Provincial Police sergeant obliged us with a lift in his van, and as it accelerated away from the river the contrast between our casual, almost crawling pace in the bush and the world racing by the van windows was mindboggling.

In Pickle Lake we were put up by a logging company while we stitched tears in clothing and packs and replaced buttons and supplies. The canoe got a face-lift too. Its hull and rivets were sound, but some of the aluminium tie-off points had been sheared off. These we replaced with superior versions made of stainless steel. Bolt holes drilled in the hull were waterproofed with a green gelatinous goo that soon hardened into a watertight seal.

A few days later we hitched back down to the Doghole River and found the place where we had left off. From here, a short portage would bring us to the Albany River, a 500-mile highway to James Bay. We found the upper Albany a chaotic snarl of rapids, and the first few white-water runs were as thrilling as any we had experienced. But after a week or so, the tense business of running serious rapids every day began to take its toll.

After a particularly tough set of rapids, we would shake with nerves and have to take a ten-minute break to calm ourselves before running the next. We learned that there were good days and bad days for rapids. On the good days we felt positive: everything seemed to click, the canoe made turns like a sports car, and rapids became simple. On other days we were mentally down and the canoe handled more like a truck ploughing through the water. When we woke in the morning, our first question was about the wind direction, and our second was whether we were 'up' for the rapids. If not, we knew we'd see many portages that day.

Indian Wisdom

One evening, while setting up camp after an especially bad stretch of rapids, we saw a group of American canoeists passing and flagged them down, always eager for company. In the course of the conversation one of them remarked, 'Can you believe it? Some bastard has tied orange ribbons to the trees upriver. I didn't come all the way up here to find that sort of crap in the wilderness.'

The bastard in question happened to be me, and the encounter was typical of the contrast in attitudes between those who visited the northern bush for a few weeks and those who lived there. This group of canoeists was seeking unspoilt wilderness, and the sight of our orange tape marking campsites or portages was enough to spoil it for them. They had removed the tape. But Pete and I didn't invent these practices; we imitated those of the Cree, the Salteaux and the Ojibway. Like us, many of these people have had to hack out a miserable campsite or portage in the rain because they couldn't find a suitable one. In national parks and wilderness areas in the USA, I'm all in favour of leaving the place as you found it. It's appropriate in such places, which tend to be heavily used escape areas for city-based outdoor-lovers. But it's not necessarily appropriate in a working environment like the northern bush, where you may travel for a month without meeting another soul. A family of Indians poling upstream to sell wild rice to the Hudson's Bay Company isn't on vacation. For them, missing a poorly marked portage may mean the loss of half a day's income.

▲ **Indians, like this Cree trapper setting off on an expedition up the river, have an intimate give-and-take relationship with the environment on which they depend.**

The Indians we met tended to keep their own counsel about the habits of visiting whites, and often they answered our questions about river conditions and local customs evasively. Rather than speaking bluntly, the Indians tend to paint a vague word picture and then leave you to interpret it. The canoeist who has 'lost' precious time from his two-week holiday because an Indian failed to connect all the dots on the word painting has missed its significance. Part of the Indian's message is that one shouldn't enter the bush without a good understanding of local topography and bushcraft. Fancy modern gear, the best maps, even the best advice are ultimately no substitute for self-reliance—that's the gist of the lesson, and too many visitors miss it completely.

The World of Spirits

As far as the Indians of North America were concerned, they were surrounded at all times by other living beings: their family and friends, plants, birds and animals, and, no less important, innumerable spirits. These included the spirits of people and animals who had died and—perhaps most surprising from a Western point of view—the spirits of the very land itself: of rocks, streams, wind, clouds and thunder. For the Indians, these spirits were not otherworldly, or supernatural; they were a normal, integral part of the natural order, and could have a profound effect on people's lives.

Among the most important spirits for many hunting Indians were the 'animal masters', who controlled the game they depended on, and who communicated with them in various ways, particularly through dreams. A hunter might dream that he heard an animal singing outside his tent; on waking he would play his drum and sing the dream song; soon he would see a brilliant vision in the centre of the drum, telling him where to hunt.

The natural relationship between people and animals was one of mutual respect: the animal masters directed the Indians to the food they needed and the Indians reciprocated by not killing more animals than necessary; they also performed ceremonies and left gifts for the masters to show their respect. Sometimes, however, this harmony was disrupted, resulting in a shortage of food. A medicine man, or shaman, would then have to question the spirits about the cause of the problem.

One of the rituals for conducting such questioning was the so-called 'shaking tent' of the Cree. The shaman, sometimes bound so that he could not move, would sit inside a specially constructed tepee and summon the animal masters to him. The tent would shake violently as the spirits entered, and their strange voices would be heard speaking to the shaman, sometimes for hours. When the ritual was over, the shaman—often exhausted by the experience—would have to rest, but eventually he would be able to explain which spirits were angry and how they could be pacified in order to ensure a plentiful supply of food.

The shaking tent was also used to help the shaman diagnose diseases and predict the future, but with fewer and fewer Indians now living in the traditional way, the ritual has largely died out.

▲ The wearer of this West Coast Indian mask would have believed he was descended from wolves.

▲ Resplendent in a bison-horn headdress, this Plains Indian is preparing for a ritual dance.

◀ A West Coast Indian totem pole, representing the animal spirits with which a particular clan or family believed they had a special affinity.

▲ Traditionally, the owner of this tepee would have been allowed to decorate his home with a leaping bison only if he had been visited by one in a dream.

▲ A rare historic photograph of a special tepee being built for the Cree 'shaking tent' ritual.

◀ Wearing a 'star blanket', this medicine man, or shaman, is enduring a four-day fast in the wilderness in preparation for an important spiritual ceremony.

CHAPTER 6

Onwards to James Bay

▲ **The author surveys a set of dangerous rapids in a novel way—from the top of a gigantic ladder improvised from coniferous trees.**

WE STOPPED ON AUGUST 1 to scout an ominous-looking set of rapids. An Ojibway family travelling upriver for the wild-rice harvest was there too, getting ready to portage. We exchanged greetings and gave them the remains of an eighteen-pound pike I had caught the day before. While the women set up camp, we helped the men to portage their freight canoe.

Later we joined them for tea, and the Ojibway shook their heads vigorously on hearing that we planned to run the rapids. They pointed to a wrecked canoe that stood with its back broken in midstream, an inverted V wedged among the rocks.

Pete voted to portage but I talked him into running the rapids. With the spray cover on, we could handle deep, powerful rapids in relative safety. This one, though, was a staircase of drops with scant water cover, littered with unseen rocks. We were likely to encounter similar rapids ahead, and I thought we needed the practice.

Careful scouting didn't provide much encouragement. Four-fifths of the rapids were wholly unnavigable, and the only safe path was an extremely narrow chute on the far side of the river. To reach the chute we would have to cut diagonally across the sloppy upper white water. There was a good chance that before we could make it, the current would push us broadside into the first stair. The Ojibway family crowded the riverbank as we pushed off.

Less than a dozen paddle strokes into the current I knew I'd made the wrong decision. Judging from our drift, the chance of reaching the chute before the first drop was slim. I wasn't alone in this realisation: two of the Ojibway sprinted for their canoe.

We bottomed out on the first shelf of the staircase with a sickening, high-pitched squeal of aluminium on rock. Water began piling up against my back as we strained against our paddle shafts to free the canoe. We broke loose, only to ground out again on the second shelf. On the third, aluminium buckled and the stern began to cave in. We dumped.

My head broke the surface in time to dodge the rolling canoe. Pete shouted from the other side and I answered. We tried to fend off the rocks with our legs, but it felt as if they were being beaten with hammers, thrashed and twisted into unnatural positions. Finally the river bottom dropped away and the current began to ease.

Then the Ojibway men were pulling us into their canoe by our collars and helping to retrieve lost paddles and flotsam. Ki would have nothing to do with a canoe; he swam straight for shore.

For the next two days we dried gear, stitched torn clothing, repaired the canoe and tended our battered bodies. Most of our camera equipment and food was ruined, but the canoe had survived amazing punishment. Though it would always be slightly lopsided, we were able to bash it back to its general shape. Pete and I had lost our boots in the spill, but other than our damaged feet and a few cuts and bruises, we were in surprisingly sound shape.

Yet in some way this spill took the heart out of us. What began as a slight nagging depression grew to dangerous proportions as the delay forced us to take stock of the expedition's progress. Vancouver was 3,200 miles behind us, but Tadoussac was still 1,500 miles ahead. We had hoped to make it by the end of this summer, but it was now August, with the first frost only weeks away. We both knew we could never reach the St Lawrence before freeze-up.

▲ The author tending fat trout over the campfire—a therapeutic activity during this testing phase of the epic journey.

The success of the expedition was never more in jeopardy than here on the Albany. We were sick of it and of each other. I believe we both wished to quit at this point, and we would have, were it not for the loss of face.

Undoubtedly the prospect of waiting out another winter and stretching the expedition well into the next year was weighing on us, even if unconsciously. Whatever the reason, we had lost our will to continue. We escaped into books and often didn't leave the tent before noon. The cuts in our feet became infected and blood poisoning further sapped our strength; we limped on swollen feet over the portages.

Strangely, we never argued during this period. If you don't care, there's no reason to argue. As at other times, Ki held us together in his blind faith that we would make the right decisions. He sat patiently by the campfire or in the canoe, his only motivation the desire to be with us.

A week after the Indian family had plucked us from the rapids, we stepped ashore at the Ogoki Ojibway settlement. It didn't do much for our spirits: the only empty cabins were owned by the chief, who was far from fond of whites, so we camped in front of the Hudson's Bay post. A further blow was finding that the post was nearly out of the supplies we'd counted on for our final 300-mile run down to James Bay, but at least we found some penicillin to combat blood poisoning.

On August 10, we moved on. The country was getting increasingly bland and ugly the closer we got to sea level, and the current was slow. No sailing—just boring, mindless, endless paddling. One change, though, was for the better. The fierce rapids of the upper Albany were a thing of the past. The next day, things improved still more. After covering thirty-three miles to reach the mouth of the

▲ Away from the pressures of city life, a fisherman finds peace on this tranquil lake.

Kenogami River, we spotted tent canvas on the far side of an island that splits the Albany at the river junction. Richard Foley, a big man with a round face and an ever-present smile, greeted us at the island's dirt landing. His group of half a dozen fishermen from Pittsburgh had flown to this isolated island for a week of trophy fishing; they were scheduled to be picked up by floatplane the next afternoon.

Cordon Bleu in the Wilderness

This group had fished remote rivers and lakes throughout northern Canada, and they provided a cheerful, upbeat atmosphere that gave us a much-needed lift. They liked to rough it, but had decided that one small luxury couldn't hurt—so they had flown in a chef from Montreal. We dined that evening beside a tin wood stove in a tent on a choice of three entrées; I had chicken cordon bleu. I barely knew what to do with the napkin to the left of my salad fork; not since Pickle Lake had we wiped our hands on anything but our trousers.

Another pleasant surprise greeted us in the morning. Fifty pounds of unused canned meat and vegetables made up for what we couldn't purchase in Ogoki. None of the fishermen wanted to fly out with the extra food, and I suspect someone had noticed our alarmingly light grub box. We were no longer restricted by weight, since the now sluggish Albany wouldn't require a single portage from here to James Bay, so we eagerly accepted the food.

Our stay with Foley and his friends seemed to leave us with fresh enthusiasm and luck. A strong tail wind grew as we loaded the canoe, and filled our sail as we set off. I doubt we paddled more than a few dozen strokes all day, yet when we pulled to shore eight and a half hours later, we were a record seventy-two miles downriver.

We were tempted to continue, calculating that if we travelled until midnight we could break 100 miles. But the wind was shifting, and heavy, charcoal-grey storm clouds were leapfrogging across the horizon. We had reached an abandoned settlement called Ghost River, so we wisely decided to camp there and explore instead. Our search for artefacts was cut short by a drenching downpour, but by the time we finished dinner the wind had blown itself out and the rain slowed to a drizzle. Pete and I sipped tea beside the spitting fire while Ki preened himself in his nest under an ancient spruce. He wanted little to do with the idiots who had dragged him away from the orgy of food at the fishermen's camp, where he could be dozing in the heat of a wood stove instead of huddling beneath a tree like a wild animal. It was the time of day when individual trees on the opposite shore dissolve into a solid grey. About 200 yards upriver, a small campfire highlighted an Indian family; while we watched, the parents left their three children in the firelight and paddled towards our camp.

After we'd said our hellos, Pete and I waited for the solemn couple to divulge the purpose of their visit. We were already sharing tea, as is customary, but when I reached for the pail to pour a second round, I saw that their eyes were fixed on the few leftover peas in our dinner pot. They accepted my offer of them and stood there eagerly sharing them in the drizzle. I wondered how hungry their children must be and, without speaking, moved my eyes from the Indians to Pete to the grub box. Pete smiled and nodded his agreement. I walked over to the box and returned with half our food. Broad smiles crossed their faces, and the man uttered the first full sentence we'd heard from them: 'We are short on food.' Then he led his wife back to their canoe. I think Foley would have been pleased about how his food was used.

▲ A strong tail wind forces Pete to make emergency adjustments to the sail.

We soon discovered that our record-breaking seventy-two-mile day was a fluke. Now only 300 feet above sea level, the Albany's current continued to decrease as the river widened to a shallow expanse. At times our paddles bumped the bottom in the centre of the river. The banks spread out onto vast mud and gravel flood plains, bespeaking the river's force in the spring floods after the breakup of winter ice. Steady head winds slowed us further, and our travel-weariness reached new lows. At times we even propped open our books with stones, so we could read as we paddled. Pete was glued to Leon Uris and I found escape in novels about nineteenth-century Southern plantation life.

Thirty miles before spilling into James Bay, the Albany fans out into a delta of as many as ten channels. Somewhere in this maze lies a small waterway called Yellow Creek, which leads to the Cree village of Fort Albany—one of the first fur posts established by the Hudson's Bay Company in the seventeenth century, and our last stop before James Bay. When we did manage to reach Yellow Creek, we were amazed to find a 'parking lot' of canoes. More than fifty ocean-going craft lay stranded on a tidal mud flat. Each parking spot consisted of four ten-foot posts driven into the mud. The rising tide would lift the canoes within their posted spaces, which kept them from drifting free or banging into each other.

When we pulled up to the Fort Albany dock, we were welcomed by Joan Metatawabin, a white schoolteacher who had worked in the village for years and had assumed a Cree name. Joan was interested in the expedition and invited us to stay at her home, which spared us the expense of the village boarding house. While lodging with Joan, we were offered the use of showers and laundry facilities at the nursing station (the village itself had no running water). This we gratefully accepted, and since it was the first time we and our clothes had been clean in a month, I imagine the townspeople were just as grateful.

We again went to work repairing and replacing clothing and gear, thanks to a crate of spare supplies, maps and film we had flown in from Pickle Lake.

Our primary task in Fort Albany was to gather information about canoe travel on James Bay, where strong winds, huge tides and heavy seas would present hazards that we had not yet encountered. It would be much more like coastal ocean travel than river paddling, and we had no experience in this area.

The usual practice of canoeists coming down the Albany was to have their canoes flown out to Moosonee, at the southern tip of James Bay, and then shipped home by rail. If they were determined to travel across the bay, they could hire an Indian guide with a twenty-three-foot canoe and a fifty-horse-power outboard to take them safely to Moosonee. Our little eighteen-footer, the locals warned, would be no match for the unpredictable conditions. The country around James Bay is lowland, and tidal mud flats extend as far as ten miles out from the coast, making camping a tricky business. Some paddlers had lost their boats to the incoming tide and had to walk out through the bush. Others had run out of food after being windbound for weeks. Lives had been lost.

Even allowing for the probability that the tales were embellished by Cree guides with dollar signs in their eyes, the 100-mile paddle to Moosonee sounded less than pleasurable. And our travel on James Bay wouldn't end there: it was another 120 miles from Moosonee to Rupert House on the Quebec shore, where we were to resume river travel.

But we didn't really see a choice. To follow the guides' advice would have meant breaking two cardinal rules of the expedition: never to travel with the assistance of a guide and never to aid advancement by motor.

Canoeing James Bay

After a four-day stopover we paddled out into James Bay, our mood the mixture of fascination and fear that a skydiver feels just before his first jump. The first day's travel presented no problems: only gentle swells and light breezes greeted our bow. But that night's camp left us wondering if we should have heeded the guides' advice.

We raced the ebbing tide at sunset to reach shore before the outflow stranded us on the mud. The 'shore' wasn't much better. It was an oozing muck of decayed vegetation, with the nearest trees more than two miles inland—a situation we were unprepared for. We found a campsite on a twenty-by-fifty-foot island of scrub willow in a sea of waving grass, and proceeded to our next lesson.

While Pete gathered driftwood for a fire, I walked inland in search of water that was neither salty nor tea-coloured. Half a mile inland I filled my bucket from a pond of reasonably fresh water, then turned back towards camp. But where was it? I squinted at the horizon, trying to discern which of a hundred thickets of scrub willow was ours. Retracing the path was out: my trail had twisted and turned during the search for water. Adding to my confusion, the tide was now many miles out and the featureless grass stretched to the horizon.

◀ **His lordship, Ki, keeps a lookout for a suitable campsite as the author drags their canoe across a sea of swampy grass.**

After a while I yelled, sheepishly at first, and heard Pete's faint answering shout from my right. I walked a few hundred yards in that direction and yelled again. This time his voice came from the left. We played this hide-and-seek game for nearly an hour, until finally I spotted a flicker of red a long way from where I expected to find our camp. Pete had stripped off his scarlet long johns and tied them atop a tall pole as a signal flag. It was a good lesson—from then on we didn't venture far across the tidal grasses without leaving marker flags.

A steady rain fell throughout the night. In the morning we learned another lesson in James Bay travel: never retire without setting the alarm clock if you plan to catch an early tide. Though we were packed and ready to depart by 7.30am, already the water's edge was more than a mile away and receding fast. There was nothing to do but sit down and wait for the evening tide.

The next lesson followed promptly. For the first few hours of the evening, the sea rocked us gently and our paddle strokes were quick and eager. But once the orange orb of the setting sun touched the horizon, the temperature took a nose dive.

As we hunched our shoulders to hide from the wind, our paddle strokes became stiff and awkward. Ki slept in a curled ball between us, apparently having given up trying to comprehend our actions.

We monitored the falling tide by measuring the water depth with a six-foot pole, and whenever the depth decreased we hustled further out to sea. Nevertheless, it soon dropped to an alarmingly shallow two feet, and rocks began to surface. The risk of being stranded on a shoal was great, yet we dared not venture further out—we were already beyond sight of land. We realised our danger suddenly and forcefully. Should a strong wind come up, especially an offshore wind, we could lose our orientation to land and have little hope of saving ourselves if we swamped.

Slowly the rocks grew into shoals and the shoals multiplied, until we were forced to climb out of the canoe and walk it through channels only inches deep. At midnight we ran out of water completely and just stopped, the canoe a shiny speck upon an endless moonscape. We were miserably cold and hungry, so I suggested that we anchor the canoe by its bow rope to a rock, split a can of stew and catch a few hours of sleep on the shoal. I estimated that the tide would

regain our shoal at 4am. Pete's face, illuminated by the late-rising moon, betrayed his doubt, but he was too tired and cold to argue. I set the alarm for three, allowing an hour's margin for error.

A wave washed over our legs at 2am. We were further offshore than I had thought. We ran round our disintegrating shoal, tossing sodden sleeping-bags into the now floating canoe and groping beneath the slapping waves for any forgotten items. Our clothing soaked through, we climbed into the canoe and paddled away. At five that morning we grounded, half a mile off a rocky protrusion called Nomansland Point. We anchored the canoe where we could retrieve it later and stumbled over the flats. Nearly twelve hours after leaving solid land, we collapsed with our packs beside a high-water wall of driftwood.

We remained on the point that day, and in the afternoon I sat by the campfire, watching the water ripple along the horizon and the first southbound flights of ducks and geese undulate across the sky. Falling into a reverie, I began to hear a chanting song drift over the water. Ki sat up, his mane bristling. I glanced over at Pete, who seemed to be having the same dream. Then I turned and stared.

Nine canoeists were paddling into our camp in a twenty-four-foot fibreglass replica of a birchbark canoe. The '*voyageurs*' wore fur tukes (close-fitting helmets with earflaps) on their heads; their red paddle blades danced in the sun's rays.

Before we could recover enough to speak, one of the voyageurs enquired, 'Are you Halsey and Souchuk, Trans-Canada?' At our affirmative nods, he then strode forward to introduce his group. 'We're Expeditions of North America—ENA. We began in Minnesota, and our destination's Moosonee.' Pete asked how they knew of us. 'We heard about you 600 miles up the Albany. You set off two days ahead of us. We've been trying to catch up.'

The speaker, Chuck Benda, and his fellow leader, Tod Spedding, then explained their trip to us. Both were counsellors for a juvenile offenders rehabilitation programme in Minnesota, helping to improve attitudes and motivation. This particular group consisted of seven bright and friendly kids ranging in age from sixteen to eighteen.

Both expeditions tried to leave on the next morning's tide at sunrise, but high winds and a heavy breaking sea stopped us cold. Even the big ENA canoe could make no headway and Pete and I actually lost ground in our little one. The wind didn't subside until mid-morning, long after the tide had peaked. Here was the Catch-22 of canoeing James Bay: if we caught the tide before it began to fall, the wind was too strong to paddle against; if wind and waves were light enough to allow progress, the tide was probably ebbing.

Stuck on the peninsula for another day, we joined forces with Chuck and Tod's gang to prepare a major feast of canned chicken and vegetables, soup, fresh-baked bannock, and pie made with ripe gooseberries from a nearby hedge. It was a special treat for the kids after a month on a freeze-dried diet.

The next morning brought a gently swelling tide and blessedly light head winds. Both canoes set off together, though the ENA group soon outdistanced us. Our speed advantage on the Albany had been due mainly to the rapids, most of which we could run while they had to portage, but in the expansive waters of the bay their craft was ideal. Eight paddle blades flashed in synchrony, while the sternman ruddered his long, sweeping paddle. They pulled ahead of us with the first few strokes, and slipped beyond the horizon within an hour.

We stayed well off the coast that day, sometimes as many as six miles out. An offshore wind suggested there might be an extra-low tide and we couldn't afford to lose more time hung up on a shoal. Paddling in the deep-water waves was a very different experience. Amid these deep rollers we would glimpse a panoramic view while topping the crests, then descend into the troughs and lose the horizon. Though large, the waves were quite safe, for they never crested. Flocks of scoters—black sea ducks with an odd whistling call—bobbed between the hills of water.

▲ **Bannock, made with oatmeal, cooks on a hot stone over an open fire.**

The wind died as the tide ebbed, and our canoe slipped over the smooth, still deeps beyond the reach of flats and shoals. The only sounds other than our voices were the occasional cries of distant shore birds. Though there was nothing behind me but the small stern deck, I distinctly heard someone back there say 'Push,' with a soft 'p' and an accented 'sh' sound. I glanced over my shoulder just in time to see an ivory hump emerge.

'Pete! Pete, look, a whale!'

'Oh, yeah, right, Halsey.'

Paddling the calm waters was boring, and Pete assumed I was trying to liven up the day with a whale hoax. Then a midsize beluga whale surfaced for air no more than fifty feet from our bow.

The white, grey and mottled belugas remained with us for an hour or so. From twelve to thirty feet long, they broke the surface as close as twenty feet from the canoe, and never further than 100 yards away. If we slowed, they slowed. Like dolphins, they surfaced side by side in pairs and threesomes; it was hard to tell how many there were in all. Far from displaying fear of us, they seemed curious. Ki was mesmerised throughout. The sight of a bear or a moose made him yap and leap, yet he didn't so much as whine at the whales. He just sat at attention, staring.

Curious to see how they would react, we stopped paddling altogether. The whales continued to swim southeast very slowly, and then paused, as if waiting

The White Whales of the Arctic

THE COLD WATERS of the Arctic are home to the beluga, the only white whale in the world. Friendly, inquisitive and playful, belugas are among the most 'talkative' of whales. They have an extraordinary range of squeaks, pops, croaks and whistles, which they use for communicating with each other, and which have given rise to their nickname, 'sea canaries'.

Every summer, thousands of belugas gather in river estuaries and other shallow waters to shed their skin by rubbing themselves against the ground. Here they become vulnerable and may fall prey to polar bears and the harpoons of Inuit hunters—the only people who are now allowed to kill them legally.

A small group of about 500 belugas also inhabits the St Lawrence River, where a more insidious threat lurks: chemical pollution in the form of pesticides and industrial effluent. About 15 of their number die each year, many of them from tumours and other abnormalities. Worst of all, the pollution is making the whales sterile, so their population is steadily shrinking.

Fortunately, the St Lawrence belugas are not being ignored. Their plight is being closely monitored not only by environmentalists and scientists, but also by many ordinary people, who love to sail out to the whales to hear them 'sing' and to watch them playing cheerfully together.

▲ **An inquisitive beluga rises to the surface to stare directly at the photographer.**

for us to catch up. Finally a hummock of water boiled against the hull and, as we watched, a large white beluga passed directly beneath us. This closest encounter may have been a final inspection. In any case, no other whales surfaced again. From below, our hull was similar to a beluga in shape, size and colour. We wondered whether we might look like an injured whale.

Normally we ate lunch in the canoe, the flats presenting a barrier between us and dry land. But the whales had steered us towards a narrow, prominent point that seemed to offer a reasonable anchorage. We beached on the flats and dragged the canoe what we guessed was a safe distance above the water line. A great heap of driftwood spanned the base of the point, promising the rare luxury of hot tea with our lunch.

Ki interrupted our second mug of tea with an unfortunate success at his latest favourite pastime: he chased and was sprayed by a skunk somewhere upwind of our lunch site. His concrete sinuses didn't seem to mind, but we preferred the fresh sea breeze and ordered him to stay well behind during our return walk to the canoe.

The coastline was wonderfully serene as we strolled along. Strands of seaweed swayed with the incoming current, shore birds flitted across the water, and two lumbering cranes heaved their awkward bodies aloft. The scene would have been perfect...had it only included our eighteen-foot canoe. We gazed around in growing panic, but did not glimpse a hint of metal in any direction. There was a light westerly breeze—an offshore wind, meaning that unless the canoe had caught upon a rock, it was probably headed out to sea. Between us we had the clothes we were wearing, an empty tea pail and mugs, a few matches and a dog. The explanation was simple: somehow the bow rope must have slipped free.

Pete ran south across what little remained of the flats; I ran north up the coast and continued running through the water after the shoreline came to a dead end in a large bay. When the water was up to my waist, I climbed onto a gravel shoal that was about to be submerged and searched the horizon. It was empty, but neither was there any sign of the canoe along the shore. However, just as I was about to jump back into the water, a rock about a quarter of a mile away began to move. The rock caught and reflected the sun, then pivoted, revealing the profile of a canoe. I closed the distance quickly, but the water was soon up to my armpits, and the tidal current swirled against my chest. The rock that held the canoe was steadily shrinking beneath the climbing tide; at any moment, the canoe would skip out to sea on the westerly breeze.

I pushed through the deep water, cursing its drag on my legs. When I was ten yards away, the canoe slipped free, then paused for an instant as if trying to decide whether to escape or stay. I reached out, grasped it by the gunwales and hauled myself in. I found Pete stranded on a spit of gravel, having waded channels and crossed shoals as I had. We couldn't see Ki but we could smell him, still off shoal-hopping. Sea water, we sadly discovered, does not reduce skunk odour.

▲ A skunk marking its territory by spraying scent on a cluster of pretty daisies. Note the skunk's extraordinarily long claws, with which it forages for insects.

However, Ki's lingering aroma soon became the least of our worries. Over the next four days we gained exactly ten miles. For two of those days we were pinned down onshore by a solid southwesterly wind. This was certainly a respite from the rigours of the bay, but we were falling ever further behind schedule. Worse, our supplies were nearly exhausted.

By the third day the wind hadn't abated and an angry sea still crashed across the flats. Launching a canoe in such surf was a dangerous business, but our supply situation was critical and we could no longer remain idle. We launched the canoe on the lee side of a string of boulders. Past this natural breakwater, waves jumped to the sky, the wind shearing off their foamy crests in showers of mist. When we passed the last boulder, the gale struck like fists.

Ki stood in the centre of the spray cover, shifting his weight on sea legs as he tried to keep his belly dry. Pete and I learned to sway our hips in time with the canoe's rocking motion. Simply reacting to the impact of big waves isn't enough—the canoe may swamp unless you anticipate the impact and shift your weight accordingly. By transferring weight you improve the canoe's balance and allow the wave to pass beneath the hull rather than sloshing over the top. Pete

◀ **The Expedition canoe moored on the featureless mudflats of James Bay. Open water may seem far away, but the tide rushes in astonishingly quickly, as the team found to their cost more than once.**

and I danced the hip-sway for three hours, at best gaining less than a mile for each hour's work. Exhausted and defeated, we finally gave up and turned towards shore, making camp a mere two miles from our departure point. It was nearly as bad the following day, eight hours of work advancing us only six miles. When the wind was too strong for paddling, we poled laboriously across the shallows.

Daytime high tides were now occurring after noon, and nearly an hour later each day. This meant we couldn't depart until past noon. Even worse, high tide in the wee hours made reaching shore at night an ordeal. We paddled until about 9pm and then, when ready to camp, anchored the canoe at the high-water mark and portaged the packs a mile or more to shore across boot-sucking flats. Every 100 yards we left a stake in the mud to mark our trail. From then until high tide we took hourly turns backtracking to the canoe by flashlight and poling or wading it to the most recent high-water line. Not until long past midnight was the canoe secured onshore. It was cold, miserable, frightening work. I have never before or since experienced such intense loneliness as I would feel standing a mile offshore in frigid water, praying to spot the canoe and longing for the warmth and security of our distantly flickering campfire.

On September 1, we spotted an indentation in the coastline that appeared larger than the usual creek entrances. As we paddled towards it, landmarks fell into place. We had reached Wavy Creek, the short cut around Ship Sands Island to the Moose River and Moosonee. Our timing was fortunate: the tide was on the rise, counteracting the river's current against our bow. At dusk, eleven days after leaving Fort Albany, we tied up to the dock in front of Moosonee.

Though our bodies, minds and nerves begged for rest, we intended to spend only one night in Moosonee before pushing on. We hadn't discussed it outright, but we both knew there was no longer any chance of reaching the St Lawrence before freeze-up—it was still over 700 miles away. We had never been so depleted of strength and will; we were afraid to discuss our doubts and seemed incapable of long-range planning. Our only thought was to push as far into Quebec as the weather would allow and then decide whether to continue overland through the winter or wait for another spring thaw.

The Ministry of Natural Resources kindly spared our wallets by providing lodging in a trailer on the outskirts of town. Once we had stowed our gear there, we set off for a long-awaited night in town. Though Moosonee's population is only 1,800 or so, its two hotels and several restaurants qualified it as a big city for us. With a choice of menus, we bypassed the fine steaks at the Polar Bear Lodge and ordered pizza instead. After months of a bland bush diet, our palates craved spice—washed down by a bottomless pitcher of beer.

Halfway through the pizza, our stomachs began warning us that they weren't prepared for such a culinary jolt. The beer hit equally hard. Finally Pete shook his head and got up to return to the trailer, silent and slightly greenish of hue. An hour later, I pushed aside what was left and weaved my way light-headedly towards the door.

A short cut, down a trail and across a creek, halved the mile-long walk to our trailer. Steady rain was falling, and my only wish was for bed. Some thoughtful soul had placed a length of sheet metal across the creek, but one step onto the metal sent my feet flying. I landed in the creek, scarcely noticing the water as all sensation focused on the searing pain in my ankle. I tried to stand but the ankle turned to jelly. Oh hell, I've sprained it, I thought.

I could see the trailer light 100 yards away through the rain and tried to crawl towards it, but altering the position of my ankle nearly made me black out from pain. By dragging myself belly down, however, I found I could keep my ankle fairly flat on the ground. Twenty feet...a rest in a mud puddle...another twenty feet. Ten feet from the trailer I shouted and threw stones at the window, but Pete was dead to the world. I climbed the trailer steps on my belly, stopping at each one to rest.

In the morning the local physician diagnosed my injury as a dislocated ankle and a spiral fracture of the fibula. He explained that at least one operation would be required to

The author and Ki enjoy the late-summer sunshine at a James Bay camp. ▼

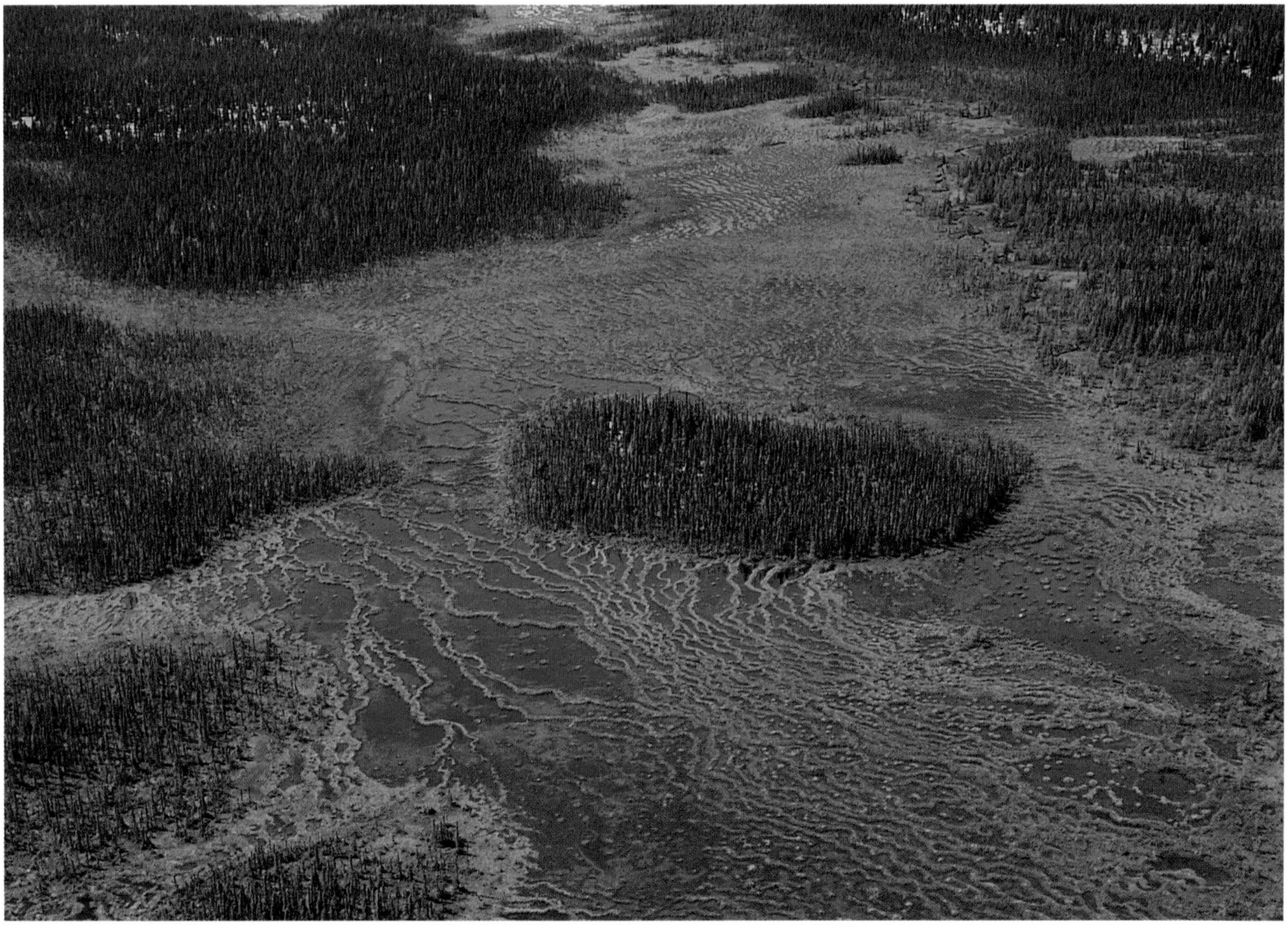

▲ An aerial view of islands of conifers standing amid intricately patterned swamp at the edge of James Bay.

put things back together properly and warned that I had little chance of escaping a permanent limp. Meanwhile, he tried to relocate the joint; I was pumped full of painkillers, and he twisted and pulled until the bones grated, without success.

Clearly there would be no bush travel for me for many months, so Pete's mother immediately flew up from Chicago to Moosonee to lend a hand. She played foster-mother to me for a few days, helping to arrange my transfer back to the United States. My feelings during this time were a black morass of shock, anger and depression, dominated by the fear that my stupid overindulgence had destroyed our chance to complete the expedition. What an ignominious ending that would be!

Despite Pete's assurances that he would be ready to start again as soon as I was, my doubts persisted. When he helped me onto the plane to Washington, I made him promise that if I couldn't continue next spring, he would find a new partner and complete the journey. Ki was accompanying me, caged in the baggage compartment; the Souchuks were flying back to Chicago. As the DC-3 swung out over James Bay before turning south, I wondered whether spring would find me again plying its waters or hobbling along some city street.

Birds of the North

OF ALL THE CREATURES eking a living from the Canadian wilderness, migrant waterfowl such as the magnificent king eider, the snow goose and the Canada goose probably have the best of it. They exploit the region's brief summer to breed on the great open spaces of the northern tundra or on the myriad pools and lakes of the boreal forest, and then migrate south when winter returns. Twice a year they recreate one of Nature's most amazing phenomena—filling the skies in their millions to fly in noisy formation between their seasonal homes.

Some birds, however, choose to brave the severe winter conditions of subarctic climes: ptarmigan, for example, which change their colour with the seasons, rather than their homes. In summer, nesting hens are arrayed in speckled brown and black to match the surrounding tundra; in winter they turn pure white to blend in with the snow. Whatever the time of year, ptarmigan are so confident of their camouflage that they will remain completely motionless even when closely approached.

Another northern bird that uses the tactic of keeping still is the spruce grouse, also called the 'fool hen' because it appears so absurdly tame. Yet it is not foolishness that has led to the demise of this bird, but extensive logging of the mature forests that are its natural habitat; spruce grouse are now rare in many areas where they were once common.

Fortunately, the reverse is true of the trumpeter swan, which was hunted to the verge of extinction at the start of the century. Its eggs were prized as a delicacy by gourmets, and mature birds were slaughtered in great numbers for their down and skin, which was used for making powder puffs. Now, thanks to careful conservation, trumpeters are recovering, and they can be found all along the west coast of Canada.

The haughty but rather dim-witted spruce grouse nests under fallen logs in mature coniferous forests. ▶

▲ This colourful king eider drake is protected from the freezing cold of Arctic seas by the finest quality down.

A resourceful Canada goose—it has made its nest on top of a strongly built, but disused, beaver lodge. ▶

▲ Drifting and settling like an early flurry of snow, a massive flock of snow geese gather together on a Quebec lake to feed and rest during one of their twice-yearly migrations between the Arctic and the southern United States.

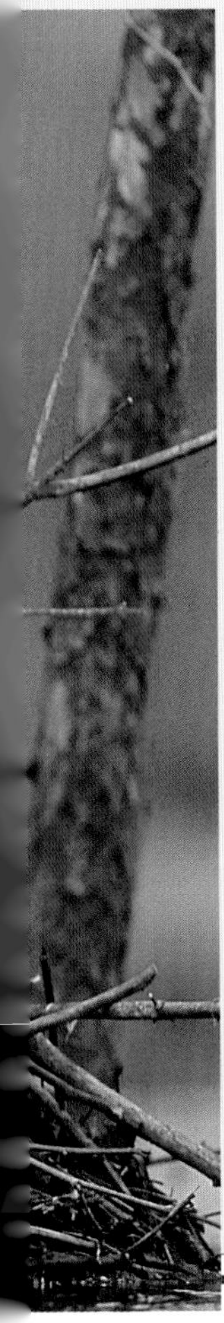

▲ This ptarmigan hen and her chick are almost indistinguishable from each other, and from their surroundings, so effective is their mottled disguise.

A graceful waterborne take-off by a trumpeter swan, the largest waterfowl in North America. The bird gets its name from its loud, resonant call. ▶

CHAPTER 7

In Pursuit of Paradise

THAT YEAR, FROM SEPTEMBER through to the end of December, I recuperated from my broken ankle at my parents' home just outside Washington DC. The ankle mended perfectly. The hospital in Washington did a great job and I did not have even the smallest trace of a limp. Clearly the doctor who had first examined me had been over-pessimistic.

My greatest worry during this time was that I would lose my acclimatisation to wilderness life. James Bay and the rivers would not be free of ice until late spring, a wait of another four months, and it seemed like an eternity. I felt as if I had left the whole centre of my identity up there. Every day I spent in the suburbs, my dream of completing the trans-Canada journey faded just a little more.

In desperation, I decided to return to James Bay then and there. Even if I couldn't travel, at least I could grapple with winter properly in some remote outpost. So I finally got in touch with people I had met in Moosonee and they helped me to contact the Cree band council—the tribal elders—at the settlement at Attawapiskat, a little place on the western shore of James Bay, about 175 miles north of Moosonee. Although they could not promise anything, a rather vague sort of permission was granted for me to live and work with Cree

With James Bay and its surroundings now dramatically transformed by winter, Cree trapper Abraham Paulmartin tows the author to the Lake River settlement further up the bay. ▶

trappers on the winter traplines at Lake River, an isolated group of cabins some 150 miles even further north.

Frankly, I don't think they believed I would ever actually turn up. It sounded just fine to me, though. Perfect, in fact. Dad understood, of course, and so did Mom, and a couple of days after my leg cast came off they put me and Ki on a plane up to Kashechewan, near Fort Albany, from where I was able to make my way north to Attawapiskat.

In Attawapiskat I met Abraham Paulmartin, an elderly, gruff Cree man who was to be my first trapping partner and tutor. We travelled north along the frozen edge of James Bay to the settlement at Lake River. Our partnership began badly. I did not look after my feet properly on the skidoo on the journey up and they froze; I lost my toenails and was laid up for several days.

Abraham did not like this. Obviously he thought he had been saddled with a pretty useless partner. Worse than that, he somehow got it into his head that I was an agent sent up by the Canadian government to spy on the Cree people, and he sent me back to Attawapiskat to stand trial before the Indian band council. Luckily I got a break: Abraham was known to the Cree as a difficult character, and a young Indian named Eli Tookate decided I was being unfairly treated. He invited me back to Lake River to work on his family's traplines.

Once Ki and I were back in Lake River the problem of where we were to live came up. I did not want to impose on Eli and his family, so I found a site about a mile upriver from the main settlement, set up a camp for myself and started to build my own cabin. It was not much of a camp, as I had no tent, and cutting the trees was hard work, with the temperatures down to thirty and forty below zero.

▲ A spruce-bough floor and wood stove are essential home comforts for Cree trappers in their tents.

The truth is, I was trying to prove something to myself and I'm not sure now that I would have made it on my own. One morning, though, Matthew and Mary Hookimaw snowshoed into my camp. They spoke no English and I was only just beginning to pick up a bit of their language, but somehow they managed to tell me that they wanted me to go and live with them in the settlement. They were getting on in years and had no children, and I think they saw me as a white boy they could sort of 'adopt'. Also, as Eli told me later, Matthew had found his father, many years before, frozen to death from sleeping out, and he and Mary were worried by the thought that that might happen to me.

In the next weeks I really worked at fitting in. Old Abraham still bitched on about me being a visitation of evil from the white man, but luckily nobody took much notice of him. Eli and his family were the only English-speaking people in the settlement, and in the evenings they tutored me in the Cree language and customs. Meanwhile Mary Hookimaw had made sure I was properly kitted out,

▲ Trapping provides not only food for Indian tribes such as the Cree, but much-needed warm clothing as well, as this trapper's splendid fur hat and waistcoat show.

chewing caribou hide for new moccasins, trimming my parka with fur and stitching a rabbit-fur blanket for my bed. Matthew was my trapping instructor, and gave me daily lessons in snaring, beaver-skinning and hide preparation. In return—and it was not much—I was able to keep them supplied with snare wire, ammunition and tobacco.

Towards the end of January the whole settlement moved about twenty miles inland, to a tent camp much closer to the traplines. Here we spent the rest of the winter. I had my own Cree tent and was given my own lines.

An Early Start

The working day began at seven, about an hour and a half before sunrise. Most mornings a faint grey light in the southeast provided just enough light for me to see without a candle. The cold was bitter. Everything in the tent was covered with quarter of an inch of hoarfrost, and my hair was matted with ice from my breath.

Heat was the first priority. Everything in the tent was geared to speed and efficiency: lying ready on the spruce-bough floor were three neat piles, one of paper wads and pine slivers, one of finger-sized kindling and one of quartered logs. Clad in two layers of long underwear and socks, I lunged from my sleeping-bag, dropped paper and slivers into the stove, then kindling and logs on top, and a tablespoon of lard for starter fuel. I struck a match on the stove and lit the paper, then put the tea pail over the stove-top hole. The pail had been filled the night before and was a solid block of ice.

I had been out of my sleeping-bag for less than two minutes but already I was aching from the cold, so I dived for my bed. The most beautiful music of the day was the sputtering of the lard as the kindling began to catch, and then the low roar of the draught hole, feeding air to the growing blaze.

Gradually the tent warmed up to about 50°F, though around the stove was a six-foot circle of luxurious 80° heat. Breakfast was usually mugs of strong tea and half a twelve-inch bannock spread with lard and jam—butter was saved for special treats. Then I got ready for work. Socks, moccasins, liners and mitts hung over the stove, thawed and dry. Foot insulation was the biggest palaver: liners and insoles went into my caribou-skin moccasins, then two pairs of wool socks over them, duffle socks, and finally a pair of rabbit skins. Over all this I put on lined moccasins, and over my underwear I wore heavy woollen trousers, shirt, sweater, scarf, and finally an outer layer of goosedown parka, hat and two more sets of mitts.

As the fire died I filled my Thermos with boiling tea and my pack with everything else I would need for the next ten hours, a twelve-mile trek along one of my traplines. Before leaving I had to tie up Ki in front of the tent—I hated to leave him but his constant bounding through the snow confused the tracks I had to decipher.

Matthew was much faster at rising than I, and was probably already a mile or two out on his own trapline, but I would often see Mary trudging back to her tent with a couple of hares slung over her shoulder, and we would wave. Then, for the rest of the day and well into the dark, I was out on my own. The main well-beaten trail ran for about five miles, with a single snowshoe trail every mile or so, angling off to north or south—Matthew's, Eli's, Eli's father's, maybe my own. These trails formed a network covering an area thirty miles by fifty—1,500 square miles.

At sunrise there was rarely any wind, but around ten o'clock it came blasting out of the east and funnelled down the Lakitusaki River, right into my face, searching out gaps in my clothing. I quickened my pace as I neared the shelter of Willow Creek and turned in, pausing to put on my snowshoes. From there on, the trodden snow of the main trail was replaced by a profusion of overlapping tracks—mouse, ermine, squirrel, grouse, rabbit, ptarmigan, mink, otter, fox, and lynx, the most elusive and valuable quarry. Each time I went out on the lines I couldn't help thinking that this would be the day I would catch a lynx.

The elusive lynx, with its luxuriantly thick fur, is the ultimate reward for the patient trapper. Normally timid creatures, lynx have been known to enter cities in search of food in years when their usual prey, the snowshoe hare, is scarce. ▼

My morning was spent going to each of my sets of traps. Many of the sets were only a few feet off my trail, but some were way back. Near the end of the line there were six baited lynx sets. Five were untouched that morning, but one had been burgled: a lynx had managed to slip in and steal the bait without tripping the snare. Annoyed as I was, at least I was obviously setting the snares in good locations. Around one o'clock, after a break for lunch—sardines and bannock, plus typical trapper's tea fortified with flour, sugar and lard—I had the six-mile hike back to camp to face, and a stack of new snares to set.

▲ **A trapper carefully arranges sticks around a lynx snare to guide an animal into the noose. The bait of fresh meat nailed to the tree has already attracted the attention of an opportunistic bird.**

The job involved choosing the best of thirty or forty good sites. A few hundred yards from my lunch spot the creek narrowed from its average width of thirty feet to about ten. The banks were steep here with thick growth on either side—a natural funnel—and lynx and fox signs were good. The idea was to span the gap with an impassable fence, leaving a six- or eight-inch hole to direct the animal into the snare. I cut willow and pine branches and planted them in the snow to form a four-foot fence, interwoven to prevent gaps. Next I anchored a stout four-foot pole vertically on one side of the hole with a bracing pole on the other side and secured the snare to the vertical pole about a foot from the snow. A brass hook attached to the bracing pole held the noose perpendicular to the trail, and sticks placed carefully above and below the snare prevented the lynx from passing over or under it.

Snare-setting is a dreadful, time-consuming chore. It made my body throb with the cold, my muscles cramp from kneeling in the snow. Often, after half an hour of painstakingly setting a snare, it didn't look right—too obvious maybe—so I would tear it down and start again. And today I was bringing back no more than a bundle of rabbits.

Swapping Trappers' Tales

Back at camp Mary had already gone into my tent, lit a candle, built a fire, filled my water pail with fresh snow and put the tea on to boil. She knew there was nothing more depressing than coming back to a cold tent and waiting, shivering and exhausted, for the stove to heat up.

Straining against his rope, Ki leapt up to greet me. I collapsed on my bed, savouring the aroma of strong tea as the stove's heat poured over me in delicious waves. Later, after I had restocked my woodpile, I thawed out a pot of leftover rabbit stew and skinned the rabbits I'd brought home for tomorrow. I was still outside, washing rabbit blood from my hands and rolling the carcasses in snow to wipe them clean, when Eli and Matthew showed up for the evening social hour. I gave the rabbit skins to Eli for the blanket that his wife was making, and the meat to Matthew for his stewpot.

Matthew began the nightly tale-swapping with an account of his day on the trapline and Eli translated where necessary. He'd had a good day: not only had he come home with two fat beavers, but he had also found another beaver lodge on a creek to the south. Everyone, he said, would have good beaver meat for supper tomorrow!

▲ The beaver's outer layer of water-repellent fur covers a dense, soft undercoat. Here, a beaver nibbles at a juicy branch—its staple diet—delicately held between dexterous front paws.

By the fourth round of tea it was time for my trapline tale of the stolen lynx bait. Matthew, thinking back to his first year of trapping, gave me a reassuring smile. Then I dug out my map of the region. Neither Eli nor Matthew had ever seen a detailed map of the area—all their lives they had navigated by memory—and examining my map had become a nightly ritual.

The evening ended with an empty tea pail around eleven o'clock. Matthew and Eli left, Ki curled up beside me, and I let the fire die while I pulled out my Cree dictionary. My eyes roamed round my food supplies as I repeated the words for sugar, lard, flour, tea, water, and wondered if I'd ever be able to speak a proper sentence in Cree. So far, any effort of more than a word or two had elicited giggles.

I understood what these people were giving me. Matthew was old enough to remember times when the Cree were treated little better than dogs, enduring starvation while white settlers continued to get regular food shipments from the south. So far I had caught no fur and I couldn't keep up with the others. I had better food, clothing and equipment than they, but I still cursed and complained when it got to forty below. Yet they had accepted me.

I also felt that they had taught me an enormous amount, which I wanted to try out on my own. In particular, I had one burning ambition: to make an overnight trapping trip. It seemed so uneconomical to return to camp each night, wasting a quarter of each day just travelling; furthermore, I was curious to see some new country beyond my traplines. But every time I brought up the idea, Matthew and Eli vetoed it. I had no idea, they said, of the hardships of winter camping without a tent.

They knew nothing about the Trans-Canada Expedition and so had no idea that Pete and I had spent dozens of nights out without a tent the previous winter. I hadn't told them about it because I doubted they would understand. What would be the point of walking and canoeing thousands of miles, unless you were trapping?

But finally, in late February, Matthew agreed to let me make a three-day exploratory trip north, scouting the area and setting snares. The weather was fine

Balancing precariously on the edge of a snowbound river, a trapper assesses the best place to set an otter trap. ▶

and clear, with moderate temperatures, and he was curious about the animal population, not having trapped that country himself for twenty years. The plan was for me to break a trail north of the treeline to a branch of the Lakitusaki River I hadn't yet seen.

A Solo Expedition

On departure day I loaded my toboggan with two days' worth of food and assorted gear, including a map and compass. Six miles of the proposed route would be on featureless tundra. I had not travelled beyond the tree line before and was both excited and apprehensive about it. For the first mile I followed

Eli's trail, the toboggan sliding easily over packed snow. The trail ended where the trees did, and before me, stretching to the horizon, was a white desert of windblown snow. Six-foot stunted skeletons of tamarack trees dotted the drifts liberally at first, then tapered off to widely scattered clumps. Ptarmigan tracks—and occasionally the trail of an arctic fox—wound round the tamaracks. Now and then the white whirr of a ptarmigan rose over the drifts, always out of range of my shotgun.

Soon I was losing sight of the trees behind me. Since from here on I would have to navigate by compass, I reached into my pocket for it. No compass—I must have dropped it in the tent. I felt a little sick at my stupidity, but as long as the sun stayed out I could use that to navigate. I just prayed that I could pick up my trail on the way back.

By mid-afternoon I spotted a telltale line of trees, the oasis along every riverbank above the tree line. Ki seemed equally pleased to see it; he'd been rather bored on the tundra with no squirrels to chase. When we reached the trees, though, they proved as much a curse as a blessing. Every few paces I had to hew a trail through the dense growth of willow and alder. Finally, two hours before sundown, we reached a narrow, meandering river.

I spent the remaining daylight setting rabbit snares, cutting firewood and building a shelter. I dug a depression in the snow for a firepit, with a shelf of snow next to it, covered with spruce boughs for seating and sleeping. Around this I built a conical hut from two dozen pine saplings, anchored in the snow and leaning inwards. With the stove roaring, I could keep the hut a comfortable 40° even after the outside temperature dropped to –20°. I felt cosy and secure, camped in an island of trees amid a sea of frozen 'barrens'.

▲ The one that got away... Otters are strong and lithe enough to break out of many snares and traps. Like beavers, they have ears and nostrils that can be closed at will, allowing them to remain underwater for several minutes at a time.

Morning light revealed a low bank of clouds on the horizon, signalling, along with the rising temperature, that a snowstorm was probably on the way. The prospect of travelling across open country in poor visibility briefly made me consider returning to the main camp before the storm hit, but unseen country is a strong magnet, so once again safety took a back seat to adventure. Leaving Ki tied to the hut, I shouldered my daypack and turned northwest up the river.

Progress was slow over the river's virgin snow, as each step had to be checked with a prodding pole to make sure the ice would support me. After a while I started paying more attention to otter signs than to the ice—not a smart idea, I realised, as a four-foot circle of ice gave way beneath my feet. Luckily, the snowshoes dispersed my weight, allowing me time to sidestep onto firm ice. Shaken but dry, I stared down into a hole full of gurgling black water.

▲ Unlike grizzlies, black bears are agile tree climbers. They spend much of the winter asleep, but do not go into full hibernation and can wake up if provoked.

Otter signs looked better than I'd ever seen, so I set half a dozen snares at den entrances. I was doubtful of any results, though, as otters are incredibly strong for their size, and chances were the animal would snap my six-strand lynx wire.

After lunch I constructed eight lynx sets along the meagre selection of trails. I was beginning to consider the whole trip a waste of time when I came across a fairly fresh set of moose tracks. Matthew would be excited to hear about this.

An even better find appeared on my way back to camp: under an overhanging ledge on the riverbank, hidden behind an uprooted tree, was the mouth of a black bear's den. A good-sized bear with his winter fat could yield 200 pounds of meat, and Matthew could get forty or fifty dollars for the hide. I inched nervously towards the den. My shotgun was loaded, but it was too dark inside to see anything. I wasn't about to poke a stick in there, and the smell of damp fur told me all I needed. I stepped back silently and returned to the trail; Matthew and I could come back later for the bear.

Back at the hut, I was disappointed to find no rabbits in my snares. I set out another twenty snares and slept peacefully through the night.

When I threw the blanket off my head in the morning, I was startled to find myself covered with several inches of new snow that had seeped through gaps in the hut. The snowfall intensified while I gulped down a hurried breakfast. I was out of food and my snares were all buried—yesterday's work wasted. I had packed little food in the interest of travelling fast; now I had to think about getting home fast.

I had no trouble finding my trail through the trees, but out in the open the wind had picked up and there was no sign whatever of my tracks. The seriousness of the situation began to sink in: with zero visibility, I could end up wandering aimlessly across the barrens. At this point Ki came to the rescue. He trotted on ahead like a homing pigeon, stopping occasionally to sniff around and then strutting cockily onwards. Lacking other options, I followed. Every four or five hundred yards, the faint impression of a snowshoe confirmed the accuracy of Ki's nose. Meanwhile the storm had grown into a fully fledged blizzard—the worst I had ever seen, much less travelled in. Only the thought that Mary and Matthew would be worried sick kept me from turning back to wait it out.

After travelling for hours I wondered why the main woods we were heading for remained out of sight. Ki was still trotting confidently ahead, but when I looked towards our back trail, I realised that we had unwittingly been snaking back and forth. Apparently Wonder Nose had lost the trail and was now just roaming around sniffing animal tracks. I sank to my knees as I tried to control the panic welling up from my stomach. I had to count on the wind; if it hadn't shifted, we were still heading generally south towards the camp. Unreliable as it was, the wind was my only source of direction.

The snow became softer as we went on. Dozens of times I fell or sank to my thighs, even with snowshoes. The chances of reaching our camp before the next day seemed slim. Then in early afternoon we came to a taller than usual stand of tamarack. Was this the edge of the heavy timber near the river? Suddenly I noticed a tree trunk with a gash where the bark had been rubbed off...where my toboggan had bumped into it two days before! Up ahead I could just make out the faint imprint of my old trail, and I set off again, marvelling at the odds of stumbling onto it after wandering directionless for hours.

Back in the trees, we raced over Eli's packed trail to the banks of the Lakitusaki River. I made a beeline for the Tookates' tent, where Eli gave me a casual hello as he poured my tea. I was rather taken aback: even in good weather they had all feared I'd kill myself, so why this unconcern now? Ice melted from my face as I sipped the gloriously hot tea and recounted the fur prospects to the north; then Eli explained his lack of surprise at my safe return. Mary and Matthew had seen the storm warnings, but Matthew had had a dream in which he saw me sleeping safely and peacefully in my hut. The dream said I was safe, so my friends promptly ceased worrying.

Alone on the Traplines

February 26 was an eventful day at Lake River. For two hours around noon, James Bay was dimmed by a solar eclipse; at our camp the air seemed heavy and grey, and no one spoke for a long time. On that day, too, the Hookimaws and the Tookates left by skidoo on a week's trip into Attawapiskat for socialising and supplies. I stayed behind with Ki to feed the dogs and tend the traplines.

I hadn't been to town in more than a month, yet the prospect of a week's quiet and solitude was more tempting than cold beer and old friends. The peace of the Lake River camp had had a dramatic effect on me, and was much more appealing than Attawapiskat with its skidoo traffic jams.

◀ **The author saws up wood for logs at the Lake River camp, in readiness for the return of Mary and Matthew Hookimaw, his Cree 'parents'.**

On the seventh day after my new friends' departure, I set off for an inspection of my main trapline, guessing I could get back in time for their imminent return. I had spent most of my time alone cutting wood, and I smiled at the thought of Mary and Matthew's surprise when they found an enormous stack of wood in their yard.

Three miles out on the line, I stopped in my tracks about 100 yards from one of my lynx sets. I started to shake with excitement as I saw lynx tracks trampling the snow and broken branches strewn around. Beneath a scrub willow twenty yards to my left, a lynx lay twisted in the snow, the wire snare and drag pole wrapped round the tree. In frantically yanking to free himself, he had pulled the noose tight and died quickly.

A lynx! After all those weeks of poorly constructed snares, I had actually set one right. I couldn't wait to show the others. It was a big animal, much bigger than any I had seen caught all winter. When measured, it came to forty-six inches (classified as extra large) and about fifty pounds. The pelt was a near-perfect salt-and-pepper and in good condition for such a late-season catch. It would certainly go for 300 dollars when Matthew sold his pelts.

Back at camp, I sat and stared at the lynx for hours—but my eagerness to share my pleasure was frustrated, as the Indians failed to arrive that day, or the next. Still more days passed with no sign of anyone, and a nagging anxiety slowly replaced my sense of peace as the quiet began to grind on my nerves.

Magical Polar Night Lights

THE EARTH'S POLAR REGIONS are often bleak and dark: for much of the year snow obliterates the colours of nature and night seems to last forever. For those who endure life at these latitudes, however, there is the occasional reward of a spectacular display of lights in the night sky.

A faint glow will appear in the heavens and spread to form an amazing array of ever-changing shapes that may have been conceived by an abstract artist. Great curtains of light may hang in the sky, to be replaced by arcs, streaks and broad sweeps—all in beautiful, luminous colours, ranging from vivid red to bluey-green. Very occasionally, enchanted observers also report hearing the faintest tinkling sound in the distance.

This is the aurora borealis, or northern lights. (The equivalent phenomenon in the southern hemisphere is called the aurora australis, or southern lights.) It arises when electrically charged sub-atomic particles released by the sun are trapped in the earth's magnetic field, where they collide with air molecules, which then radiate light. The Indians of Hudson Bay, however, have an altogether more poetic explanation: for them, the lights of the aurora are spirit torches that guide the dead to a land of light lying beyond the black shell of the sky.

A great sweep of brilliant, turquoise light from the aurora borealis transforms the muted colours of a winter night. ▶

Even so, I had my hands full keeping up with the rabbit snares, and I set a personal record of eleven trophies in a day. This was good news for Ki and the other dogs, who had been living on oats and lard.

One still night as I lay in my tent reading, I was distracted by an unfamiliar sound—something like the shattering of thin crystal a great distance away. I cautiously slipped out of the tent to find an incredibly brilliant display of northern lights rippling across the sky, sheets of colour climbing and descending in an intricate dance. Every few minutes the colours changed partners and began a new dance. The performance went on for several hours, but the unearthly music lasted only half an hour, during the most elaborate show. To hear the music of the aurora borealis is a once-in-a-lifetime experience, and many spend their entire lives in the north without ever hearing it.

▲ **The tools of the Cree trapper's trade are silhouetted against the warm, ethereal glow from inside his tent.**

I spent the afternoon of the fourteenth day hunting and checking snares, returning to camp to find fresh skidoo tracks running past my tent. Quickly seeing that Matthew and Mary were not back, I raced downriver to the Tookates' tent. There were Eli and his wife Phemi unloading their machine and grinning from ear to ear.

After presenting me with my long-awaited box of groceries and mail, Eli and Phemi came up to my tent for a pot of tea. As I reached for the tea pail, Eli shook his head and smiled. 'I thought you would like to help me with this,' he said, pulling a quart of Canadian Club whiskey from his pocket. For the next several hours the bottle went to and fro as I ran down the events of the last two weeks and, for the climax, brought forth my lynx. Eli just sat there, grinning hugely. He hadn't caught any lynx himself that winter, so was all the prouder of my accomplishment. 'Ha!' he shouted. 'Abraham will not believe this. He will think you stole it! Ha!'

Eli did most of the talking from then on, with occasional nods and murmurs from Phemi. He said the Indians in town harassed and abused his family because he refused to take welfare money. Disgust welled up in me as he explained that many were afraid the government would cut off the welfare funds if it saw that a family could, in fact, live well off a trapline. Eli, it seemed, was setting a poor example. The bottle was nearly empty now, and Eli was getting groggy. He began telling bizarre stories, usually leaving them unfinished, and recited old Cree spells and incantations. This drew glares from Phemi, who clearly felt that he was saying too much. Though I was fascinated, it made me uncomfortable too.

That night Eli and Phemi decided that it was time to end the trapping season, which had been poor for them, and return to town. My eyes filled with tears as I realised this was the beginning of the end of my life at the camp. As I watched them pack the next day, I thought of our first days together in January, of our late-night conversations round the oil-drum stove, fantasising about bumper hauls of beaver and scheming over new lynx-set designs. Now they were leaving. After several yanks on the starting cord of his recalcitrant skidoo, Eli turned and embraced me, saying he had never had a closer friend. We would have to trap together one day.

On the sixteenth day, I was out cutting wood when I heard the faint rev, choke and race of Matthew's skidoo. I dashed back to my tent to restore some kind of order to my bachelor existence. It was a joyful reunion, with Matthew nearly speechless, clapping me on the back and repeating, 'Heh, heh!' and Mary babbling incoherently. In a cascade of rabbit pelts, she hoisted her 200-plus-pound frame from the toboggan and began gesturing for this box and that to be unloaded.

Matthew pointed to one apparently important box and signalled for a warm-up round my stove. Over tea, I opened the parcel, their gift to me of a cornucopia of store food: pork sausage, chicken, doughnuts, cheese, and canned stew that contained not a scrap of rabbit. Then it was time for my gift to the Hookimaws; I presented the lynx with a flourish as Mary clapped and cheered and Matthew launched another round of 'Heh, heh!' He seemed especially pleased that the animal had been properly snared round the neck, rather than in a fur-damaging body snare.

From now to spring there would be just the three of us. To celebrate our reunion, I proposed a dinner party in my tent. Promptly at 6pm Mary and Matthew arrived in formal dress. Mary had combed out her hair and, carrying her bag, walked daintily down the trail in her finest calico dress and moccasins, Matthew beside her in a clean white shirt with all the original buttons. I had laid a new spruce-bough floor in my tent for the occasion and covered my bench with a towel. Silverware wrapped in freshly laundered bandannas lent an air of elegance. A heaped bowl of Spanish rice kept warm by the stove as chicken sizzled in the skillet.

We were a little stiff over the grapejuice cocktails, preoccupied with table etiquette. While serving dinner I began sniffing the air, trying to place an unfamiliar scent. As Matthew sat up prim and proud and Mary broke into giggles, I recognised it as aftershave, and we laughed through the rest of the evening. The dinner cemented my already close bonds with the Hookimaws, yet our laughter was partly a way of escaping the knowledge that we would soon part.

Activity at the camp tapered off over the next couple of weeks, and towards the end of March we began pulling up traps and snares in preparation for returning to the cabins at Lake River. Matthew and I retraced my journey north, but found all my snares empty and the den of the hibernating bear vacant. With little else to do, we spent much of the time stockpiling wood for the spring beaver camp: in June, Matthew and Mary would come back to the tents to hunt beaver by shotgun from a canoe. Matthew would see the long-awaited breakup of ice on the Lakitusaki River, but not I. His snowshoes would be hung from the rafters until next winter, while mine were destined for the customs office, a plane and finally a garage in the suburbs of Washington. It was time to return to the reality of the expedition.

The End of Winter

The day before we left for the cabins, March 23, I went out to pull up the last of my snares, taking Ki with me this time as it no longer mattered if he messed up the tracks. I vividly remembered setting each snare in February's bitter cold. It didn't seem fair that I had to leave just as I was mastering the art of trapping.

After two months in a tent, cabin life was not as pleasant as I remembered. Without the ventilation of canvas walls, the air was stale and heavy with the accumulated smells of smoke, beaver grease, dogs, gasoline and human bodies. The plywood floor was never really clean, no matter how much I swept, and I thought back fondly to my spruce-bough floor, always fresh-smelling.

There were a few chores to complete before returning to Attawapiskat: packing gear, washing clothes and drying the last beaver pelts. Matthew spent exasperating hours piecing together a working carburettor for his skidoo from pieces of a dozen defunct ones.

◀ **Evidence of a successful winter on the traplines—rows of beaver skins stretched out to dry inside wooden hoops.**

During our last few days together I sometimes walked into their cabin to find Mary sobbing and Matthew wiping his cheek. They showed me snapshots of their wedding and their relatives in town, while I tried with sketches to describe my family and our life. They didn't understand why I had to leave, why I could not remain as one of the family. In a very real sense they had become second parents to me, and I was haunted by the thought that I was abandoning them.

One morning, shortly before we were due to make the trip to town, we woke to find wolf tracks—the first we had seen all winter. This was bad news, for our game snares as well as for our dogs, the wolves' favourite food. For the next five nights their howling began just after dark and continued long into the night. Mary, wide-eyed with fright, would dash outside at the first sound and herd the dogs inside like a mother hen. Matthew and I, on the other hand, would grab our shotguns and unleash a five-minute salvo on the pretext of protecting our homes and property—when in reality it was just an excuse to raise a little hell and waste ammunition without getting a scolding from Mary.

We never saw the wolves and certainly never came close to hitting any, though when we recounted our heroic deeds to Mary their snapping jaws were always mere inches from our gun barrels.

The books say that wolves, unless threatened or rabid, won't harm humans—which I tend to believe. But I disagree with the books that say a wolf will avoid man at all costs; my experience suggests that wolves will sniff your toes out of curiosity if they think they can get away with it.

Mary Hookimaw giggles with delight, sandwiched between her fond husband and the author. ▶

The number and variety of tracks outside our cabins led us to estimate this pack at a population of six or seven. Apparently they weren't looking for trouble; they seemed to be just checking out the situation and hunting for scraps of food. We were more ambitious: with wolf pelts fetching sixty to eighty dollars apiece, Matthew saw the potential for income, and we hurried to block every wolf trail with an extra-sturdy snare. Traps would have been better, but we had none big enough. The snares remained empty, though, as the animals always found a new route through the bush to bypass the booby-trapped trail.

If the old belief of the Cree and other tribes is true, that all forms of life are spiritually related, then I would guess that wolves and men have a lot in common. One evening after supper, as a large moon rose over the spruce and the wolves began their nightly chorus, I left the cabin and settled in among the willows along the riverbank. This spot gave me a wide view of the river, lit by the moon; with the wind in my favour and a bit of luck, I hoped to catch a glimpse of the pack. My shotgun lay in my lap, mostly for the illusion of comfort, as it was loaded only with birdshot. Occasionally a howl would drift down the valley.

▲ A handsome wolf—potent symbol of the wild north. North America's largest wolves live in Canada, where their howls can be heard at a distance of ten miles.

I heard the wolves before I saw them. A pant and a whine, the faint sound of crystallised snow being compacted underfoot. Three dark shapes slipped out of the trees and down onto the frozen river, great graceful hulks in the dim light.

To me, the three wolves strolling along within a stone's throw of my hiding place represented all that I was seeking to learn at Lake River. In cunning and strength they are the kings of the fur-bearing animals. They are the embodiment of Nature's secrets, and Nature had been kind in permitting me to view them at such close range.

Some day I might be granted one of their pelts—not for the sake of tacking it to a wall in pride, but as a reward for learning an animal's habits well. Neither the animal lover who is against trapping, nor the hunter who sees animals only through a rifle's sights will ever gain this knowledge. The Indian who finds a fur in his snare has not 'conquered' the animal. No battle has been won. He has been given the pelt as a reward for his understanding of natural relationships. No human is closer to the animal than that man.

The wolves were nearly out of sight now. I stood up from my nest in the willows, stretched and gazed up at the sky, then closed my eyes to bring back their images. I walked slowly back to the cabin, somehow convinced that they had been aware of my presence as well.

Canada's Cree Indians

THE CREE ARE THE MOST WIDESPREAD Indian tribe in Canada, with communities dotted across the country from the Rockies to Quebec. Before the arrival of Europeans, the Cree had lived for some 5,000 years as migratory hunters, pursuing moose, caribou and other game in the vast forests and barren lands of subarctic Canada. During this time they had evolved a successful way of life which allowed them to survive in one of the harshest inhabited environments on Earth, while maintaining its natural ecological balance. With immense ingenuity they made use of limited resources to provide everything they needed: animals gave them meat for food, hides for clothes, blankets and tents, and bones for tools and weapons; birch bark was made into huts, canoes and containers; even the windswept tundra yielded wholesome berries and medicinal plants.

European contact quickly threw this way of life into disarray: epidemics of smallpox, measles and the common cold cut a swathe through the native peoples, in some communities killing over 80 per cent of the population; fur traders introduced guns, metal tools and traps, sparking off furious competition between tribes as they vied for trade, and leading to the rapid depletion of fur-bearing animals in many areas.

Today, many Cree have been settled in permanent villages with schools, a store and other facilities, but this has often led to the collapse of their culture and acute problems of welfare dependence, alcoholism, family violence and suicide. As a result, some communities have returned to the old hunting and trapping way of life, finding a valuable sense of continuity and cultural identity in following venerable traditions.

▲ This landscape near James Bay may look empty, even bleak, to an outsider, but the Cree have lived here for thousands of years, obtaining almost everything they need from hunting and trapping.

▲ As a Cree hunter waits patiently for a flock of geese to pass, the tension becomes too much for his catapult-wielding young son.

Setting off for a distant trapping ground in the middle of winter. ▼

▲ Sitting on a floor of spruce boughs and caribou hides, a Cree family enjoys some music-making in their winter tent. Note their outdoor clothes hanging up to dry.

◀ In this northern Quebec school, Cree children are taught how to make snowshoes using traditional materials: a wooden frame, interlaced with strong leather thongs.

▲ In the time-honoured manner, a Cree fisherman hangs out his catch to dry. In the background is a smokehouse, providing another method of preserving fish for winter.

CHAPTER 8

Rivers to the Sea

▲ Spring breakup, when the ever-warmer sun splits the solid ice of winter into a million angular fragments.

AFTER EIGHT MONTHS on dry land, the paddle shaft felt awkward in my hands. It would take at least a week of accumulated calluses before the handle and shaft would be comfortable again. Our paddle strokes had lost their smooth coordination, and the canoe no longer seemed to steer itself. Still, it felt good to hold a paddle again, to be moving east towards Tadoussac.

When Pete had arrived in Moosonee on May 8, a week earlier, it was more than a reunion—it was the rebirth of the expedition. Before my broken ankle had intervened, the prognosis for our success had seemed poor. Back in early September, we were near the end of our endurance, with two months of autumn travel ahead and another 700 or more miles to our destination. Reaching the St Lawrence River by the end of the year had been virtually impossible, and if we had failed, I doubt we'd have come back for another try.

But the accident that I feared would be a fatal blow had instead given the expedition new life. Pete had enjoyed his time back in the city and had worked to raise money for us. I had found my escape in Lake River, where no telephone calls, letters, equipment lists or budgets could reach me. The delay had left us both rested and eager to return to the trail. Pete looked rugged and ready: no extra inches round his waist, no city-pale complexion.

The remaining 120 miles of James Bay travel to Fort Rupert would present a new challenge: ice. During spring breakup on the bay, the pack ice recedes from shore, moving generally west to east, pushed by the prevailing winds. Travelling in the same direction, we would progress as quickly as we could find passage through the ice barrier. The solid pack would split into massive floes and bergs, these ruptures beginning as thin cracks in the pack, or leads, through which we could pass, depending on luck and timing.

Our room at the Polar Bear Lodge was quickly converted into a command centre and storage warehouse—maps strewn on the beds, hip-waders draped over the shower curtain, hundreds of pounds of supplies scattered across the carpet. Word of our plans spread through town, and it seemed that everyone wanted to get in on the act. The school donated materials for a new canoe mast; pilots gave us reports on ice conditions in the bay; the local meteorologist shared statistics on warming trends and wind direction. Rarely did we pass any of the Cree canoe-taxi drivers without receiving some advice on bay travel.

Mere hours before we pushed off from the dock, the latest updates on weather and ice conditions were ominous. Pilots who had scouted the coast reported solid pack ice all the way down to the southernmost tip of James Bay. A narrow lead along the shore had been sighted, but no one knew if it was navigable water or just tidal overflow. The canoe-taxi drivers urged us to postpone our departure until June, past all danger of being stranded by ice. But a forecast of northwest winds to fill our sail was too tempting. What we failed to realise was that those same winds would carry more ice down from the north.

As we headed towards the mouth of the Moose River, I felt a familiar satisfying jolt as our unfurled sail caught the following wind. We turned into a modest tack, and I watched Moosonee shrink and then disappear behind a string of islands. Pete was in the bow, adjusting the tack ropes; Ki napped in his accustomed place on the spray cover. I sat back in the stern with an arm draped over the rudder, smiling at the sun, the billowed sail and our reunited team.

Our first obstacle was wood: a logger's boom had burst a few days earlier, sending tens of thousands of logs down the river. Pete kept us on a zigzagging course through the 'wood-bergs', but this was just practice. Near the mouth of the river some ice did block our path, and we began learning the exhilarating game of ice roulette. Sailing at six to eight miles per hour through a four-foot gap between converging ice floes is a trick that leaves little margin for error. To complicate matters, our sail blocked 90 per cent of my forward vision, so split-second blind turns through an icy obstacle course proved as stimulating as any difficult rapid.

As we swung out onto the expanse of James Bay, fifteen miles from Moosonee, the drifting ice and floes became so thick that we had to lower our sail and pole our way through. Sometimes a half-hour struggle to penetrate the maze would bring us to a dead end, leaving no choice but to turn round and seek a new route. After a few hours, we realised that the ice ahead was solid pack. The only visible path through the mass was a meandering lead three or four miles offshore. It looked inviting, but the Indians had warned us about offshore leads: how the wind can suddenly shift and blow the pack straight out to sea.

▲ A huge consignment of logs is held in place by a great boom, itself made of logs. Timber is big business in Canada, where there are over 1,000 million acres of forest.

Deterred, we started looking for a campsite, but the receding tide and impassable ice left us with few choices. We scanned a moonscape of mud and ice, trying to will a good site into being, but the nearest trees and dry ground were more than a mile inland. Between ice and trees was nothing but spongy, boot-sucking ground and what looked like thousands of years' accumulation of seaweed and goose droppings.

After staking the canoe at the high-water mark, we began the ritual, familiar from last August, of relaying equipment through the mud and tidal pools to a fifty-foot-square island of semi-firm ground. We had looked forward to our first camp back on the trail, with town treats, cold beer, a blazing fire. Reality brought drizzle that turned to sleet as the temperature dropped. Finding little dry wood on the flats, we retreated to a tent with our macaroni and cheese.

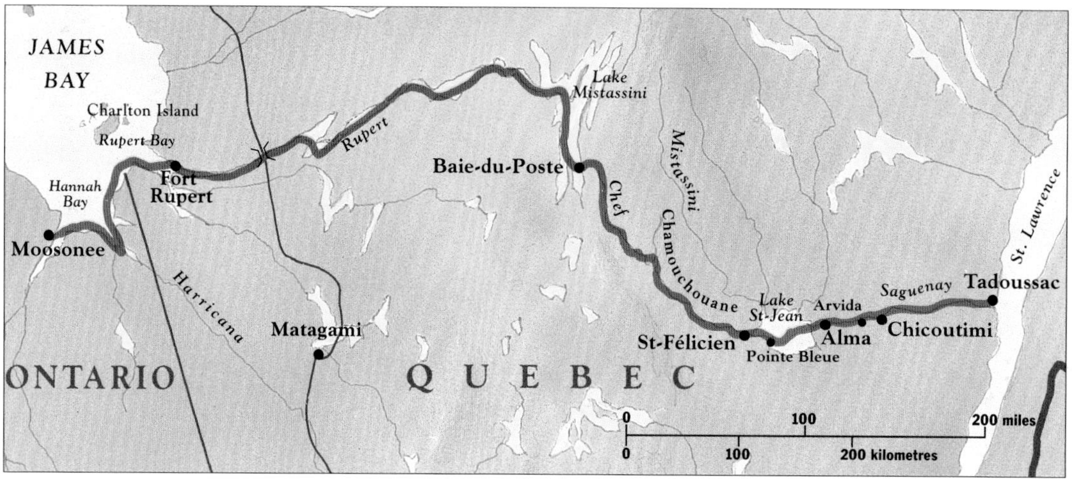

The final leg of the journey made by the Trans-Canada Expedition, taking the team from Moosonee to Tadoussac, on the St Lawrence River. ▶

In the morning, over a bottle of beer and half a dozen eggs each, we decided our first priority would be to find a good base camp with plenty of firewood and fresh water. From there we could make scouting trips down the coast to determine the extent of the ice, and wait as long as need be for an opening. Netitishi Point, five miles down the coast, seemed a likely spot, but we'd have to portage the whole distance.

Luckily, we didn't have to go that far. As we crossed a creek a mile from camp, we spotted a canvas tent tucked back in the trees about a mile from the coast. Following the creek inland, we found an abandoned Cree goose-hunters' camp. Dozens of roughly hewn decoys were piled in a corner of the main tent along with a collection of foam pads, blankets and sleeping-bags. A family of weasels had moved into that corner, but we took possession of the rest, which looked far more comfortable than our tiny two-man shelter. The freshwater creek was a mere 100 feet away, and driftwood was plentiful.

Stranded by Ice

The ice remained jammed up for four days. Each day we took turns scouting for any newly opened leads. But the south winds stayed away and the ice remained solid. Whenever the frigid air over the pack ice met warmer inland air, we witnessed spectacular illusions: great pillars of cloud climbed hundreds of feet above the ice, and shiplike apparitions rose up on the horizon, then vanished. The pack itself seemed to grow into towering cliffs of ice that shimmered and danced like the northern lights.

There was little else to do but eat and read, and the frustration of being stranded began to wear on our nerves—especially Pete's. The months of quiet at Lake River had trained me to a slower pace, and I welcomed the chance to sit and reflect. I spent some time inventing new creations from our standard fare of salt pork and potatoes, and many hours just viewing an entertaining parade of daydreams. I built a wilderness cabin for myself, worked on this book, planned my life year by year up to 2003. Ki seemed to share my philosophy: he was happy enough to doze in the sun, occasionally opening an eye to watch for passing ground squirrels. Pete, on the other hand, was fresh from the city and, without a book or a chore to attend to, he seemed lost.

On May 21, a full week after leaving Moosonee, we had no more than a few days' food left. Our alternatives were to continue down the coast and hope to find some, or to accept the dangers of offshore travel and paddle eighteen miles straight across Hannah Bay to the Quebec border. We decided on the latter, but the danger couldn't be ignored. Waves wouldn't be a problem, as the ice would keep the sea calm, but timing would be critical. Wind, and drift from a running tide, were the key factors.

We plotted our course, examined maps, studied the offshore leads and noted the fluctuations in wind direction. Our route would take us past three bale-out points where we could abandon the crossing if the wind shifted and the lead we were following closed. If the wind shifted during one of these shoal-hops, and ice bullied us past them, we might never reach land again.

We spoke little as we paddled towards the first stop-off point, a large grounded iceberg. We had planned as well as we could; the success of the crossing now rode on the luck of the winds. I had left two letters in the Cree tent: one to the tent's owner, with money for the food and fuel we had used, and another to a potential search party, with a map of our route in case we didn't make the crossing. Every few minutes we heard the distant thunder of massive floes colliding, one buckling up on top of the other. I couldn't erase the vision of a canoe caught between floes in such an encounter.

Four miles offshore we found an iceberg encased in a mile-wide belt of wedged floes—too solid to pass through yet too unstable to climb over—and our

◀ The author scratches his head in bewilderment at the thought of trying to find a way through this mayhem of jagged ice floes on James Bay. The dirty, grey colour of the ice is caused by sediment held in suspension since the water froze the previous winter.

plan collapsed before it was barely launched. We headed back to shore and for two more days waited out the ice in an abandoned trapper's shack. It was far from perfect, but with our sail in place of the missing door and a stove fashioned from discarded sheet metal, we managed to stay warm and dry. The snow was quickly receding under the late May sun, and the first unwelcome flies of the season appeared.

Late on the second day, two canoes slipped in and out of the ice on our horizon, one towing the other. I met them in my hip-waders 400 yards from shore. A man who had been poling off ice raised a hand to greet me; two Cree women with a ground sheet over their shoulders sat between the men, and children peered over the gunwale. They were leaving their camp on the Harricana River to purchase supplies in town. During breakup, outlying camps are stranded for up to six weeks, and this was the start of the Indians' spring exodus from bush to town.

They shook their heads when I described our shoal-hopping idea. 'Even a fool would not make that crossing this time of year,' the poler said. 'Better to stay by the coast. You only have five more miles of ice! But hurry; the lead is bad and it will close with the afternoon tide.' He dug his ice pole into a floe and left us with a final tip: 'You will probably find Indians with food on the Harricana River, around Francis Island.'

The team's aluminium-shod paddles come in useful for testing the strength of ice floes. ▼

It seemed we were destined to hug the coast after all, though our food situation was still dire. As we poled through the ice, the cries of sea ducks echoed off the bergs. We dug with our paddles to get within range, and as I yelled *'Fire!'* Pete dived to the deck to stay beneath the shot pattern. Firing over your bowman is hardly an advisable hunting practice, but sometimes we had to stretch the rules. Two ducks lay in the bottom of our canoe by the time the others caught on and took flight.

About halfway through the remaining ice we reached a spot where the floes were packed solidly together. We chose the likeliest-looking crack for a test of the canoe's icebreaker potential and built up some speed on the approach. At the last second before the crash, Pete yelled for a slight left turn. It was perfectly timed: the canoe's double-riveted bow cut into the ice, wedging its nose far enough into the crack to part the floes. We leaned on our paddles, their aluminium shoes cutting into the surface, and drove the canoe further into the gap. Like a steel wedge splitting a log, the canoe's thrust continued to widen the opening; aluminium ground against the floe with the screech of fingernails on a blackboard. After a thirty-foot struggle, we slipped out from between the floes into the next pool. The test had been a success, and the canoe had suffered no structural damage—only a few cosmetic gouges in its hull.

Icy James Bay

THE ICE PACKS of James Bay are not for the fainthearted, as Captain Thomas James—after whom the bay was named—discovered in 1631. James had set out from England at the behest of King Charles I to search for the elusive Northwest Passage to the Orient. His small ship and hand-picked crew reached Hudson Strait, where sea ice forced them into Hudson Bay, and then ever further south into James Bay.

Realising that they were going to be stranded for the winter, James beached the ship on Charlton Island and immediately organised the building of a wattle shelter, using the mainsail as a roof. Here he and his crew survived for the entire winter with the loss of only two men—a remarkable achievement, as the area is renowned for icy weather and cutting winds more typical of regions hundreds of miles further north. Only 11 years earlier, the Danish Captain Jan Munk had lost 13 of his 16-man crew while wintering in Hudson Bay.

James concluded that if there was a Northwest Passage it would have to be further north and that arctic conditions would probably make it unusable. This so discouraged the merchants who were backing exploratory voyages that they financed no further expeditions for several decades.

▲ **Massive icebergs such as this must have been an awesome hazard for the small wooden ship of Thomas James (inset).**

We continued to make progress through the morning. Many of the 'open' pools were navigable yet not really open; the temperature had dropped the night before, leaving a skin of new ice. I enjoyed looking back at the pattern traced by our stern's wake through the delicate layer of crystal.

Around midday an odd shimmer caught my eye. I stood up in the canoe and looked out, all the way to the horizon—across open water! Waves licked the surface—waves created by wind unhindered by breakwaters of ice. We dragged the canoe onto a small floe at the edge of the open water for a celebratory lunch. Ki rolled in the snow to scratch his back as Pete and I sprawled on the ice with the last of our garlic sausage and raisins.

We lounged a bit too long, though. Without the protection of surrounding ice, the floe was being quickly eaten away. Suddenly a crack developed beneath the canoe, and we began to list. As waves washed over the ice and lapped our boots, we frantically grabbed the remains of lunch and jumped into the canoe.

We sailed south for the next ten miles, making good time. Three miles short of the mouth of the Harricana, which flows into the south end of Hannah Bay, the wind shifted and rose, throwing waves into us broadside. The waves soon had us outclassed, forcing us to turn back. Low tide stopped us a mile from shore, so we staked the canoe and started on the familiar hike inland.

▲ With open water now in sight, Pete uses the canoe paddle to forge a route between the thinning floes.

After an hour of weaving back and forth over the flats and around tidal pools, we reached a few clusters of scrub willow on patches of semi-dry ground. A nearby swamp offered passable drinking water, better if disguised as tea. While I plucked our sea ducks, Pete left on the three-mile round trip to the canoe for a second load. At suppertime our first bite of sea duck told us why no one hunted these birds. All in all, it was a dismal ending to a long day.

Our camp on the flats was the most miserable of any in the journey. Mud was everywhere—in our boots, on our faces, in our hair.

Next day the wind abated just enough to tempt us into leaving. Scouting the west side of Francis Island, at the mouth of the Harricana River, we found an Indian camp that had been inhabited just days earlier. Was this where we had been told we could buy food? Picking through the garbage pile, I found a glass jar containing a few handfuls of rice. This would be our supper.

On May 29, about fifteen miles up the east coast of Hannah Bay, we came to the Missisicabi River and another camp, hidden back in the trees with only a radio tower sticking up to reveal its presence. This was a well-established camp where American hunters paid for the privilege of roughing it in half a dozen cabins circling a clearing. The cabin doors were locked but the windows, decorated with football-team logos, were open. Though we found the radio inoperable, we did get away with some booty: a handful of loose tea, a pound of lard, a few cheese crackers, a little sugar and macaroni.

That evening we had visitors: four Indians in a canoe loaded with shotguns and fishnets. They were low on food too, they said, and couldn't afford to sell us any. The spring goose flight had been the worst in decades and the whitefish weren't running. We were more concerned about ice conditions than hunting prospects, but they could not tell us the extent of the ice further north. They wished us luck and, as they pushed off from shore, tossed us a freshly killed goose. We declared the evening a mini-vacation and lounged on foam mattresses reading dogeared copies of *Playboy* while picking goose meat from our teeth.

A Visit from the Police!

Our luck seemed to be improving. Our grub box was growing heavier rather than lighter. When we stopped to help some Indians dislodge their scow from a sandbar, we were rewarded with cans of bacon, beef stew and peaches—the best food we had seen since Moosonee. We passed more ice as we worked our way north, but never as much as we had battled on the west coast. Every time we thought we were running into pack ice, a new lead would open up and allow us through. Far offshore, aircraft carriers of ice, towering up to twenty feet above the water, cruised by in defiance of the warm sun. White beluga whales and their grey offspring surfaced between the floes, sometimes as close as fifty feet from our canoe, and seals dozed on the ice.

▲ This young harp seal pup appears untroubled by the attentions of the photographer. It will soon shed the fluffy, white coat that has helped disguise it from predators during its first weeks of life.

May 31 was our last day in Ontario. As we completed the three-mile crossing of Gull Bay, we entered the tidal waters of Quebec. A light, quartering head wind sent ripples across the bow, and I stripped to my underwear in the seventy-degree heat. We were paddling two miles offshore to avoid shoals, marvelling at the variety of passing ice formations, when we heard the drone of an aircraft. After several passes, the plane circled and buzzed us, then turned into the wind to land on the water. Eagerly speculating that it might be a newspaper or television crew who had tracked us down for a story, Pete and I sat up from our slouch and dug deep with our paddles, trying to look as macho as possible.

But no cameras clicked from the windows; no microphones were proffered. Instead, an officer of the Ontario Provincial Police stepped down onto the pontoon. 'You boys OK?'

We assured him that we were fine, if a bit hungry. Neither he nor the pilot had thought to bring so much as a candy bar. They had been dispatched from South Porcupine, Ontario, after getting a radio report from Moosonee that Indian hunters had spotted us caught in the ice. They offered to return with food, but I proudly declined (and would kick myself for it afterwards). After bringing us up to date on the news, the officer promised to phone our parents and climbed back into the plane.

A chance to check the canoe's bearings when the Ontario Provincial Police fly in, alerted by reports that the team might be in danger. ▶

Our first camp in Quebec, on Pointe Mésaconane, was among the most beautiful we had seen. Almost exactly at the Quebec border, the tidal flats of James Bay's west coast gave way to the magnificent country of the eastern shore. Instead of miles-wide flats, clean sand and gravel shores rose steeply from the water. The land was higher and drier here, and grassy knolls backed by tall spruce replaced the dreary swamp landscape.

Next morning our luck held, and the modest head wind changed to a substantial tail wind. With the sail up, we practically flew along the coast, at one point covering four miles in twenty-five minutes, without paddling! We were about to round the Ministikawatin Peninsula, where our heading would change from northeast to east-southeast, and I feared that our rig wouldn't handle the new tack. But again the wind shifted in our favour as we made the turn.

Near a place inappropriately called Consolation Point, the lively weather turned suddenly fierce, and rain hammered our backs as we raced past granite cliffs. We had a decision to make: turn south at the point and hug the coast for safety, or cross the open water of Rupert Bay to Stag Island, eight miles out. The latter route could save a day's travel, and our growling stomachs made the decision.

The instant we passed the point we were committed. The wind shifted again to the southwest and lashed out with new strength. Its force snapped the sail taut and jolted the canoe nearly onto its side. I had to lean all my weight against the rudder paddle to keep us from flipping over. Both of us were leaning far out over the water, yet still we rode at a forty-five-degree angle.

Our speed slowed on this difficult tack. My hands ached and my arms were cramped from gripping the rudder; my jaws hurt from clenching my teeth. We hadn't had time to put on life jackets, but it hardly mattered: in water just a few degrees above freezing we wouldn't last more than a few minutes, with or without them.

The wind shifted even more to the south. We were sliding too far north; we would miss the island! Ki began to panic and run back and forth on the deck to escape the waves breaking over him.

It's hard to sail a canoe in a wind much over twenty miles per hour. Later we learned that the winds that day reached forty. The waves were close to six feet, black walls of water towering over us and burying our bow much of the time.

Finally the bow swung back towards the island and now we were sailing at uncontrollable speed towards a wall of rock surrounded by tremendous breaking surf. Just as it seemed we must crash, we glimpsed a sand beach tucked between massive boulders. At this critical moment, our canoe performed brilliantly. Instead of wallowing in the surf, she rode the tops of the waves as gracefully as a surfboard and we coasted in safely, jumped out and pulled her up on the beach.

Two days later, after inching the rest of the way across Rupert Bay against strong head winds, we landed in front of a cluster of Cree cabins and tents. Dogs charged through camp to announce our arrival, and a huge Indian stepped from a tent. Six children hid behind him, sneaking peeks at us around and through his legs.

This was Roderick Stevens, a trapper from Fort Rupert. Our arrival was timely, since his table was already crowded with food, but he grunted to his wife for even more.

Our meals for the last two days had consisted of water, oats and onion broth, and the spread nearly overwhelmed us. We ate smoked whitefish, Spam sandwiches, potatoes, bread, and fruit cocktail, and drank quarts of tea with sugar and canned milk—and then we ate some more, until Roderick was satisfied that we had eaten our fill.

As the canoe rounds Consolation Point, high winds and a heavy swell throw fresh challenges at a weary team. ▼

We declined his offer to stay the night. Fort Rupert was only ten miles away, a three- or four-hour paddle, and I was eager to turn our bow into the Rupert River and bid farewell to James Bay. The bay had done its best to beat us: to sink, starve, freeze or drown us. But the battle was over and we had survived it.

Paddling Uphill on the Rupert

No one in recent memory had paddled a small canoe from Moosonee to Fort Rupert, so our arrival provoked much curiosity. Before docking, Pete and I slicked our hair down and jammed our shirt-tails into our trousers to give an impression of casual competence, but I doubt if anyone was fooled. Our strained faces, torn clothing, chafed skin and sunken cheeks were giveaways.

Apparently a rumour had reached town that we were lost in the bay and had probably perished in the ice; the Cree men who crowded round our canoe poked the spray cover and sail and asked questions faster than we could answer them, but their expressions were noncommittal.

There were no reservations, though, in the welcome we got from John and Hazel Pearson, who immediately sat us down to a fortifying dinner of shepherd's pie and beer. Childhood sweethearts from the Shetland Islands, they had worked at Hudson's Bay Company posts all over Canada. John was a bluff, blond, bearded Viking type. He evinced a child's excitement about our journey and eagerly pressed us for details. The next morning, as we reviewed plans for our ascent up the Rupert, he shook his head and commented that no one had canoed *up* the Rupert for years.

'You do have some work ahead,' he said. Then he brightened up perceptibly: 'Say, La Sarre Airways flies all the HBC freight for me. The bloody thieves charge enough—they owe me a few flights. Tell 'em Pearson said to fly you upriver to scout the rapids.'

Thus originated a network of connections that was to prove invaluable throughout this difficult part of the trip. As John had warned, we did have our work cut out for us. Ascending the Rupert made going up the Berens look like child's play. A few statistics tell the tale: the Berens gains elevation at a modest 1.4 feet per mile, while over the Rupert's first 100 miles that average shoots up to eight feet per mile. Walking along a trail, this elevation gain would be too slight to notice, but on the water it's a very different story. Even a single foot of altitude per mile is a struggle.

We met pilot Georges Boucher at the La Sarre Airways trailer, and he happily agreed to help with the aerial scouting. In fact, he was just on his way to a small lakeside settlement about ninety miles east of Fort Rupert to pick up supplies, and we were welcome to ride along. Georges flew the round trip from town six times daily; so he could not only take us on recce flights, but could easily track our progress once we set off on the river.

Pete wanted to photograph around town, so I went on the first flight with Georges. It was an interesting trip. I didn't learn the identity of the supplies we were to pick up (2,300 pounds of bagged cement) until Boucher's obnoxiously loud, rattling, single-prop plane landed on the lake. The forklift on hand was a

◀ Looking down from Georges Boucher's plane on a picturesque village built on a calm stretch of the Rupert River.

primitive model (the two-armed, sore-back design, ie me)—so much for my free ride. Once the stuff was loaded, Georges taxied the length of the lake and ordered me into the back. In response to my puzzled look, he said as an afterthought, 'Oh, I forgot to mention: this plane's maximum cargo capacity is 1,800 pounds. I'll need you back there to adjust the load till we fly level.'

The lake was nearly a mile long, and our pontoons left the water no more than 200 yards from the far shore. Once we were airborne (if our gasping, treetop-scraping progress deserved that term), I dived for the rear and began shifting bags of cement until Georges shouted the OK. I expected him to fly at a safe 1,000 feet or so on the way back, but he obviously wanted to give me a close-up view of the rapids, so we followed the Rupert at about 100 feet most of the way, sometimes as low as twenty feet. Georges held the plane tightly to the river course, banking at each bend like a sports car carving up a country road. This wasn't just showing off; if we had veered from the river channel, we would have struck trees. I tried to take notes on the white water, but from this perspective most of the rapids defied navigation, and I was reduced to noting possible portage routes.

By June 9 Pete and I were ready to get going. From here to Tadoussac on the St Lawrence River we would be on rivers all the way, except for a few lakes and innumerable portages. John and Hazel, along with a few friends, met us at the first rapids, two miles from town, for a final farewell party, preceding us upstream in their outboard-powered rubber boat. Aside from this, day one on the Rupert was a total disaster. The current was about half as fast again as it had been on the lower Berens, and we failed in our attempt to line and wade up the first mile-long set of rapids. As on the Berens, we found that upriver travel by pole, line and paddle was nearly extinct, and we were again forced to blaze our own trail through a maze of brush. We camped the first night on an island only six miles from town.

New problems arose as we struggled on. Whereas we were used to paddling through stretches between rapids on the Berens, on the lower Rupert even the flat water was too swift for us to make progress by paddling. Other options were equally limited: the water was often too deep to advance by poling, and the banks were either sheer rock covered by matted growth or else choked with dense brush, both impractical for lining from the shore.

Most often we resorted to a method we called 'willow walking', which consisted simply of pulling ourselves hand over hand by overhanging branches, while remaining in the canoe. It was a painfully slow form of progress, our gains measured in scant yards per hour, and the willow exacted its price in countless slashes across arms and cheeks.

The week following our departure from Fort Rupert was one of exhausting river travel. We had committed ourselves to a schedule that would put us in Tadoussac on August 17, and plans had been set in motion for an arrival celebration. Meanwhile, though, it was a terrible grind, and it was not helped by the blackflies. In comparison it seemed as if we had had no bugs last summer. They came in clouds—getting into our eyes, ears and hair. We inhaled them when we breathed and swallowed them when we opened our mouths. Repellent had no effect. The only respite was to light a fire and sit in the smoke.

However, on June 17, five miles before reaching the Rupert River Bridge, we had a pleasant surprise. A plane circled and landed on the river, and out jumped six of our friends from Fort Rupert. We all climbed onto a beaver lodge, tied up the plane and canoe, and had quite a party with the goodies they brought.

Battling to Keep a Deadline

The next five miles turned out to be some of the worst, with three rapids and no portage trails. With the blackflies, it was living hell heaving the canoe through the bush and wading up to our waists in the still-icy water.

We were going through a bad patch. After reaching the Rupert River Bridge I felt like an old man. I hate to say it, but there was little joy in the trip any more. The thought of missing our August 17 deadline was overwhelming and we just kept going, seven days a week, ten to twelve hours a day. I didn't have time to fish, and we didn't even enjoy camps, just lit a fire, wolfed down dinner, read in the tent for half an hour, then collapsed. Still, each time we went hungry or dumped in a rapid I reckon we learned a little more and grew a bit stronger.

As we approached Lake Mistassini things got easier. The landscape flattened out and the river widened into a system of narrow lakes with connecting channels. Here the tough portages and rapids were interspersed with sections where we could make good time with the sail up or by paddle.

We had planned for Lake Mistassini to be the turning point in this section of our trip. Once past the lake we would be heading downriver for the rest of the way to the St Lawrence. Typically, though, somewhere between Moosonee and the Rupert River Bridge we had lost the large-scale maps for this last leg of the journey. They were important—the headwaters of the river were a mess—so at the Rupert River Bridge I wrote a letter home to Dad, asking for a duplicate set.

It eventually arrived by one hell of a roundabout route. Dad shipped the maps by air to Boston, from where they were flown to Montreal, then forwarded by a smaller carrier to Val-d'Or in Quebec, and on by ground transport to La Sarre, near the Ontario border. There La Sarre Airways and Georges Boucher took over, flying them to Fort Rupert and then on by helicopter to where we were camping, staked out at an abandoned goose-hunting camp. They were just in time. We were at the limit of the helicopter's range and another day's travel would have put us out of reach.

On entering Lake Mistassini our plan had been to travel down towards Tadoussac on the beautiful Mistassini River. Now, though, poring over the charts, we totted up the number of rapids we would have to negotiate and came to the conclusion that we could not do it in the time. Instead, we continued

◀ Serene Lake Mistassini here mirrors every detail of the landscape and clouds in its still waters.

down to Baie-du-Poste and on to Lake File Axe, from where we could join the Chef and Chamouchouane rivers.

By August 2 we had reached the Chamouchouane River and were back in the white water. The upper twenty-odd miles of the Chamouchouane were thick with rapids, and late on August 3 we came to a testing set of five. Everything had been going well, so well that we thought we'd have plenty of time in the last couple of hundred miles to the St Lawrence to relax and drift with the river. Meanwhile, our blood was running—we were in the mood for rapids.

The first was fine, but as we neared the second I started having bad feelings. The stage was set for a dump. We were running unscouted water, the light was fading and a steady drizzle kept visibility to a minimum.

My uneasiness grew as half a dozen nighthawks appeared, diving as close as a paddle's length from the canoe. I had never seen birds act like this. The water had turned inky black, shiny in the dim light. Of course, the Indians would say that the nighthawks and slick water were signs of nature, warnings of danger. They would never travel another foot after seeing such signs. But we were white men and knew that such things were foolish. We should have learned, but apparently we hadn't. We turned the canoe, pointing the bow upstream to stand and scout the rapid. It seemed to present no problems; it looked tough but fun and not too dangerous, the kind of rapid I most enjoy: deep standing waves mixed with quick, critical turns.

Fifty feet into the only navigable route, the current slammed into a rock wall, slipped round a jagged corner and disappeared in an avalanche of cascading white. If we didn't cut that turn perfectly, we wouldn't see the rest of the rapid—

A promontory jutting into the Chamouchouane provides an ideal campsite with spectacular views of the river's raging white water. ▼

or anything else beyond. Once round the turn, though, we simply had to keep the bow into the deep stuff and maintain pressure on the rudder to keep the canoe from rolling in crosscurrents. It was my job to feel the constantly shifting current which can change direction three or four times in seconds.

We cleared the rockface beautifully, with room to spare. The canoe leaned into the turn and we hit the first wave perfectly, taking a little wash over the spray cover. Ki suddenly rolled off. We lost sight of him behind rock and spray but soon spotted him dashing along the shore rocks after us.

▲ **Ki in a meditative mood—perhaps reflecting on the many near-disasters his companions have led him into.**

So Ki was safe and we had only three or four big waves to go. We ploughed into the first, and as we began the descent we got our first full view of the next wave. What had appeared to be just another four-foot wave loomed now, less than a paddle stroke away, as a ten-foot fang of white and grey. This was because the base of the wave was a black hole six feet beneath the surface, invisible unless you were looking right into it. After so many miles of paddling we had finally encountered one of the worst hazards of a river: a recirculating hole, so called because the combined pressure of the current and the height of the wave behind it can trap an object so that it never breaks free of the hole but endlessly climbs and descends the same wave. There was no way our eighteen-foot canoe would survive a head-on collision with a ten-foot wall of water without upending in a spectacular somersault. Yet there was no time to avoid it; any attempt would have taken us into it broadside—in which case our bodies and the canoe would probably recirculate until ice from the next spring's breakup forced us out.

My thinking hadn't progressed this far when we began our descent into the hole. At such times I imagine that thoughts are crowded out of the mind by sheer awe. Probably in the last second I shouted some vital instruction to the bow, such as, 'Oh, hell!'

The fact that we hesitated probably saved us. Earlier, I would have said that speed might be one's only chance to clear such a rapid, but in this case a spurt of speed would have been just the thing to complete the somersault and leave us keel-up. As the bow rose and cleared the crest, the canoe stood nearly vertical. We couldn't climb over it, nor did the wave have quite enough force to flip us. So we compromised by sliding backwards. At the bottom, the stern slammed into the rock from which the wave originated.

The rear third of the canoe, where I sat looking up at Pete, was underwater, as was I from the rib cage down. Then we rebounded and began to climb the wave a second time, without any help from our paddles. Again the bow cleared the crest, and again we slid back into the 'death hole'—the name that came soonest to mind. There is no feeling more revolting and gut-wrenching than to slide backwards into the bowels of a rapid.

As we slammed into the rock a second time I screamed to Pete, '*Paddle! For God's sake, paddle!*' This seemed to rouse Pete and he dug for life. Later he told me he thought the hull had been pierced and we were taking in gallons of water. In two short paddle strokes it was almost over; we emerged back into life-giving daylight and out of the wave. We were still too busy to celebrate, but within seconds we had cleared the last waves, veered into a back eddy and ground ashore, as if we had imagined the whole thing.

We ran upriver shouting for Ki and found him on a small beach. He bounded towards us joyfully, coughing a few times to clear water from his lungs. The canoe was basically sound, too, and after a short calm-down session we paddled back into the river and through a last minor rapid.

▲ **A waterfall in a verdant Quebec forest near Lake St-Jean—seen here without the hordes of sightseers that so depressed the author.**

All I could think of was how beautiful everything was. The sky was a deeper blue than I had ever seen. Each tree, each passing rock was full of unspeakable beauty. I kept thinking that we shouldn't be seeing these things—we should still be in the hole.

The Last Lap

The remainder of the trip down the Chamouchouane was relatively uneventful, except that the deep wilderness gradually began to show signs of civilisation—the occasional railway track or road. These should have made me excited but instead, for some reason, they got me really depressed. I don't think Pete and I talked much during those last two weeks.

About twenty-five miles from St-Félicien we camped at a series of waterfalls, the Bear Falls. We were unprepared for the ugly sight that greeted us—crowds of families with transistor radios, fishing and picnicking while their children played rowdy games. The parking lot was filled with cars and overflowing garbage cans.

In the middle of all this, though, millions of sweet wild blueberries were growing. We picked loads, camped a little distance downriver and feasted on blueberry pancakes. That was the day, I think, when we both faced the fact that our trip was nearly over.

We spent August 6 and 7 in St-Félicien, resting and stoking up on good food. We were right on schedule, ten days from our planned arrival date, and I called home to alert my parents that it was time for them and Pete's mom and dad to leave for Canada. They had said they wanted to be in Tadoussac a few days early, to organise the landing celebration.

Then came our last major lake crossing. Lake St-Jean, thirteen miles wide and some twenty-five miles long, was a formidable challenge: not only was it notorious for its high winds, it also had a heavy traffic of massive boats laden with aluminium ore that could plough us under without even noticing. We set out on the morning of August 8, sailing straight across the lake. Visibility was good, there were no ore boats, and we made about five miles under sail before the wind suddenly strengthened and we nearly flipped over. There was no going on so we made a right-angled turn south and managed to paddle to shore, landing at a spot called Pointe Bleue, where we were forced to be patient.

A few days later the wind calmed down and we made the crossing in one long tack, finding a landfall near Pointe-à-la-Savane on the eastern shore.

Sailing parallel to the lake's northeastern shore, we continued on and camped at the mouth of the Saguenay River, just below the town of Alma.

There we had a unique experience. The river at Alma is entirely blocked by a dam that provides hydroelectric power for processing the aluminium brought by the ore ships, and we had to portage the canoe down nightmare steps against its cold concrete face. It wasn't something we would care to do again in a hurry.

The riverbanks were heavily built up along this section of the Saguenay, through the towns of Arvida and Chicoutimi—the biggest along our route since Kamloops, back in British Columbia—and we had to portage round two more dams. We were now less than 100 miles from our destination.

Before it joins the St Lawrence, the lower half of the Saguenay turns wild again. As the canoe sailed down this broad, majestic stretch of river, lined on both sides with high cliffs, I had plenty of time to daydream. Nearly 5,000 miles and now this—there had been so many times during the journey when reaching Tadoussac had seemed impossible, yet after all our adventures it wasn't going to be quite the thrilling arrival I had imagined. I talked a bit with Pete about making another expedition, maybe going east to west and further north, but he didn't seem keen, so I stopped mentioning it. Maybe I was suffering from something the experts call post-traumatic stress, the letdown felt after a long period of high excitement.

The majestic granite cliffs of Cape Trinity, rising over 1,600 feet above the Saguenay River, lifted the spirits of the team on the final home straight. ▼

On the far side of a continent: Tadoussac, for so long just a remote name on a map, was a fittingly beautiful place for the team's 4,700-mile dream to come true. ▶

At any rate, the day before our arrival, our parents and a reporter from the *Toronto Star* came upriver by motorboat to spend the evening at our last campsite. They brought a bottle of champagne and discussed the arrangements for the final landing ceremony. I did my best to be enthusiastic, but Dad told me later that he'd noticed I was low.

When Jacques Cartier explored up the St Lawrence River back in the 1530s, there was an Indian village on the site of present-day Tadoussac. Its location, on the north bank of the St Lawrence, just where it joined the Saguenay, was strategically perfect. The village soon became a trading centre for furs and fish, and later, in 1600, the first French-Canadian trading post on the river. Today Tadoussac boasts a year-round population of only about a thousand, but it's a very popular summer resort with a proud place in the history of Canadian exploration.

Whales come up the salty St Lawrence to the Saguenay and beyond, and whale-watching excursions are popular tourist attractions. One of these excursion boats, along with a small flotilla of other small craft—rowing boats, kayaks, canoes—was ready for us when we rounded the last promontory above the small beach in Tadoussac.

We had been waiting behind this promontory, Pete and Ki and I, Canadian and US flags flying from our bow and stern, for the time to be right. Now it was coming up to 2pm, the day was August 17, and we were dead on schedule.

Dad was out on a breakwater with his binoculars, waving. A foghorn on the south bank tooted a greeting and the welcoming escort of boats gathered round to offer congratulations. On shore scores of people were cheering beneath a huge welcoming sign. It was an emotional moment.

As we approached the beach the water got shallow and our paddles scraped the bottom. When we hit land we both stood up slowly. The problem of who should get out first was solved by Ki, who hopped out and stood on the beach, wagging his tail. Cameras clicked as we hugged our families and each other, posed for photos, yelled for Ki, drank champagne and pushed our way through the cheering crowd.

The formal part of the celebration was laid on in the Tadoussac Hotel. The mayor of the town, Octave Caron, made a welcoming speech in French and English, and presented us with commemorative plaques carved by a local craftsman. Then Pete and I made our thankyou speeches, trying to remember to mention all the generous people along the trail who had made our journey possible. Then it was time for the banquet.

I have to admit that I went through all this in a kind of fog. I didn't quite believe in our success. But I was back with my family now, and that was important. They had shared in my journey almost mile by mile and their support had often kept the expedition going when it might have faltered. There were articles to write for magazines, and then this book.

Above all, of course, there were places that would stay in my memory for ever: a wind-blown ridgetop in British Columbia, a campsite on the Athabasca River, a run-down cabin in Saskatchewan offering shelter after a day of bitter cold, a stand of trees near a branch of the Lakitusaki River. Most especially, perhaps, I would remember the Cree friends I had made, and the warmth with which they had taken me into their lives and treated me as one of their own.

▲ The author and Pete, and a slightly bemused Ki, relishing their triumph.

Through the Great Canadian Wilderness—Travel Tips

▲ **A crimson-coated Mountie (a Royal Canadian Mounted Policeman) stands guard at Ottawa's government buildings.**

Preparing to Go

Options Many of Canada's scenic treasures are readily accessible to the visitor. The mountains, east and west coasts, lake regions and several cities are major attractions. Distances are huge, so it is impossible to cover the whole country during a short stay. Organised tours may save much time and frustration, and several companies offer adventure trips. For the independent traveller, provincial tourist offices in Canada are excellent sources of information.

Travel Most Canadian cities are served by the major international airlines. The most expensive times to fly are from July to mid-September and over the Christmas period.

Once you have arrived, driving is often the only way of getting to rural areas. Fly-drive options are available, or you can make your own arrangements, such as hiring a car in one city and dropping it off in another—though this may involve a substantial drop-off charge. An International Driving Licence is strongly recommended.

The Canadian public transport system offers various alternatives. Domestic flights are the easiest method of covering large distances. Freedom-of-travel passes, allowing unlimited travel for a fixed period, are available for long-distance buses, trains or certain domestic flights, but note that some of these passes have to be purchased prior to arrival in Canada. Canadian trains are comfortable but rail services are generally limited. Some rail journeys are wonderfully scenic, such as the ride through the Rocky Mountains from Vancouver to Jasper.

Practicalities Check with your travel agent or local Canadian tourist office about current entry restrictions. Nationals of the European Community and most Commonwealth countries do not need visas. Visitors are usually granted stays of three months, but must have proof of onward travel and may have to prove they have sufficient funds for their trip. Traveller's cheques in Canadian dollars are accepted like cash in most shops, restaurants and filling stations. Take at least one credit card (essential for hiring a car). Travel insurance is strongly recommended. No vaccinations are required for travel to Canada, but make sure you are up to date with boosters such as tetanus.

Language Canada has two official languages: English and French. English predominates, but French is the main tongue of the province of Quebec and parts of New Brunswick, though even there you can usually get by with English.

When to go Canada has a continental climate, with hot summers and cold (in many places bitterly cold) winters. Only the west coast escapes sub-zero temperatures between November and March; southwestern British Columbia generally has the mildest climate, but rainfall is high, especially in winter.

The archetypal splendour of the Rockies—a pristine wilderness of rugged mountains, cool, dark forests and pellucid lakes. ▼

The Rockies fill up with sightseers and walkers in summer, and with skiers in winter. New Brunswick, like much of eastern Canada, is popular in summer, but also has very attractive autumn colours. Ontario and Quebec can be uncomfortably hot in summer, but have pleasant autumn weather.

Accommodation Luxury hotels cater for the top end of the market, while bed-and-breakfast accommodation is available in most towns and cities. Motels, found in towns as well as in some rural areas, are modestly priced; rates are for the room, regardless of how many people use it. Campsites are abundant: all national parks and most provincial parks have them, but reservations are advisable in July and August. Rough camping is possible in many wilderness areas (often owned federally), but ask permission if possible.

▲ **A tourist boat takes visitors into the perpetual mists at the foot of Canada's 177-foot-high Horseshoe Falls, one of the two mighty cataracts that form the Niagara Falls.**

Where to Go

Canada is one of the best-organised countries for enjoying the outdoors. Permits for fishing and camping in the wilderness must be obtained from information centres in Canada's 35 national parks. The parks themselves are strongly orientated towards exploration, and many have guided nature walks and talks. Black bears and grizzlies may be encountered in the mountains and forests: they are dangerous and should not be approached, but will not generally attack humans unless startled. In the summer, insect repellent may be useful, and walkers should cover bare legs. Lyme ticks are a pest in many southern regions: their bites give unpleasant flu-like symptoms. Black flies are rife from April to June in areas near water throughout much of northern Canada; then, from July to October, the mosquitoes take over!

Mountain adventure Mountain hikes are available for all levels of fitness and experience—from short, level trails to demanding long-distance treks such as the 53-mile Cottonwood Trail in Kluane National Park in the Yukon. Walkers must be adequately shod and carry sufficient food, drink and clothing for everything the climate might throw at them.

National parks in the Rockies—the big four being Banff, Jasper, Kootenay and Yoho—have some of the country's best walks and most scenic roads, passing canyons, glaciers, lakes and waterfalls. Icefields Parkway, in Jasper National Park, is a particularly fine drive: its highlight is a trip by 'snow shuttle' onto the Athabasca Glacier. In the same park, the spectacular Maligne Canyon is the deepest gorge in the Rockies. Also abounding throughout the area are magnificent trails for horse riding.

Numerous provincial parks, such as Manning near Vancouver and Wells Gray near Kamloops, also offer plenty to tempt the hiker. Further east, some of the best walking is in Quebec—Forillon and La Mauricie parks, for example—and in Ontario, where Lake Superior and Algonquin parks offer rewarding hikes.

River adventure Ontario has outstanding canoeing, notably in the Algonquin, Killarney and Quetico provincial parks. The Rideau Canal, from Kingston to Ottawa, is one of the easiest routes, while the Ottawa River is very popular for white-water rafting. British Columbia is also excellent for white-water canoeing and rafting. Many establishments provide instruction as well as equipment hire.

Whale-watching Whale-watching cruise boats are a popular tourist attraction, with trips lasting hours or even days. August and September are the best months for watching whales in eastern Canada, while in March and April grey whales can be seen migrating along the west coast. Orca and porpoises are visible along the northwest coast of British Columbia between June and September.

Visiting the cities In the province of Quebec, **Montreal** and **Quebec** possess many cultural attractions, and both are close to fine outdoor scenery. Of the two, Montreal is the more cosmopolitan; Old Montreal, once a walled city, retains numerous old buildings reminiscent of Paris. Quebec is even more French in character, with cobbled streets, stone buildings and attractive squares spread beneath an imposing chateau.

In Ontario, **Toronto** is the largest and most culturally diverse of Canada's cities, with many fascinating ethnic districts. It also provides access by bus to the ever-popular **Niagara Falls**. Boats, helicopters and cable-cars offer rides right up to the Falls, while observation towers and a tunnel passing directly behind the Falls give further spectacular views.

On the west coast, **Vancouver** is widely considered one of the world's most beautiful cities. The Museum of Anthropology has a superb collection of artefacts, while the historic area of Gastown and the Chinatown district are interesting to explore on foot. On nearby **Vancouver Island**, Cathedral Grove offers a walk through a forest of gigantic red cedars and Douglas firs. In Alberta, the oil-boom town of **Calgary** is a popular point of departure for the Rockies. The city has a strong Wild West flavour: the Calgary Stampede, held in July, is one of the best rodeos in North America.

Index

and Acknowledgments

Note: page numbers in **bold** refer to captions for illustrations. British Columbia is referred to as BC, and David Halsey is referred to as DH throughout the index.

Acknowledgments

The editors gratefully acknowledge the use of information taken from the following books and articles during the preparation of this publication:

The Age of Leif Eriksson by Richard Humble, Franklin Watts 1989
The American Heritage Book of Indians by the editors of American Heritage, American Heritage Publishing 1961
The American North Woods by Percy Knauth and the editors of Time-Life Books, Time-Life 1982
America's Fascinating Indian Heritage, The Reader's Digest Association Limited 1978
America's Hidden Wilderness, National Geographic Society 1988
Book of North American Birds, The Reader's Digest Association Limited 1990
Canada's Fur-Trading Empire by Peter C. Newman, National Geographic, August 1987
Canada's Wilderness Lands, National Geographic Society 1982
Canada: This Land, These People The Reader's Digest Association Limited 1968
Canadian Book of the Road The Reader's Digest Association Limited 1979, 1991
The Changing World of Canada's Crees by Fred Ward, National Geographic, April 1975
Company of Adventurers by Peter C. Newman, Penguin Books 1985
The Encyclopaedia Britannica
The Eskimos by Ernest S. Birch Jr, Macdonald & Co 1988
Explorers and Exploration by Ian Cameron, Bison Books 1991
The First Americans by Robert Claiborne and the editors of Time-Life Books, Time-Life 1973
Fodor's Canada, Hodder and Stoughton 1985
Heritage of Canada Canadian Automobile Association in conjunction with The Reader's Digest Association Limited 1978
A Historical Atlas of Canada by Professor D.G.G. Kerr, Thomas Nelson & Sons 1960
The Illustrated History of Canada edited by Craig Brown, Lester Publishing 1991
Insight Guides: Canada edited by Hilary Cunningham, APA Publications 1993
The Native Americans: An Illustrated History by David Hurst Thomas et al., Virgin Books 1994
North American Wildlife The Reader's Digest Association Limited 1982
Northwest Passage by Edward Struzik, Blandford 1991
The Outdoor Traveller's Guide: Canada by David Dunbar, Stuart, Tabori & Chang 1991
Panoramic Canada by Heike and Bernd Wagner, Ziethen-Panorama 1993
The Penguin History of Canada by Kenneth McNaught, Penguin Books 1988
People of the Totem by Norman Bancroft-Hunt and Werner Forman, Orbis Publishing 1979
The Plains Cree: An Ethnographic, Historical and Comparative Study by David G. Mandelbaum, Canadian Plains Research Center 1990
The Royal Geographical Society History of World Exploration edited by John Keay, Paul Hamlyn Publishing 1991
Scenic Wonders of Canada The Reader's Digest Association Limited 1976
The Taming of the Canadian West by Frank Rasky, McClelland and Stewart 1967
The Times Atlas of World Exploration edited by Felipe Fernández-Armesto, Times Books 1991
Viking Expansion Westwards by Magnus Magnusson, Bodley Head 1973
Wild Animals of North America National Geographic Society 1987
The World Atlas of Exploration by Eric Newby, Mitchell Beazley Publishers Ltd 1975
The Wildlife Year The Reader's Digest Association Limited, 1991

Picture Acknowledgments

T=top; *C*=centre; *B*=bottom; *L*=left; *R*=right; *I*=Inset

Cover *Spine* Paul von Baich *L(T–B)* Norman Kerr, Bruce Coleman Ltd/John Shaw, National Archives of Canada, Bruce Coleman Ltd/Allan G. Potts, Bryan & Cherry Alexander *R* Tony Stone Images **2** ZEFA **3** Bruce Coleman Ltd/Stephen J. Krasemann **5** Bruce Coleman Ltd/Stephen J. Krasemann **6** First Light/Chris Harris **7** Norman Kerr **8–9** COMSTOCK/Malak **12** *TL* COMSTOCK/E. Otto *C* Bruce Coleman Ltd/Bob & Clara Calhoun **12–13** *T* Réflexion Photothèque/Anne Gardon *B* First Light/Mark Burnham **14** *BR* NHPA/John Shaw **14–15** *T* Bruce Coleman Ltd/Fred Bruemmer **15** *C* Bruce Coleman Ltd/Erwin & Peggy Bauer *CR* Bruce Coleman Inc/L. Rue *B* Oxford Scientific Films/Stan Osolinski **16** *T* Bryan & Cherry Alexander *B* Planet Earth Pictures/John Eastcott & Yva Momatiuk **16–17** *T* Bryan & Cherry Alexander **17** *BL* Bryan & Cherry Alexander **18–19** Paul von Baich **20** *BR* First Light/Todd Korol **20–21** Courtesy of the Royal Ontario Museum, Toronto, Canada **21** *TR* ZEFA/Dr H. Gaertner *BR* The Mansell Collection **22** *T* AKG London/Oslo, Nasjonalgaleriet *CL* Knudsens Fotosenter/Bakken *BL* Knudsens Fotosenter/Henden-BF **22–23** *B* First Light/Greg Locke **23** *TL* Knudsens Fotosenter **24** *TL* The Bridgeman Art Library/City of Bristol Museum & Art Gallery *C* Réflexion Photothèque/Tibor Bognar **24–25** *T* First Light/Thomas Kitchin *B* Explorer/Robert Harding Picture Library/Jean-Loup Charmet **26** *BR* Peter Newark's Western Americana **26–27** *T* Buffalo Bill Historical Center, Cody, WY, Gift of Mrs Karl Frank **27** *TR* Jean-Loup Charmet/Bibliothèque des Arts Décoratifs *BR* Le Musée des Augustines de L'Hôtel-Dieu de Québec (Canada) **28** *TR* Tate Gallery, London *CL* AKG London/British Museum, London *B* Royal Geographical Society **29** *TL* Fred Bruemmer *BL* AKG London **30** *BR* Réflexion Photothèque/Patricia Halligan **30–31** *T* Bruce Coleman Ltd/Wayne Lankinen **31** *TR* Survival Anglia/Des & Jen Bartlett *BR* The Mansell Collection **32** *BR* Fridmar Damm **32–33** *T* National Gallery of Canada, Ottawa, Transfer from the Canadian War Memorials, 1921 (Gift of the 2nd Duke of Westminster, Eaton Hall, Cheshire, 1918) **33** *CR* Fridmar Damm *B* The Bridgeman Art Library/British Library, London **34–35** COMSTOCK/B. Rose **36** *TR* ZEFA/Damm **36–37** *B* Range Pictures Ltd **37** *T* AKG London *CR* Range Pictures Ltd **38** *I* Panos Pictures/Penny Tweedie **38–39** *T* Bryan & Cherry Alexander *C* Panos Pictures/Penny Tweedie **39** *C* The Hutchison Picture Library/Brian Moser *BR* Bruce Coleman Ltd/Hälle Flygare **40** *TL* Réflexion Photothèque/M. Gascon *C* Robert Estall *I* First Light/Larry J. MacDougal **40–41** *T* Oxford Scientific Films/Tom Ulrich **41** *BL* Bruce Coleman Ltd/Jeff Foott **42–43** Tony Stone Images **46** Réflexion Photothèque/Bob Burch **47** Pete Souchuk, F22, Inc **49** First Light/Chris Harris **51** Réflexion Photothèque/Patricia Halligan **52** Oxford Scientific Films/Stan Osolinski **53** First Light/Trevor Bonderud **54** Pete Souchuk, F22, Inc **55** COMSTOCK/B. Rose **56** *TL* ZEFA/Allstock/J. Randklev *BL* Bruce Coleman Ltd/John Shaw **56–57** *T* ZEFA/Damm **57** *CR* Bruce Coleman Inc/Hälle Flygare *BL* Bruce Coleman Ltd/Stephen J. Krasemann *BR* Ardea, London/Kenneth W. Fink **58** First Light/Chris Harris **59** Pete Souchuk, F22, Inc **60** Mary Evans Picture Library **61** The Bridgeman Art Library/Royal Geographical Society **62** Pete Souchuk, F22, Inc **63** Bruce Coleman Ltd/Steve Kaufman **64** COMSTOCK/H. Georgi **65** Pete Souchuk, F22, Inc **68–69** Bryan & Cherry Alexander **70** *T* Publiphoto/Pierre Bernier *C* Bruce Coleman Ltd/Jeff Foott *BL* First Light/David Nunuk *BR* Robert Estall **71** *TL* First Light/Thomas Kitchin *B* First Light/Darwin R. Wiggett **72** Pete Souchuk, F22, Inc **74** Colorific!/Alon Reininger/Contact **76** First Light/Darwin R. Wiggett **77** Réflexion Photothèque/Perry Mastrovito **78** Pete Souchuk, F22, Inc **79** Bryan & Cherry Alexander **80** First Light/Thomas Kitchin **81** Pete Souchuk, F22, Inc **83** Pete Souchuk, F22, Inc **84** The Hutchison Picture Library **85** Colorific!/Sylvain Grandadam **87** Bruce Coleman Ltd/Fred Bruemmer **89** Bryan & Cherry Alexander **90** First Light/Patrick Morrow **91** Pete Souchuk, F22, Inc **92** *TL* Oxford Scientific Films/E.R. Degginger *CL* Bruce Coleman Ltd/Wayne Lankinen *BR* Bruce Coleman Ltd/Erwin & Peggy Bauer **92–93** *T* First Light/Thomas Kitchin **93** *TR* Bruce Coleman Ltd/Fred Bruemmer *BL* Oxford Scientific Films/Stouffer Productions *BR* Heather Angel **95** Pete Souchuk, F22, Inc **96** First Light/Stephen Homer **97** The Hutchison Picture Library/Titus Moser **98** 'Windigo' by Norval Morrisseau, 64.37.9, Glenbow Collection, Calgary, Canada **99** Pete Souchuk, F22, Inc **100** Pete Souchuk, F22, Inc **102** Survival Anglia/A. & D. Anderson **103** Pete Souchuk, F22, Inc **104** Bryan & Cherry Alexander **106** Dave Halsey **107** Pete Souchuk, F22, Inc **108** *T* First Light/Patrick Morrow *B* First Light/A.E. Sirulnikoff **108–109** *B* NHPA/Gerard Lacz **109** *TL* Royal Geographical Society/Frank Hurley *TR* Royal Geographical Society/Frank Hurley *BR* COMSTOCK/M. Beedell **111** COMSTOCK/G. Hunter **112** Pete Souchuk, F22, Inc **113** Pete Souchuk, F22, Inc **114** Robert Estall **117** Bryan & Cherry Alexander **118** Pete Souchuk, F22, Inc **119** First Light/Benjamin Rondel **120** Pete Souchuk, F22, Inc **121** First Light/Dave Reede **122** COMSTOCK/M. Beedell **123** COMSTOCK/H. Georgi **126** Publiphoto/Pierre Pouliot **127** Bryan & Cherry Alexander **128** *L* Paul von Baich *R* COMSTOCK/S. Vidler **129** *TL* Robert Harding Photo Library *TR* COMSTOCK/E. Hayes *BL* First Light/Brian Milne *BR* American Philosophical Society/Alfred Irving Hallowell **130** Pete Souchuk, F22, Inc **131** Pete Souchuk, F22, Inc **132** ZEFA **133** Pete Souchuk, F22, Inc **135** Pete Souchuk, F22, Inc **137** Publiphoto/J.P. Danvoye **138** Bruce Coleman Ltd/Jeff Foott **139** NHPA/T. Kitchin & V. Hurst **140–141** Pete Souchuk, F22, Inc **142** Pete Souchuk, F22, Inc **143** First Light/Stephen Homer **144** *TR* Bruce Coleman Ltd/Stephen J. Krasemann *BL* Bryan & Cherry Alexander/Wayne Lynch **144–145** *B* Oxford Scientific Films/Richard Day **145** *T* First Light/J.F. Bergeron *BC* First Light/Brian Milne *BR* Oxford Scientific Films/Stan Osolinski **146** Dave Halsey **147** First Light/Stephen Homer **148** Publiphoto/J.P. Danvoye **149** NHPA/John Shaw **150** Publiphoto/Fred Klus **151** First Light/Wayne Wegner **152** Publiphoto/Fred Klus **153** Bruce Coleman Ltd/Jeff Foott **154** Oxford Scientific Films/Judd Cooney **155** Dave Halsey **156** Oxford Scientific Films/Norbert Rosing **157** Bryan & Cherry Alexander **159** Bryan & Cherry Alexander **160** Dave Halsey **161** First Light/Thomas Kitchin **162** *T* The Hutchison Picture Library/Sabine Pusch *BL* Publiphoto/J. Wenk **162–163** *B* Bryan & Cherry Alexander **163** *T* First Light/Jerry Kobalenko *CL* Bryan & Cherry Alexander *BR* First Light/Stephen Homer **164** First Light/John Sylvester **165** ZEFA **167** Pete Souchuk, F22, Inc **168** Pete Souchuk, F22, Inc **169** ZEFA/Reinhard *I* Mary Evans Picture Library **170** Pete Souchuk, F22, Inc **171** Oxford Scientific Films/Daniel J. Cox **172** Pete Souchuk, F22, Inc **173** Pete Souchuk, F22, Inc **175** Pete Souchuk, F22, Inc **177** Publiphoto/Pierre Bernier **178** Pete Souchuk, F22, Inc **179** Dave Halsey **180** Publiphoto/P. Brunet **181** Robert Harding Picture Library **182–183** *T* Publiphoto/Paul G. Adam **183** *BR* Norman Kerr **184** *T* Réflexion Photothèque/Perry Mastrovito *B* NHPA/John Shaw **185** Tony Stone Images/Mike Vines

SEPARATIONS David Bruce Graphics, London
PRINTING AND BINDING Toppan Printing Co. (S) Pte Ltd, Singapore

Saratoga Springs, N.Y.
30 May 1998

SpecialTeas

SPECIAL TEAS

M. Dalton King

Photography by Katrina De Leon

Prop Styling by Jane Panico-Trzeciak

Food Styling by Marianne S. Twohie

SMITHMARK

A KENAN BOOK

This edition published in 1996 by SMITHMARK Publishers, a division of
U.S. Media Holdings, Inc.,16 East 32nd Street, New York, New York 10016

SMITHMARK books are available for bulk purchase for sales promotion and premium use.
For details write or call the manager of special sales, SMITHMARK Publishers,
16 East 32nd Street, New York, New York; (212) 532-6600

ISBN 0-7651-9744-8

SPECIAL TEAS
was prepared and produced by
Kenan Books, Inc.
15 West 26th Street
New York, New York 10010

Editors: Sharon Kalman and Sharyn Rosart
Art Director/Designer: Robert W. Kosturko
Photography Editor: Anne K. Price
Photographs © 1992 Katrina DeLeon
Prop Styling by Jane Panico-Trzeciak
Food Styling by Marianne S. Twohie

Typeset by Classic Type Inc.
Color separations by Colourmatch Graphic Equipment & Services
Printed in China by Leefung-Asco Printers Ltd.

10 9 8 7 6 5 4 3 2 1

Dedicated to Timothy, for keeping the faith.
With special thanks to:
Judie Choate, Dan Green, and Pam Long.

C O N T

E N T S

INTRODUCTION

When my partner and I started to put our tea catering service, SpecialTeas, together, we discovered that there are as many approaches to and ideas about Tea as there are types of tea. Our basic idea was to translate the time-honored British Cream Tea tradition into an American equivalent. We wanted to take the basic idea of Tea and make it suitable for any occasion. Our research showed that this was quite an easy thing to do and has been done for centuries.

Tea is more than lovely cut sandwiches, scones, and delectables. It is an occasion of warmth and sociability between two or more people. It provides the setting for problems to be solved, gossip exchanged, and comfort given.

In initiating SpecialTeas I thought of the many occasions of Tea with friends, some planned and formal, others developed at the spur of the moment. I thought it interesting that the memories of these times were always kind. One in particular kept coming back to me. I was baby-sitting an ill godchild. He had one of those flus children often fall prey to, and was lying bundled on the sofa, feeling small and isolated in his misery. There seemed to be no comfort I could offer him. Juice and ginger ale had lost their appeal. Then I remembered his mother said he could have weak tea with milk and honey. I asked him if he would like to try a "cuppa." A tiny little voice answered yes. I brought him his tea, and as he sat there with the warm cup between his hands and sipped, he began to perk up. He asked for a second cup, but wanted to help make it. While he made the tea I found some saltines. We sat together in the light of the kitchen, sipping, munching, and talking, both of us feeling better. Since that time, whenever we are together, we share a cup of tea.

This atmosphere of shared warmth and camaraderie is what any Tea giver strives for. Unfortunately, many people are a little wary of having Tea. They don't have the familiarity of the everyday to aid them as the British do, thus it becomes an occasion and has the semblance of a mystery. In fact, it's really very easy.

The table you set and the foods you choose are indicators to your guests of the pleasure you receive from their company. The setting can be achieved by using your finest china cups and prettiest linens. Fresh flowers are always lovely. If you have silver, use it, but remember, formal tableware is a plus, not a necessity. A skillful use of the tools at hand will do this nicely. If you are doing a "theme" Tea, use a bit of whimsy. The idea is to establish an atmosphere of conviviality. Think of it as creating a stage for the star of your production—the tea.

That is where this book comes in. The emphasis here is on the food. In putting this service together we decided to use the structure of the British Cream Tea as our model. It is based on a combination of practicality and fun. The sandwiches and tea provide the nourishment, the scones and desserts the fun. Using this three-course meal as a guideline, we have found that it can be adapted to any situation. We provide you with the choices: sandwiches, scones, muffins, biscuits, cakes, and tarts, you make your decisions based on the tastes of you and your guests.

We start out by giving you a good example of a British Tea and then show you how to customize it. We'll show you how to throw a Tea for holidays, children's parties, and for dinner. You'll see that it can be the perfect answer for after the theatre or a late-night "something."

We hope you will come to see Tea as a delight and a wonderful alternative to other types of entertainment. To the British it is a necessity, to us a gift.

M. DALTON KING

CHAPTER ONE

TEA — THE DRINK

A Perfect Pot of Tea

A Perfect Cup of Tea

Iced Tea

Sun-Brewed Iced Tea

Mint Tea Juleps

Lemonade Tea

Serves 6.

TEA FIRST CAME TO THE COLONIES IN AMERICA around 1650 on Dutch ships carrying the "new" drink to the Dutch colony of New Amsterdam. It took another twenty years for the rest of the colonies to become acquainted with tea. Even then, no one really had an idea of how to use it properly. People would let the tea brew and stew for hours, creating a dark, bitter drink. They also salted the used leaves and ate them on buttered bread. It wasn't until 1674, when the British took over New Amsterdam, renaming it New York, that the custom of tea drinking as we now know it was begun.

Prince of Wales Tea: ready for milk, sugar, or lemon.

TYPES OF TEA

Although tea has been sipped in North America for over three centuries, it is much older than that; in fact, over 4,000 years old. And while tea bought at the store is usually a blend of several of the 3,000 varieties available today, there are only three basic types of tea: black, oolong, and green. From these come the blends and varieties.

All tea comes from a single source, an evergreen bush that is a member of the *Camellia sinensis* (tea plant) family. From this bush comes the leaf that is processed into the three types of tea.

BLACK TEA is a completely fermented tea. This is achieved by first oxidizing the leaves, which turns them a beautiful copper color. The leaves are then fired, a process of treating them with blasts of very hot air. Black teas produce the rich, hearty brews popular in this country.

OOLONG TEA is a compromise between black and green teas. It is a partially fermented tea whose leaves are greenish black. The brew produced is lighter in both flavor and color.

GREEN TEA is not oxidized at all. The leaves are steamed after picking to prevent fermentation. These leaves produce a delicate brew that is very light in color. Mothers have used green tea for centuries to help upset stomachs, and there is increasing medical evidence that drinking green tea provides unsuspected health benefits.

Best grown in tropical or subtropical climates at varying altitudes, teas are often named after the region in which

they are grown, such as Assam or Ceylon. Tea leaves are either used singly or mixed with other leaves to form a blend. The combinations are endless. Some of the better known teas and blends are as follows:

BLACK TEAS

Assam: Grown in Northeast India, usually in low altitudes. It is most often used in blends. Rich in color, this is a strong, full-bodied tea loved by some as a morning pick-me-up.

Ceylon: Grown in Sri Lanka, this tea is often labeled "high grown" because it is cultivated at an altitude of 4,000 feet (1,219 m). Mostly used in blends, this is a strong, rich, full-bodied tea of light golden color.

China Black: A blend of tea from Keemun and the China mainland. A mellow tea with a distinctive smoky taste.

Darjeeling: Known as the "champagne of teas," it is grown in the Himalayan foothills and is available only three to four weeks a year. A very expensive tea, mostly used in blends. Famous for its fruity bouquet and light, full-bodied taste.

Earl Grey: A blend of Chinese and Indian black teas scented with oil of bergamot, a citrus fruit. An incredibly fragrant, full-bodied tea.

English Breakfast: A blend of Ceylon and Indian teas. A full-bodied "typical" English brew, popular as a breakfast tea.

Irish Breakfast: A blend of Assam and Ceylon teas. A strong, sharp brew, gives a "full cup of tea."

Keemun: The best of the China blacks, it is called the "burgundy of teas" by connoisseurs. Superior flavor with a wonderful flowery aroma.

Lapsang Souchong: A large-leaf black tea from the south of China. It has an unusual deep, rich, smoky aroma and flavor.

Prince of Wales: A blend of the finest Keemun teas. A robust tea with rich, golden color.

LAPSANG SOUCHONG/EARL GREY TEA

This blend gives a wonderfully smoky, fragrant cup of tea. It is an old recipe that catches people by surprise with its rich fullness.

Follow the directions for a perfect cup of tea. The measurements for this brew are half and half: half a teaspoon of Earl Grey and half a teaspoon of Lapsang Souchong per cup. If you are using tea bags, you will have to make at least two cups to get the measurements right. We like to drink this tea with milk; sugar seems superfluous. Serve hot.

OOLONG TEAS

China Oolong: A partially fermented tea. A light brew with a lovely fragrance.

Formosa Oolong: Native to Indochina, this tea is only available five weeks a year. An amber-colored broth, delicate in taste, and considered to be the best of the oolongs.

Mainland Oolong: A delicate Chinese tea with a beautiful aroma, sometimes scented with flowers.

GREEN TEAS

Gunpowder: A grade of tea in which the leaves are rolled into small pellets. Produces a clear, aromatic brew, which can sometimes be bitter.

Hyson: A "pan-fried" tea. A clear, light, gentle brew that leans toward being sharp or bitter.

Orange pekoe (pronounced peck-ō, and meaning "white hair"), is a grade of tea, referring to the size of the leaf. Orange pekoe is used in blends to give life or body to the infusion. The flavor varies with the place of origin or the processing involved. It is thought that at one time it was flavored with orange—hence its name, orange pekoe.

With the ever-increasing popularity of tea, three variations of traditional tea have come into vogue:

Specialty Teas The Chinese flavored their teas centuries ago. Specialty teas have black tea for a base and are flavored with spices, fruit, or other ingredients such as almond, cinnamon, lemon, or mint. These teas are distinguished from herbal teas by the fact that they contain caffeine. Specialty teas are finding increasing favor as morning or after-dinner drinks, particularly the fruit teas. These are refreshing, clear the palate, and are wonderful as dessert teas. Made with distilled essences of the fruit and/or fruit oils, these teas are available in a large variety of flavors.

For the best brew, it is best to buy fruit teas rather than try to make them yourself, since the process involved in creating your own fruit teas is not easy. Simply adding a concentrate or fruit juice does not achieve the desired effect and it will dilute the flavor of the tea. However, there are two possible alternatives to making fruit teas:

- Put a spoonful of fruit preserves in your cup before adding the tea. Bear in mind that doing this will sweeten the tea.

- Put a slice of lemon or orange rind (a two-by-one-quarter-inch slice per cup) in the teapot with the tea leaves. Pour in boiling water and

let the mixture steep for five minutes. The boiling water will release the fruit oil, thereby lightly flavoring the tea.

Decaffeinated Teas Tea contains less caffeine than coffee; coffee has one and a half grains of caffeine per cup, tea has less than one grain. Nevertheless, many people have decided to eliminate caffeine from their diets entirely. In recognition of this, most tea companies are producing decaffeinated teas.

Today, most tea manufacturers no longer decaffeinate their teas through a chemical process—they use sparkling water instead. Those who use this process let you know, so read the box labels.

Decaffeinated teas are also being produced by not using tea at all. Rather, a compilation of herbs that simulate the taste of tea are substituted. A word of caution. If the box lists "maté" in its ingredients, the tea has caffeine—maté is a South American caffeine plant. Herbal teas do not use black teas and are naturally caffeine-free.

Herbal Teas To the purist, herbal teas are not really tea at all. They are considered to be infusions, or in Europe, tisanes. An herbal tea is made from a combination of herbs, leaves, flowers, plants, berries, and spices. They are naturally caffeine-free, provide a wonderful alternative to caffeinated drinks and carbonated sodas, and are good both hot and cold.

Traditionally used as "medicines," herbal teas can act as mild digestives, help lift depression, soothe you to sleep, and slenderize the physique. The myriad benefits of herbal teas also carry with them an element of caution. Exercise care in the amounts and kinds of herbal tea you drink. In the interest of safety, you should limit your intake to two or three cups per day, moderation being the key. Not all herbal teas are safe to drink as a beverage. Read labels. If you prepare your own mixes, use only those herbs that are beverage-safe.

BEVERAGE-SAFE HERBS

Listed below are those ingredients safe to drink as a beverage. We suggest seeking expert advice before using herbs and plants not listed.

Alfalfa	Lemongrass
Catnip	Linden flower
Chamomile	Nettle
Chicory root	Peppermint
Elder flowers	Rosehip
Fennel	Red and Black raspberry
Fenugreek	Red clover
Ginger	Spearmint
Goldenrod	Slippery elm bark
Hibiscus	Yarrow

TEA RECIPES

A Perfect Pot of Tea

THE ROUND SHAPE OF THE TEAPOT WAS designed by the Chinese, who used a musk melon as the model.

To brew a perfect pot of tea, boil fresh, cold tap water in a kettle. (Cold water is essential because it has a greater oxygen content and gives the tea a fuller flavor.) While the water is boiling, warm the teapot with hot water. Once the teapot is warmed, pour out the water and put in the tea. Use one teaspoon of leaves or one tea bag per cup of tea. Some people like to add one extra for the pot. Once the water is boiling, bring the teapot over to it and pour it in the teapot immediately. Boiling water drops in temperature the moment you lift it from the flame, so by bringing the teapot to the kettle rather than vice versa, you have the hottest water possible. Let the tea brew three to five minutes. For reliability in flavor, always "brew by the clock, not the color." Serve hot.

A Perfect Cup of Tea

TEA BAGS WERE INVENTED BY MR. Thomas Sullivan of New York City. Sullivan was a coffee and tea merchant who wanted to send samples of his tea to customers in the hope of generating sales, so in 1904, he had little white silk bags made up and filled them with tea. To his surprise, orders for tea poured in, but they wanted it delivered in the bags. Ladies had found they could make a wonderful cup of tea by pouring boiling water through the bags.

To make a perfect cup of tea, you need the following:

1 tea bag
1 cup
Boiling water

Place the tea bag in a cup. A 10-ounce cup is best, but lesser amounts, such as an 8-ounce cup, work fine. Heat cold, fresh tap water in a kettle until it boils.

Bring the cup over to the kettle and pour boiling water over the tea bags, leaving enough room in the cup to accommodate milk or lemon. Dunk the tea bag once or twice. Let the tea brew for 3 to 5 minutes. As a tea bag can hold up to 7 times its weight in water, squeeze the bag as you remove it from the cup. Serve hot.

Iced Tea

MAKES 8 12-OUNCE GLASSES (WITH ICE).

Of the 45 billion cups of tea consumed each year in the United States, 37 billion are sipped in the form of iced tea. Iced tea was invented in 1904 at the St. Louis World Fair by an English tea merchant who was there to introduce Americans to Eastern teas. It was a hot day and fair-goers bypassed his pavilion for those who served cold drinks. In desperation, he poured his tea into ice-filled glasses. It was an instant hit, and has remained so.

2 quarts cold, fresh tap water
12 tea bags (your choice)

The rule of thumb when making iced tea is to use 50 percent more tea than when making hot tea. This amount of tea gives you a flavor that is not diluted despite melting ice. Pour 1 quart of water into a saucepan and 1 quart of water into a 2-quart pitcher. Heat the water in the pan until boiling. Remove the pan from the heat, add the tea bags to the pan, and let sit for 10 minutes.

Remove the bags from the pan and pour the tea concentrate into the pitcher of cold water. Cover and refrigerate until cold, approximately 2 to 3 hours.

Because of tea solids, tea made this way sometimes becomes cloudy. The flavor isn't affected, but if this bothers you, pour a small amount of boiling water into the tea. This should clear it up.

SUN-BREWED ICED TEA

MAKES 4 12-OUNCE GLASSES (WITH ICE).

1 quart cold, fresh tap water
6 tea bags (your choice)

Place the cold water in a glass container. Put the tea bags into the water. Cover and set out in the sun for 2 hours.

Serve over ice or refrigerate until ready to use.

MINT TEA JULEPS

MAKES 4 12-OUNCE GLASSES.

6 tablespoons sugar
6 tablespoons water
12 large mint leaves, approximately (depending on your personal taste)
Sun-Brewed Iced Tea, chilled
4 straws

Put the sugar and the water in a small pan and bring to a boil. Continue to boil for 2 minutes. Remove from the heat and cool to room temperature.

Fill 4 12-ounce glasses halfway with ice. Tear mint leaves with your fingers and put them over the ice (3 leaves per glass). Spoon 2 tablespoons of syrup into each glass.

Pour iced tea into the glass, filling it. Stir. Place a straw in each glass. Serve.

LEMONADE TEA

MAKES 4 12-OUNCE GLASSES.

2 cups lemonade, approximately
1 quart cold, fresh tap water
4 tea bags (your choice)
2 lemon tea bags

Fill ice cube trays with the lemonade. You will want approximately 6 ice cubes per glass of tea, so adjust the lemonade measurement as necessary. Freeze until the lemonade cubes are hard.

Meanwhile, put the cold water in a glass container and add the tea bags. Place the container in the sun and let brew for approximately 2 to 3 hours. When the tea is brewed let it chill in the refrigerator for at least 1 hour.

Fill a 12-ounce glass with lemonade cubes, then pour the chilled tea over the cubes until you have a full glass. Serve.

You can make up the cubes several days in advance and store them in plastic bags in the freezer. The tea can be made the day before and stored, covered, in the refrigerator.

Sun Brewed Iced Tea: cold and refreshing on a summer's day.

CHAPTER TWO

House SpecialTeas

Clove-Studded Lemon Wedges

Welsh Currant Cookies

Clotted Cream

Alice Paradis' Peach Preserves

Strawberry Jam

Fruit Butters

Serves 6.

AT SPECIALTEAS, WHENEVER WE PLAN A TEA FOR A client, there is always an in-depth discussion of the food preferences of both the client and their guests. This is important, for the primary rule of thumb at a Tea is for everyone to derive great satisfaction from the meal before them. The meal should be well prepared, appealing to the eyes, and pleasing to the palate. Keeping this in mind, there are preparation practices we always adhere to:

❁ Use fresh, thinly sliced bread. Normal slices of bread change the taste of the sandwich because it increases the ratio of bread to filling, and you cannot achieve the delicate look or taste that Tea sandwiches have.

❁ Every slice of bread used for a sandwich should be covered with a very thin coating of butter. This stops the filling from leaking through, thus preventing the bread from becoming soggy. Use real butter, not margarine or a mixture of butter and margarine. Butter adds a richness and substance to each sandwich that is evocative of Tea as a whole.

❁ Plan on a total of two whole sandwiches or eight sandwich pieces per person. It sounds like a lot, but the bread is thin and once the crusts are cut off, the size of the sandwich is greatly diminished. Guests tend to approach Tea sandwiches with a healthy appetite. Because they are so small, most people aren't really aware of how many they are eating. If there are some left over, have a small Tea for yourself the next day. They will keep.

❁ We generally cut each tea sandwich in one of four ways.

—into four small squares, achieved by cutting two intersecting lines (as in the shape of a cross) in the sandwich;

—into four small triangles, achieved by cutting two intersecting lines (as in the shape of an X) in the sandwich;

—into three parallel pieces, achieved by three lengthwise cuts in the sandwich, making sure the pieces are of equal size. In England toast is often cut in this manner to eat with boiled eggs and the pieces are called egg soldiers;

—the exception to the above would be to cut your sandwiches into different shapes, such as stars and hearts, by using cookie cutters. Depending on the size of the cutters, you will have to adjust the number of sandwiches you need to make to fulfill your serving requirements. The disadvantage to cutting your sandwiches this way is that there will be a certain amount of waste of both filling and bread.

❁ Always serve cucumber sandwiches. They are refreshing and cut through the richness of the other foods. This is not reflected in the menus; however, two different recipes for cucumber sandwiches are provided if you choose to follow our custom.

❁ Always serve jam and clotted cream with the scones. This is only a suggestion, however, because some people prefer to keep things simple and have their scones plain or with butter.

❁ Because people have a tendency to eat so many sandwiches, their appetites lose their edge when it is time for the scones. For this reason we keep the scones small. Large scones are simply too much for people to each once they are covered with jam and cream. In this case less is absolutely best.

Ceylon tea served with slices of pound cake.

❁ What applies to scones also applies to pastries. If you are making individual tarts and cakes, keep them small.

It has been our experience that people generally know what to expect at a Tea. They are familiar with the basics. What they don't know and want to see are the extras. What additional treats will there be? What kind of jam? Will there be clove-studded lemons? We think these little frills are important. At any Tea we serve, we make sure the following are available:

❁ clove-studded lemon slices
❁ Welsh currant cookies
❁ clotted cream
❁ a choice of two of the following
—homemade peach preserves
—strawberry jam
—fruit butters

These small touches add the finish to your Tea—they are the *"je ne sais quoi"* of the tea table.

Russian tea, to be served with cherry preserves, lemon and sugar, and Tea Cakes.

Tea break!

SERVING THE TEA

In the following chapters are recipes for tea and food. Before you read them it would be helpful for you to know a few of the Tea "procedures." Then, as you read the recipes and plan your Tea, it will be easier to create a mental picture of how it all will come together.

The first thing to do is to make two decisions: Are you serving brewed tea or using tea bags, and, is your Tea going to be served buffet-style or is it to be a "seated" Tea?

TEA BASICS

Plan on serving two to three cups of tea per person. Each person should have a cup, a saucer (if necessary), and a spoon. Since people take their tea in one of six ways—plain (often called black), with milk, with sugar, with milk and sugar, with lemon, and with lemon and sugar—make sure you have all of these accompaniments on hand. The sugar can either be cubes or granulated, although cubes are less messy. If you have tongs for the cubes, even better. The lemon should be set on a plate with a small fork. Some people serve lemon with tea by putting it in the cup and pouring the tea over it, but we prefer to place the lemon on the side (on the saucer) and let the guest add it. As an extra treat, we stud some of our lemons with cloves (see recipe, page 26) for added taste and fragrance.

BREWED TEA

If you are serving brewed tea, use a large enough teapot (two if necessary) so that all your guests are accommodated in a single pouring. As they are drinking the first cup, replenish the pots. It is wise to have help: one person to be the pourer and another to keep the kettle boiling, replenish the brew, and bring in the food. You can do all of this yourself, but you may decide you don't want to keep leaving your guests. Enlist a friend to help or hire someone for a few hours.

When the teapot is not in use, cover it with a tea cozy to keep it hot. If you don't have a cozy, an attractive tea towel, folded and placed over the spout and lid, will help. Keeping the tea hot is not as much of a problem with a silver service, since the metal retains the heat.

When you serve brewed tea you need an attractive strainer to prevent the leaves from going into the cup. Place the strainer in a small bowl by the pourer. Place the strainer on top of each cup before the tea is poured, then remove it and put back in the bowl. Excess leaves can be tipped into the bowl to prevent the strainer from clogging. The pourer then asks each guest what they would like in their tea, adds whatever is desired, and hands the cup to the guest. This continues until each guest is served. This is the standard method for a seated Tea. If you are having a buffet-style Tea, you may still want to have a pourer or you may choose to let the guests serve themselves.

As said before, always keep a kettle—or two—boiling while the party is in full swing, thereby insuring that fresh, hot pots of tea are no problem. Simply dump out the used leaves, put in fresh leaves, and pour in the water. A friend of ours bypasses the need for using a tea strainer by brewing her tea with a Melita-type drip coffee maker. The measurements are the same as those used for a regular pot of tea. She puts the tea in a paper filter and pours the water over the leaves, letting it drip down into the container. A low flame keeps the tea hot until the dripping process is finished. The tea is then transferred to the serving pot. This method produces a good cup of tea and eliminates some of the fuss.

The key to having a Tea is to be organized and prepared. Make sure everything is set up beforehand and it will be very easy to keep the pots filled and the flow of the party going.

From the Thanksgiving Tea: Red Cabbage and Bacon Vinaigrette Tarts served with Assam tea.

TEA BAGS

If you choose to use tea bags, make sure you have enough for each guest to use a fresh bag for each cup of tea. Arrange the tea bags on a small platter or in a bowl. Using tea bags gives you the opportunity to provide your guests with an assortment of teas from which to choose. Place the hot water in an attractive urn or china pot that can be refilled as necessary.

Tea Food

The food you serve at a Tea is the same whether it is served buffet-style or seated. You will need a fork, knife, plate, and napkin for each guest. If you serve buffet-style, set the food out on a table and let the guests help themselves. We always put the jams and clotted cream in bowls with spoons, which facilitates putting these toppings on the scones.

Serving the Food

There is a correct order in which the food should be eaten. First the sandwiches, followed by the scones (which are lovely cut in half, spread with jam, and topped with a dollop of clotted cream, or vice versa), and lastly the sweets, with cups of tea offered throughout. A buffet offers guests more freedom of choice, so don't be surprised if some disregard this prescribed order.

When you serve people who are seated, the Tea foods should be served in the order mentioned above. The jams and cream should be placed on the table and left there throughout the meal. The food is brought to the guests on platters or trays and passed by the hostess or server. Make sure each guest has had their fill of a course before passing the next one. Cookies and small cakes can be placed on the table, allowing the guests to help themselves while the hostess or server passes around the larger desserts.

The important thing to remember in all of this is that you and your guests should enjoy the occasion. Do not be frightened by the ceremony; relax and let the party flow. The more Teas you give, the more effortless they will become. You do not have to follow anyone's rules: make your own, create your own traditions. Simply remember to have fun making the food, serving your guests, and collecting compliments.

The following recipes are the little extras that can be served at any tea. Finally, since it is your Tea, it is important to remember that what we are giving you are the guidelines; it is for you to decide what suits you and your guests best. It may mean you choose to pull a Tea together from several different menus, serve less of one sandwich and more of another, or none at all. Do whatever you choose to insure that both you and your guests are delighted with your special Tea.

Filled Chinese Pancakes.

Clove-Studded Lemon Wedges

MAKES 8 WEDGES.

1 medium-size lemon
Whole cloves
Toothpicks

Early in the day of your Tea, wash a lemon under warm water with a vegetable brush. Dry the lemon thoroughly.

Using a sharp paring knife, draw 8 equally spaced lines from the top of the lemon to the bottom. Going down the length of these lines, puncture continuous holes with a toothpick. Push a whole clove into each of these holes until you have 8 complete lines. Place the lemon aside until Tea time.

While you are boiling the water for the tea, cut the wedges by centering a knife between 2 rows of cloves and slicing. Continue until you have cut out all 8 wedges.

Welsh Currant Cookies

MAKES APPROXIMATELY 6 1/2 DOZEN COOKIES.

4 cups flour
1 3/4 cups sugar
4 teaspoons baking powder
1 teaspoon cinnamon
1/4 teaspoon nutmeg
1 cup shortening (such as Crisco)
1 cup milk, approximately
1 10-ounce package currants

Mix the dry ingredients together in a bowl. Cut in shortening. Pour in milk, a little at a time, mixing to make a firm dough. If necessary, add more milk (up to 1 cup), being careful that you don't end up with a sticky dough. Add the currants.

Roll out the dough on a floured surface to 1/4-inch thickness. Cut out the cookies with a 2-inch biscuit cutter or glass.

Over low heat, cook the cookies on an ungreased griddle or skillet until very brown, about 2 minutes per side. Cool and serve. The cookies can be frozen.

Clotted Cream

MAKES 1 1/3 CUPS; SERVES 4 TO 6.

THE CREAM USED IN ENGLAND IS NOT available here, although there are a number of substitutes and facsimiles available. We use the following:

1 cup heavy cream, at room temperature
1/3 cup sour cream, at room temperature
1 tablespoon confectioner's sugar

One hour before serving, pour the heavy cream into a bowl and whip until soft peaks form. Whisk in the sour cream and sugar, continuing to beat until the mixture is very thick.

Place in the refrigerator and chill until it is time to serve.

If you want to make this ahead of time, it should last 4 to 6 hours in the refrigerator.

ALICE PARADIS' PEACH PRESERVES

MAKES 4 PINTS.

- **2 quarts peaches (approximately 6 to 8 peaches per quart, depending on the size)**
- **1/4 cup lemon juice**
- **7 cups sugar**
- **1 teaspoon cinnamon**

Peel and pit the peaches. Place in a large saucepan and sprinkle with lemon juice (this protects the peaches from browning). Mix in the sugar. Cover the pan and let stand overnight.

The next day, bring the mixture to a boil over medium-high heat. Once the mixture has boiled, turn the heat down to low and simmer slowly until the syrup thickens and the peaches are clear. Add the cinnamon, stirring well. Skim any bubbles off the top, making sure all the foam is removed.

After skimming, crush the peaches in the saucepan using a potato masher.

Pour the peaches into 4 hot, sterilized pint-size mason jars. Fill to 1/2 inch from the top. Wipe the tops of the jars with a clean, damp cloth. Screw the lids on tightly. Turn the jars upside down, allowing the lids to heat and seal.

After the jars have cooled, return to the upright position and let sit for at least 24 hours. Label and date.

Store in a cool, dry place. The jam will have a shelf life of approximately 1 year.

STRAWBERRY JAM

MAKES 8 HALF PINTS.

- **9 cups fresh strawberries**
- **2 tablespoons lemon juice**
- **8 cups sugar**

Wash, dry, hull, and halve the strawberries. Put them with the lemon juice in a large pot. Heat over medium heat until the mixture begins to simmer. Cook at a simmer until the fruit becomes soft, approximately 15 minutes.

Add the sugar, stirring until dissolved. Raise the heat to high and bring the mixture to a boil. Continue cooking for 30 minutes or until thick. Remove from heat, skim off any foam, and let sit for 5 minutes.

Pour the jam into hot, sterilized mason jars. Fill to 1/2 inch from the top. Wipe the tops of the jars with a clean, damp cloth. Screw the lids on tightly. Turn the jars upside down, allowing the lids to heat and seal.

After the jars have cooled, return to the upright position and let sit for at least 24 hours before using. Label and date the jars. Store in a cool, dry place.

The jam will have a shelf life of approximately 1 year. Should you open a jar and find any sign of mold or encounter a peculiar odor, discard it immediately.

FRUIT BUTTERS

MAKES APPROXIMATELY 1 1/2 CUPS.

- **1/2 pound butter, at room temperature**
- **1/2 cup of your favorite fruit preserve**

Place the butter and preserves in a bowl. Using a mixer, a food processor fitted with the metal blade, or a blender, whip the 2 ingredients together until well blended.

Spoon the butter into a serving dish or ramekin. Chill until ready to serve.

CHAPTER THREE

A British Cream Tea

Smoked Salmon and Dill Sandwiches

Curried Egg-Mayonnaise Sandwiches

Cucumber Sandwiches

Roquefort, Walnut, and Cognac Sandwiches

Currant Scones

Scottish Petticoat Tails

Fruit Tarts

Classic Sponge Cake

Prince of Wales Tea (or your choice)

Serves 6.

When Anna, the seventh Duchess of Bedford, made her first eloquent request for afternoon refreshment, she started a tradition that is still beloved a century and a half later. The British Cream Tea is the epitome of this afternoon pleasure. A Cream Tea is so called because it is just that, a Tea with clotted cream and the products of milk: butter, whipped cream, and custards. These, and a wonderful array of sandwiches, scones, cookies, cakes, and pastries, grace the tea table. The combinations are endless.

Mind you, the British do not indulge in a Cream Tea every afternoon; it is as much an occasion for them as it is for us. Their daily Teas are considerably pared down. They may be as simple as tea and toast, crumpets heated over the fire, or slices of a simple cake.

But when the British do a Cream Tea, it's heaven. There simply is no comparison, as we found to our delight. Their Teas are remarkable not only in the choices available but for the freshness and wonderful quality of the foods they serve: the swirling richness of the cream, the buttery crispness of shortbread, and the melting appeal of cakes that are both substantive and light. We have tried to remain faithful to the memories of these Teas by choosing those foods that are classics.

Smoked Salmon and Dill Sandwiches

MAKES 12 PIECES.

6 thin slices wheat bread
Unsalted butter
3 ounces smoked salmon, sliced
1 teaspoon chopped fresh dill

Spread each slice of bread with a thin coating of butter. Divide the smoked salmon evenly between 3 slices of bread. Sprinkle 1/3 teaspoon of fresh dill over each sandwich. Cover the sandwiches with the remaining bread slices. Trim the crusts. Cut each sandwich into 4 pieces.

Curried Egg-Mayonnaise Sandwiches

MAKES 12 PIECES.

4 thin slices white bread
4 thin slices wheat bread
Unsalted butter
Curried Egg Salad

Spread each slice of bread with a thin coating of butter. Divide the Curried Egg Salad between the 4 slices of white bread and spread evenly. Top the white bread with the wheat bread. Trim the crusts. Cut the sandwiches into 3 parallel pieces.

Curried Egg Salad

MAKES 3/4 CUP.

2 hard-boiled eggs, peeled
1/2 cup mayonnaise
1/2 teaspoon curry powder

Finely chop the eggs. Mix in the mayonnaise and curry powder, making sure all the ingredients are combined.

This will keep in the refrigerator, well covered, for 3 days.

Cucumber Sandwiches

MAKES 12 PIECES.

1/2 medium cucumber, peeled and thinly sliced
1 tablespoon apple cider vinegar
Unsalted butter
6 thin slices white bread
Salt (to taste)
Pepper (to taste)

Combine the cucumber and vinegar in a bowl. Toss to blend. Let sit for 1/2 hour. Drain off excess liquid.

Spread a thin coating of butter on each slice of bread. On 3 slices of bread, place the cucumber slices, making sure the bread is well covered (you'll need 6 to 8 slices of cucumber). Salt and pepper each sandwich. Cover with the remaining slices of buttered bread. Trim the crusts. Cut each sandwich into 4 pieces.

Currant Scones with jam and clotted cream (see recipe on page 32).

ROQUEFORT, WALNUT, AND COGNAC SANDWICHES

MAKES 12 PIECES.

- **1/2 cup walnuts**
- **1/4 pound Roquefort cheese, at room temperature**
- **2 tablespoons cognac**
- **6 thin slices white bread**
- **Unsalted butter**

Toast the walnuts under the broiler for approximately 8 to 10 minutes or until golden brown. Cool and finely chop.

While the walnuts are toasting, blend the cheese with the cognac.

Spread each slice of bread with a thin coating of butter.

Spoon the cheese mixture, dividing evenly, on 3 slices of bread and spread over each slice. Sprinkle a full tablespoon of nuts over the cheese. Top each sandwich with the remaining bread slices, pressing down firmly.

Trim the crusts. Cut each sandwich into 4 pieces.

CURRANT SCONES

MAKES APPROXIMATELY 10 TO 12 SCONES.

- **2 cups flour**
- **1/4 cup sugar**
- **2 teaspoons baking powder**
- **1 teaspoon salt**
- **3 tablespoons unsalted butter, cold**
- **3/4 cup milk**
- **1 egg**
- **1/2 cup currants**
- **1 egg yolk**
- **2 tablespoons cold water**

Preheat oven to 350° F.

Sift the dry ingredients together. Using a pastry blender or 2 knives, cut the butter into the dry ingredients until the mixture is crumbly.

Beat the milk and egg together. Pour into the dry ingredients and stir until well blended. Add the currants, stirring until well combined.

Prepare a flat surface by flouring it well (the dough will be slightly wet and will absorb the flour quickly). Place the dough on the flat surface. Knead briefly (once or twice) and pat the dough until it is 3/4 inch thick. Cut out the scones with a 2 1/2-inch biscuit cutter and place on a greased baking sheet.

Beat the egg yolk with the cold water. Using a pastry brush, glaze each scone with this mixture. Bake for 25 to 30 minutes or until golden brown. Serve hot or cold, with jam and clotted cream, if desired.

SCOTTISH PETTICOAT TAILS

MAKES 8 OR 16 WEDGES.

- **2 cups sifted all-purpose flour**
- **1/2 teaspoon baking powder**
- **1 cup unsalted butter**
- **1/2 cup sugar**
- **1 tablespoon grated lemon rind, optional**

Preheat oven to 300° F.

Sift together the flour and baking powder. Put the butter in a food processor fitted with the metal blade and cream. Add sugar to the butter and process for 30 seconds or until well blended. Add the flour and baking powder, processing until a dough is formed. Do not overwork. Put in the lemon rind (if using) and pulse the processor until just blended in.

Remove the dough from the food processor and put it in a greased 9-inch pie plate. Pat the dough down with your fingers, distributing it evenly over the bottom of the pie plate.

With the back of a knife, carefully cut the dough into either 8 or 16 pie-shape wedges. Prick each wedge in several places with a fork. Bake for 30 minutes or until golden brown. Remove from oven. The wedges will run together while cooking, so retrace the original knife cuts while the shortbread is still hot. Let the cookies cool completely.

When cool, remove the first wedge carefully. The petticoat tails will stay fresh for a week if stored in an airtight container.

NOTE: If you choose not to use a food processor, just follow the instructions and mix by hand.

Prince of Wales Tea and Scottish Petticoat Tails garnished with orange and strawberry.

Fruit Tarts with lemon curd.

Fruit Tarts

MAKES 6 TARTS.

Sweet Pastry

MAKES ENOUGH DOUGH FOR 6 TARTS.

1 cup all-purpose flour
2 tablespoons sugar
$^1/_4$ teaspoon salt
$5^1/_2$ tablespoons butter
1 egg, slightly beaten

Combine the flour, sugar, and salt in a food processor fitted with the metal blade and pulse 2 or 3 times. Process in butter until the dough is crumbly. Add enough of the egg, approximately one half, to form a dough. Wrap the dough in plastic wrap and chill for 1 hour.

Preheat oven to 350°F.

Roll out half of the dough on a lightly floured surface. Cut out 6 4-inch circles. (Freeze the remaining dough, well wrapped. It will last 3 months.)

Place a dough circle in each of 6 fluted tart pans, 3 inches in diameter and $^1/_2$ inch high. Press down and around gently. Remove any excess. Gently prick the dough with a fork.

Bake in a preheated oven for 15 to 30 minutes or until starting to brown. Cool in the tins until ready to use.

Judie's Lemon Curd

MAKES 2 CUPS.

$1^1/_4$ cups sugar
4 eggs
Juice of 4 lemons (approximately $^1/_2$ cup)
12 tablespoons unsalted butter
Grated rind of 2 lemons (optional)
Fresh raspberries (for final step of assembly)

Beat the sugar and eggs until light and fluffy. Blend in the lemon juice.

Pour the mixture into a saucepan and heat over a low flame until hot. Add the butter, 1 tablespoon at a time, until completely melted and blended. Raise the heat to medium and cook until thick. Stir well as it thickens to prevent sticking and burning. Fold in the rind, if desired. Cool.

To assemble the tarts, fill each shell with 2 tablespoons of Judie's Lemon Curd. Starting in the center and working outward, cover the top of the tarts with fresh raspberries, approximately 20 per tart. Refrigerate until ready to serve.

These tarts are best if made within 24 hours of serving.

Classic Sponge Cake

MAKES 1 9-INCH LAYER CAKE.

2 eggs
2/3 cup sugar
1 cup self-rising cake flour
4 tablespoons unsalted, melted, cooled butter
1/2 cup milk
1 teaspoon vanilla
1 cup damson plum preserves (or your favorite)
Confectioner's sugar

Preheat oven to 325°F.

Beat the eggs in a mixer on high speed until they are thick and lemon-colored, approximately 5 minutes. Gradually add the sugar, continuing to beat until the mixture is very thick and falls in thick folds when you lift the beaters from the batter. Add the flour, beating just until well blended. Combine the butter, milk, and vanilla. Add to batter. Mix until well combined. Do not overbeat.

Pour batter into a greased 9-inch cake pan. Place in the preheated oven and bake for 25 to 30 minutes or until golden brown and a toothpick inserted in the center comes out clean.

Let cool in the pan for 10 minutes, then turn the cake out onto a cake rack and cool completely. When cake is cool, slice into 2 even layers. Gently spread the preserves evenly over the bottom layer. Replace the top of the cake. Dust the top with confectioner's sugar.

This cake tastes best when made and eaten the same day.

Classic sponge cake filled with preserves.

CHAPTER FOUR

AN AMERICAN CREAM TEA

Roast Beef Sandwiches with Horseradish Sauce

Waldorf Chicken Salad Sandwiches

Goat Cheese and Sun-dried Tomato Tartlets

Curried Tuna Salad Sandwiches

Walnut Scones

Ginger Snaps

Tangy Lemon Bundt Cake

Vanilla Custard Fruit Tarts

Ceylon Tea (or your choice)

Serves 6.

On December 16, 1773, when the colonists dumped tea overboard at that famous tea party in Boston, they were revolting against the taxes that came with the beverage, not against the tea. This act led to a deep schism between the American colonists and Britain. It didn't actually stop people from drinking tea; it just stopped them from having tea with the Brits. Two hundred years later, this, of course, has changed. The wounds have healed and the two countries now refer to each other as cousins. The bonds between the two countries are so firmly established that their cultures often overlap.

Of the many wonderful gifts the British have given us, Afternoon Tea is clearly a favorite. Americans often call this meal "High Tea," pointing out the aura of majesty and mystery with which Americans view Tea. (High Tea is something else entirely that we will explain in a later chapter.)

An American Cream Tea can be very simple. Following the British example—for we consider its basic design and variations perfect—it is easy to convert this custom to American tastes. We stick to the structure of a three-course meal. Our variations come in the food choices we make, borrowed from the myriad of cultures that flourish in North America, and from American classics such as Thanksgiving.

Roast Beef Sandwiches with Horseradish Sauce

MAKES 16 PIECES.

2 tablespoons mayonnaise
1 tablespoon prepared horseradish
8 thin slices white bread
Unsalted butter
4 ounces thinly sliced roast beef
Salt (to taste)
Pepper (to taste)

Combine the mayonnaise and horseradish in a small bowl. Set aside.

Spread each slice of bread with a thin coating of butter.

Put 1 ounce of roast beef on each of 4 slices of bread, folding it to conform to the size of the bread. Season with salt and pepper. Spoon a teaspoon of the horseradish sauce over the beef on each sandwich.

If you would like a sharper taste, use $1\frac{1}{2}$ teaspoons of the sauce. Top the sandwiches with the remaining bread slices. Trim the crusts. Cut each sandwich into 4 pieces.

Waldorf Chicken Salad Sandwiches

MAKES 12 PIECES.

Salad

3 cups cooked chicken, medium diced
3/4 cup walnuts, coarsely chopped
3/4 cup Granny Smith apples, small diced
1/2 cup golden raisins
1/2 cup celery, small diced
2 scallions, finely sliced
Salt (to taste)
Pepper (to taste)

Dressing

1 cup mayonnaise
1/2 cup sour cream
1/4 cup cider vinegar
1 tablespoon honey
6 thin slices whole wheat bread

Butter

Place the salad ingredients in a large bowl, tossing to combine.

In a smaller bowl, whisk the dressing ingredients together. Pour the dressing over the salad and mix well. Season with salt and pepper. Chill about 2 hours.

To assemble the sandwiches, spread the bread with a thin coating of butter.

Spread 2 to 3 tablespoons Waldorf Chicken Salad on each of the 3 slices of bread. Top the sandwiches with the remaining bread. Trim the crusts. Cut each sandwich into 4 pieces.

GOAT CHEESE AND SUN-DRIED TOMATO TARTLETS

MAKES 8 TARTLETS.

Tartlet Shells

MAKES 8 SHELLS.

8 thin slices white bread
2 1/2 tablespoons melted butter

Preheat oven to 350°F.

Cut 1 circle out of each slice of bread with a 3-inch round biscuit cutter, preferably with crimped edges. Lightly brush melted butter on both sides of each round. Press each round into a cup in a cupcake tin. The edges of the bread rounds will come up the cup sides slightly. Bake for 10 to 15 minutes. Watch the shells closely, as you want them golden brown. They have a tendency to become too dark.

These shells can be stored up to a week in an airtight container.

Goat Cheese and Sun-Dried Tomato Tartlets served with Roast Beef and Waldorf Chicken Salad Sandwiches.

Goat Cheese and Sun-Dried Tomato Spread

MAKES 1/3 CUP.

1/4 cup goat cheese, at room temperature
2 tablespoons heavy cream (milk can be substituted)
2 tablespoons minced sun-dried tomatoes
2 sun-dried tomatoes, each cut into 8 thin slices

Combine the goat cheese and heavy cream until smooth. Add the minced sun-dried tomatoes, mixing thoroughly. This spread can be kept in the refrigerator, covered, for 3 days.

To assemble the tartlets, fill each shell with the goat cheese and sun-dried tomato spread, dividing it evenly between the 8 shells. On top of each shell crisscross 2 slices of sun-dried tomatoes.

CURRIED TUNA SALAD SANDWICHES

MAKES 12 PIECES.

1 3 1/4-ounce can solid white tuna, drained
1 tablespoon finely sliced scallion
3 tablespoons currants
3 tablespoons finely chopped walnuts
1/2 cup mayonnaise
1 1/2 teaspoons curry powder
3 thin slices white bread
3 thin slices wheat bread

Butter

Put the tuna in a small bowl, flaking with a fork to separate the meat. Add the rest of the ingredients and mix well. You can use for sandwiches immediately. Making it the day before allows time for the flavors to meld. This salad will stay in a refrigerator for a maximum of 3 days.

To assemble the sandwiches, spread 3 thin slices of white bread and 3 thin slices of wheat bread with a coating of butter.

Divide the Curried Tuna Salad between the 3 slices of white bread, spreading it evenly. Cover each sandwich with the wheat bread slices.

Trim the crusts. Cut each sandwich into 4 pieces.

Walnut Scones and tea.

WALNUT SCONES

MAKES APPROXIMATELY 10 SCONES.

2 cups flour
1/4 cup sugar
2 teaspoons baking powder
1 teaspoon salt
3 tablespoons unsalted butter, cold
3/4 cup milk
1 egg
1/2 cup walnuts, coarsely chopped
1 egg yolk
2 tablespoons cold water

Preheat oven to 350°F.

Sift the dry ingredients together. Using a pastry blender or 2 knives, cut the butter into the dry ingredients until crumbly. Beat the milk and egg together. Pour into the dry ingredients, stirring until a dough is formed. Add the chopped walnuts, combining well. Using an ice cream scoop, form the scones and place on a greased baking sheet.

Beat the egg yolk with the cold water. Using a pastry brush, glaze each scone with this mixture. Bake for 25 to 30 minutes or until golden brown.

Serve hot or cold with jam and clotted cream, if desired.

GINGER SNAPS

MAKES APPROXIMATELY
4 DOZEN COOKIES.

This is a 100-year-old recipe.

- **1 cup molasses**
- **1/3 cup shortening (such as Crisco)**
- **3/4 teaspoon baking soda**
- **1 teaspoon dry ginger**
- **1/4 teaspoon salt**
- **2 3/4 cups flour, approximately**
- **Sugar**

Preheat oven to 350°F.

Pour the molasses into a medium-size saucepan and bring to a boil.

Add the shortening, baking soda, ginger, and salt to the pan and stir well. When shortening has melted, turn off burner. When the mixture has cooled slightly, add enough flour so that the dough comes away from the sides of the pan. The dough is very elastic and will not require much flour.

Place the dough on a lightly floured surface and roll out very thin. Cut dough with a 2 1/2-inch round cookie cutter and place on a greased cookie sheet. Sprinkle each cookie lightly with sugar.

Bake until the cookies are firm and start to brown, approximately 10 minutes. You will be able to smell these cookies very strongly as they get done.

Cool on a rack.

Stored in an airtight container, these cookies will last up to 2 weeks.

TANGY LEMON BUNDT CAKE

MAKES 1 10-INCH BUNDT CAKE.

- **3 cups self-rising cake flour**
- **2 1/2 cups sugar**
- **4 large eggs, at room temperature**
- **1/2 cup milk, at room temperature**
- **1 tablespoon vanilla**
- **3 1/2 sticks unsalted butter, at room temperature**
- **1 1/2 tablespoons grated lemon peel**
- **2/3 cup fresh lemon juice**

Preheat oven to 350°F.

Sift together flour and 1 1/2 cups of the sugar. Beat eggs, milk, and vanilla together. Cut butter into pieces and add to dry ingredients along with 1/3 of the egg and milk mixture. Beat on medium until smooth, about 3 minutes. Add another third of the egg and milk, beating just until blended. Pour in remaining egg and milk and lemon peel. Mix just until blended. Pour into a 10-inch greased cake pan and press down with a spoon to push out air pockets. Bake 45 minutes to 1 hour, or until cake is golden brown and a toothpick inserted in the cake comes out clean.

Shortly before the cake is done, combine the lemon juice and remaining sugar in a small saucepan over high heat and cook until the sugar is dissolved. Lower the heat and cook for 2 minutes.

When the cake is done, remove from the oven and place on a cake rack. Spoon 1/2 cup of the glaze over the exposed part of the cake (this is actually the bottom of the bundt) and let it sit for 10 minutes. Remove from rack. Coat a piece of wax paper with a light layer of cooking spray and place on the cake rack. Turn the cake onto the wax paper. Using a pastry brush, cover the top and sides of the cake with the rest of the glaze. Cool thoroughly. Remove cake to a platter and serve.

Wrapped well and refrigerated, this cake will last for at least 3 days. It can be frozen but must be well wrapped.

VANILLA CUSTARD FRUIT TARTS

MAKES 6 TARTS.

Follow the procedure for Fruit Tarts in the British Cream Tea (page 41), substituting this recipe for Judie's Lemon Curd.

- **1/2 cup sugar**
- **4 tablespoons all-purpose flour**
- **1/4 teaspoon salt**
- **1 1/2 cups milk**
- **2 egg yolks, beaten**
- **2 teaspoons vanilla**
- **1 tablespoon unsalted butter**

Combine sugar, flour, and salt in a medium-size saucepan. Mix together the milk, egg yolks, and vanilla. Whisk the milk mixture into the flour mixture. Cook over low heat, stirring constantly, until the custard starts to thicken, about 5 minutes. Add the butter. Let the custard cook until very thick, 2 minutes. Remove from the heat and cool to room temperature. Fill the pastry shells with the custard.

CHAPTER FIVE

A Southern Tea

Fried Chicken 'n' Biscuit Sandwiches

Cajun Shrimp Sandwiches

Potato Salad in Cucumber Compotes

Ham Salad in Corn Muffin Cups

Coconut Cake

Pecan Scones

Sour Cream Sugar Cookies

Sun-Brewed Iced Tea

Serves 6.

THE AMERICAN SOUTH HAS ALWAYS EVOKED THOUGHTS OF GRACIOUSNESS and gentility. It is easy to conjure up images of ladies in large hats and white gloves sitting on the veranda having Tea. One senses balmy days and fragrant breezes floating about them as they sip delicately and eat sandwiches. It seems dreamlike.

The cuisine of the South consists of substantive foods that have become national favorites. Light, flaky biscuits (which are, by the way, first cousins to scones), tender, juicy fried chicken, and tall, moist cakes.

The Southern diet is one that has evolved over two centuries. It never strays very far from its origins, for Southerners are loyal people and these foods have always suited them and their way of life.

It suits us well, too. We've designed our Southern Tea to include all of our favorites. Nothing is nicer on a summer day than fried chicken and potato salad. We've changed the form but the essentials are there.

Everything can be prepared in advance, including the tea. Set out your Tea and as your guests begin to serve themselves, sit back and relax with a tall glass of iced tea.

As a change from iced tea, try a cup of Coronation tea.

FRIED CHICKEN 'N' BISCUIT SANDWICHES

MAKES 12 SANDWICHES.

Renny White's Biscuits

MAKES 1½ TO 2 DOZEN BISCUITS.

- **2½ cups sifted all-purpose flour**
- **5 teaspoons baking powder**
- **2 tablespoons sugar**
- **1 teaspoon salt**
- **5 tablespoons unsalted butter or shortening, cold**
- **1 cup milk**
- **2 tablespoons melted unsalted butter**

Preheat oven to 425°F.

In a medium-size bowl, combine flour, baking powder, sugar, and salt. Using a pastry blender or 2 knives, cut in the shortening until the mixture is crumbly.

Pour in the milk and mix until a dough is formed. Place the dough on a lightly floured surface and pat it out until it is ½ inch thick.

Cut out the biscuits using a 2-inch biscuit cutter and place them on a greased baking sheet. Lightly brush the top of the biscuits with melted butter. Using a pastry brush, cover the tops of the biscuits with melted butter.

Bake for approximately 15 minutes or until golden brown.

Fried Chicken Nuggets

MAKES 12 PIECES.

2 cups flour
3 teaspoons paprika
1 teaspoon salt
1 teaspoon garlic powder
1 teaspoon ground black pepper
2 eggs
1/2 cup milk
2 pounds boneless chicken breasts, washed and dried
4 tablespoons unsalted butter
8 tablespoons vegetable oil

In a small bowl, combine the flour, paprika, salt, garlic powder, and pepper.

In a separate bowl, beat the eggs. Add the milk. Lay the chicken breasts on a cutting board and apart so they lay flat. Cut the breasts into 2-inch-square pieces.

Heat the butter and oil in a skillet until hot. While the skillet is heating, dip the chicken pieces first in the egg mixture and then coat with the flour mixture. Place the nuggets in the hot skillet and cook until golden brown on each side, about 5 minutes. Remove from the skillet and place on paper towel.

To assemble the sandwiches, cut the biscuits in half. Butter each side lightly. Place a Chicken Nugget on each of the biscuit bottoms. Replace the biscuit tops.

NOTE: These can be put together earlier in the day, refrigerated, and reheated in a microwave on high for approximately 30 seconds, or warmed in a 325°F oven, loosely covered with aluminum foil, for approximately 10 minutes.

CAJUN SHRIMP SANDWICHES

MAKES 12 PIECES.

1/8 teaspoon onion powder
1/8 teaspoon garlic powder
1/8 teaspoon cayenne pepper
1/8 teaspoon ground black pepper
1/4 teaspoon paprika
1/4 teaspoon salt
1 tablespoon unsalted butter
1 cup fresh tiny shrimp, peeled, cooked, and drained
1 teaspoon grated orange peel
6 thin slices white bread
Unsalted butter

Combine all the seasonings and set aside.

Heat the butter in a skillet until hot and foamy. Pour in the seasonings and cook at medium-high heat for 1 minute. Add the shrimp and orange peel and cook until all the liquid is absorbed, about 2 to 3 minutes. Cool to room temperature.

Spread each slice of bread with a thin coating of butter.

Divide the shrimp mixture between 3 of the bread slices. Top the sandwiches with the remaining bread. Trim the crusts. Cut each sandwich into 4 pieces.

NOTE: If you cannot find fresh tiny shrimp, it is best to buy them frozen rather than canned.

Cajun Shrimp Sandwiches and Sour Cream Sugar Cookies.

POTATO SALAD IN CUCUMBER COMPOTES

MAKES 6 COMPOTES.

1 hard-boiled egg, peeled
2 cups cooked potato (approximately 2 large potatoes), medium diced
1 cup mashed potato (approximately 1 large potato)
½ cup finely chopped sweet pickles
1 finely chopped scallion
1½ cups mayonnaise
½ teaspoon prepared yellow mustard
½ teaspoon celery seed
Salt (to taste)
1 cucumber, approximately 6 inches in circumference, peeled
Paprika

Put the egg in a medium-size bowl and finely chop. Add the potatoes, pickles, and scallion to the egg and mix very well.

In a small bowl, mix together the mayonnaise, mustard, celery seed, and salt to taste. Pour this mixture over the potatoes. Using a fork, blend the salad and dressing together. Don't be shy about whipping vigorously with your fork, as this is a creamy potato salad. Chill well before serving (approximately 2 hours).

To assemble, cut 6 1-inch thick slices from the cucumber. With the small end of a melon baller, hollow out the cucumber slices, making sure to leave the walls solid and enough on the bottom to sustain the filling. Fill the hole with 1½ teaspoons of potato salad. The filling will come up over the top, so mound it nicely. Sprinkle each slice with paprika.

NOTE: Because biscuits and muffins are so filling, we make a smaller number of compotes (1 per person). There is enough potato salad to increase this number if you choose, simply by cutting additional cucumber slices.

HAM SALAD IN CORN MUFFIN CUPS

MAKES 6 MUFFIN SANDWICHES.

Corn Muffins

MAKES APPROXIMATELY 1 DOZEN MUFFINS.

1 cup flour
1 cup cornmeal
3 tablespoons sugar
1 tablespoon baking powder
1 teaspoon salt
1 egg
1 cup milk
4 tablespoons melted, unsalted butter, cooled to room temperature

Preheat oven to 350°F.

Mix the dry ingredients together in a bowl.

In a separate bowl, beat the egg, then beat in the milk. Add the egg mixture to the dry ingredients, mixing until well blended. Pour in the melted butter, beating until it is incorporated into the mixture.

Fill 12 greased muffin cups one half full. Bake in the preheated oven 15 to 20 minutes or until the muffins are golden brown. Cool.

These muffins can be made the day before, and stored in an airtight container, or wrapped in plastic wrap.

Ham Salad

MAKES 1⅓ CUPS.

1 cup cooked ham, medium diced
¼ cup red bell pepper, finely diced
1 tablespoon scallion, finely sliced
4 tablespoons mayonnaise
1 tablespoon honey mustard
2 green olives

Place the ham, bell pepper, and scallion in a bowl and toss to combine. Add the mayonnaise and mustard. Mix well.

This salad lasts well in the refrigerator for 5 days.

To assemble, scoop out the center and sides of each muffin with a melon baller or teaspoon to make a cup. Be careful not to scoop out too much or the muffin will collapse; you want to be able to hold each muffin securely in your hand with no breakage. Fill the muffins with the ham salad. Cut 2 green olives into 3 slices each. Place 1 slice in the center of each muffin.

Potato Salad in Cucumber Compotes, Ham Salad in Corn Muffin Cup, and Fried Chicken 'n' Biscuits.

Luscious Coconut Cake decorated with Strawberries.

COCONUT CAKE

MAKES 1 9-INCH LAYER CAKE.

This is a great example of an "old-time" cake.

Summer Sponge Cake

MAKES 2 9-INCH LAYERS.

1 cup flour
1/2 teaspoon baking powder
1/2 teaspoon salt
6 large egg yolks
1 cup sugar
1 tablespoon vanilla
6 large egg whites
1/8 teaspoon cream of tartar
6 tablespoons coconut milk or coconut drink

Preheat oven to 350° F.

In a small bowl, combine the flour, baking powder, and salt. Sift. In a large bowl, beat the egg yolks and 1/2 cup of the sugar until the mixture is light in color and very thick. (The batter should fall in ribbons when the beater is lifted.) Beat the vanilla into the egg yolks.

In another bowl, beat the egg whites with the cream of tartar until soft peaks start to form. Gradually add the remaining sugar and beat until the egg whites are stiff. Fold the egg whites into the egg yolks, alternating with the dry ingredients.

Divide the batter between 2 greased 9-inch cake pans. Bake for 25 to 30 minutes or until golden brown and a toothpick inserted in the center comes out clean. Remove from the oven and let sit in the pans on cooling racks for 5 minutes.

Remove from pans and let cool completely.

When the cakes are cool, spread 3 tablespoons of coconut milk or drink on each layer and let sit until absorbed.

Boiled Frosting

MAKES 4 CUPS.

- **1 1/2 cups milk**
- **1/2 cup butter**
- **1 cup shortening (such as Crisco)**
- **2 cups sugar**
- **1 teaspoon vanilla**
- **1 7-ounce package sweetened coconut**
- **7 large strawberries**

In a saucepan, heat the milk to boiling. Cool.

In a large bowl, combine butter, shortening, and sugar, beating for 5 minutes until light and fluffy. Slowly pour the milk into the bowl, beating while you do, and continue beating for an additional 5 minutes. Add the vanilla, beating for 2 additional minutes.

NOTE: This is a wonderful frosting that holds up exceptionally well on hot days.

To assemble the cake, place 1 layer on a plate or serving platter. Frost the top of the layer with 1 cup of Boiled Frosting. Place the second layer on top of the first. Frost the cake with the remaining frosting. Sprinkle the top and sides of the cake with all of the coconut.

Cut 6 strawberries in half and place evenly around the rim of the cake. Holding the seventh strawberry in your hand, hull side down, cut slices to three-quarters of the way down. Fan out the strawberry in the center of the cake. Serve.

PECAN SCONES

MAKES APPROXIMATELY 10 TO 12 SCONES.

- **2 cups flour**
- **1/4 cup sugar**
- **2 teaspoons baking powder**
- **1 teaspoon salt**
- **3 tablespoons unsalted butter, cold**
- **3/4 cup milk**
- **1 egg**
- **1/2 cup chopped pecans, medium chopped**
- **1 egg yolk**
- **2 tablespoons cold water**

Preheat oven to 350° F.

Sift dry ingredients together. Using a pastry blender or 2 knives, cut butter into dry ingredients until mixture is crumbly. Beat milk and egg together. Add pecans. Pour into the dry ingredients and stir.

Prepare a flat surface by flouring it well (the slightly wet dough will absorb the flour quickly). On the flat surface, knead the dough briefly (once or twice) and pat it until it is 3/4-inch thick. Cut out the scones with a 2 1/2-inch biscuit cutter and place on a greased baking sheet.

Beat the egg yolk with the cold water. Using a pastry brush, glaze each scone with this mixture. Bake for 25 to 30 minutes or until golden brown. Serve hot or cold with jam and clotted cream, if desired.

SOUR CREAM SUGAR COOKIES

MAKES APPROXIMATELY 3 DOZEN COOKIES.

- **1 cup shortening (such as Crisco)**
- **2 cups sugar**
- **2 eggs, slightly beaten**
- **1/2 teaspoon baking soda, dissolved in 1 cup sour cream**
- **6 cups all-purpose flour, approximately**
- **2 teaspoons baking powder**
- **1/4 cup golden raisins**
- **Sugar**

Preheat oven to 425° F.

Cream shortening. Add the sugar gradually, beating until fluffy. Add eggs and baking soda dissolved in sour cream. Sift together the 5 1/2 cups of flour and the baking powder. Add to the shortening mixture and blend well to make a very wet dough.

Flour a flat surface well and place dough on it. Add enough flour (approximately 1/2 cup) for the dough to be malleable. Knead quickly. Roll out the dough until it is 1/4-inch thick. Cut out circles with a 3-inch round cookie cutter and place them on a greased cookie sheet. Place 3 raisins in the center of each cookie and sprinkle the cookie with a small amount of sugar, approximately 1/2 teaspoon per cookie. Bake for 10 to 15 minutes or until the cookies are puffed and brown on the bottom and edges. Cool on a rack. Store in an airtight container. These are best if eaten within a week.

CHAPTER SIX

HIGH TEA

Shepherd's Pie

Raisin and Onion Chutney

Strawberry-Raspberry Cobbler

English Breakfast Tea (or your choice)

Serves 6.

HIGH TEA IS A MEAL THAT OCCURS BETWEEN FIVE AND SIX P.M. IN Victorian times it was known as the working man's Tea. It was a convenient time, after work and before an early bedtime, for a hardy meal. Its hardiness distinguishes High Tea from Afternoon Tea. High Tea is the equivalent of supper.

There are no hard and fast rules regarding the bill of fare. In England it can be as simple as a "fry up," but often extends to meat pies, slices of roast, vegetables, and casseroles. There are loaves of fresh bread, wedges of cheese, condiments, and cakes. People have a tendency to empty the larder and the meal often becomes a patchwork quilt of food.

Our High Tea would be best as supper in the fall or winter. It is a warm, cozy meal that provides comfort and nourishment against a cold, rainy, or snowy day.

It can all be done the day before. In fact, the Shepherd's Pie tastes better the next day. Warm it in the oven or heat it in the microwave before serving. Buy the bread and pop it into a hot oven ten minutes before you serve the meal. The green salad we leave to you. A combination of your favorite greens and a simple dressing will do nicely.

While everyone is eating the main course, put the cobbler in a low oven and let it warm. We serve both of the "afters" at the same time, creating a large, informal last course. We suggest pears, apples, and a wedge of sharp cheddar cheese. Place both the fruit and cheese on a cheese board with a small selection of plain crackers. Give everyone a fresh plate and let them serve themselves. One final word about High Tea: Cups of tea are served with and throughout the meal, so get the kettle boiling and keep the brew coming.

SHEPHERD'S PIE

MAKES 1 10-INCH PIE.

Crust and topping

5 cups mashed potatoes (approximately 5 potatoes)
1 egg yolk
1 tablespoon melted unsalted butter

Filling

2 tablespoons unsalted butter
1 tablespoon vegetable oil
1 clove garlic, minced
1/2 cup finely diced shallots
2 cups clean, dry, sliced mushrooms
1 10-ounce package frozen spinach, thawed, and squeezed dry
1/2 pound ground beef
1/2 pound ground pork
1/2 pound ground lamb
Salt (to taste)
Pepper (to taste
3 tablespoons flour
1 1/4 cups chicken broth
1/4 cup white wine or vermouth
1/2 teaspoon dry tarragon

Preheat oven to 350°F.

Coat the inside of a 10-inch deep dish pie plate with cooking spray.

Mix together 2 cups of the mashed potatoes with the egg yolk. Spoon this mixture into the pie plate, spreading it evenly over the bottom and sides of the plate. You may find it helpful to wet the spoon with water as you spread the potatoes.

Place the pie plate into the oven and cook for 15 minutes. Remove and let cool as you continue to work on the filling.

Melt butter and the vegetable oil in a skillet over medium-high heat until hot.

Add the garlic and shallots to the pan and cook until translucent. Sprinkle in the mushrooms. Mix well with the garlic and shallots and continue to cook until the mushrooms begin to brown.

While the mushrooms cook, put the squeezed spinach into a medium-size bowl and flake with a fork until it is well separated.

When the mushrooms are browned, remove the vegetables from the pan and add to the spinach. Set aside.

Return the pan to the heat and crumble in the beef, pork, and lamb; cook until brown. Season with salt and pepper.

Remove the meat from the pan and add to the spinach mixture, being careful to leave the drippings in the pan. Keeping the heat medium-high, whisk the flour into the drippings.

Pour the broth and wine into the roux, whisking continuously until you have a thick, smooth gravy. Add the tarragon, and season with salt and pepper. Pour over the meat and spinach mixture, mixing well.

To assemble, spoon the meat mixture into the pie plate, packing it down well. Dot the remaining mashed potatoes over the top of the meat. Use a spoon to smooth it out, making sure the entire top of the dish is covered with the potatoes. Brush on the melted butter. Furrow the top of the pie with a fork.

Place in the preheated oven and bake for 45 minutes until the top is brown. Let sit for 10 minutes before serving.

Raisin and Onion Chutney.

RAISIN AND ONION CHUTNEY

MAKES 1 CUP.

2 tablespoons unsalted butter
2 cups thinly sliced onion
1½ cups chicken broth
3 teaspoons honey
½ cup golden raisins
Salt (to taste)

Melt butter in a medium-size skillet. Add the onion and cook over medium-high heat until translucent and beginning to brown, about 5 minutes. Pour in the chicken broth and honey, and cook, covered, until most of the liquid has evaporated and the mixture has thickened, about 10 to 15 minutes.

Add the raisins and continue to cook until they have plumped, about 5 minutes. Season with salt.

Serve warm or at room temperature. The chutney should last in the refrigerator for at least 1 week.

This is a wonderful accompaniment for the Shepherd's Pie as well as other types of poultry and meat.

Shepherd's Pie, cheeses, and English Breakfast Tea.

STRAWBERRY-RASPBERRY COBBLER

SERVES 6.

❀

- **3/4 cup unsalted butter, at room temperature**
- **1 1/2 cups sugar**
- **1 1/2 cups all-purpose flour**
- **3 cups fresh or frozen raspberries**
- **2 teaspoons cornstarch**
- **1/4 teaspoon salt**
- **4 cups fresh strawberries, washed and hulled**
- **1 tablespoon fresh lemon juice**
- **1/8 cup sugar mixed with 1 teaspoon cinnamon**

Cream the butter in a medium-size bowl until light. Gradually add 3/4 cup of the sugar and beat until light and fluffy. Gently mix in the flour until well blended.

Take a sheet of aluminum foil, and with a knife point, gently mark out an 8-inch square. Lay the dough within this area and pat out evenly with your hand until you have an 8-inch by 8-inch square of dough. Fold the excess foil over the square and place in the refrigerator until cold and firm.

While the dough is chilling, place 1 cup of the raspberries in a small bowl and crush.

Combine the remaining sugar, cornstarch, salt, and the crushed raspberries in a medium-size saucepan.

Heat the mixture over medium heat, stirring constantly, until boiling. Add the strawberries and continue to boil until the mixture has thickened, approximately 5 minutes. Let cool to room temperature.

Preheat oven to 375°F.

Mix the remaining 2 cups of raspberries and lemon juice into the fruit mixture.

Pour the fruit into a greased 9-inch square baking dish.

Remove the crust from the refrigerator, unwrap it, and carefully place on top of the fruit. Sprinkle the sugar and cinnamon mixture evenly over the crust.

Bake for 35 to 45 minutes or until the crust is golden brown and the fruit is bubbling.

Serve warm or at room temperature with heavy cream or ice cream.

Strawberry-Raspberry Cobbler served with whipped cream.

CHAPTER SEVEN

THANKSGIVING TEA

Turkey and Stuffing Sandwiches

Turkey Sandwiches with Basil Mayonnaise

Red Cabbage and Bacon Vinaigrette Tarts

Cranberry Scones

Gingerbread with Fruit Sauce

Assam Tea (or your choice)

Serves 6.

THANKSGIVING IS A SPECIAL HOLIDAY THAT EMPHASIZES FOOD AND THE communion that comes with a shared meal. We love the idea of a day set aside for appreciation and thanks. The traditional Thanksgiving meal is one we look forward to all year. Outside it may be cold and crisp; inside, the warmth and the smell of roasting turkey wafts through the house.

The curious thing about Thanksgiving is, while we look forward to the dinner with all the trimmings, and are always stuffed at the end of it, what we really want is the next meal. The one made with the leftovers. This is the time when we can go into the kitchen and use food that has already been prepared to create another meal. It is a perfect scenario for a Tea.

A Thanksgiving Tea provides a wonderful opportunity to retain our sense of the holiday without having to spend several more hours cooking. Everything in this Tea, except for the clotted cream and the tea, comes from the main holiday meal or can be made a day or two in advance. You might even want to incorporate the cabbage and bacon vinaigrette into your Thanksgiving dinner. Similarly, if you want to delete or change some items (for instance, serving your pies instead of gingerbread), do so. Remember, these are just suggestions.

RED CABBAGE AND BACON VINAIGRETTE TARTS

MAKES 6 TARTS.

Cheese Tart Shells

MAKES APPROXIMATELY 12 SHELLS.

2 cups all-purpose flour
1/4 teaspoon salt
1/2 cup sharp cheddar cheese, firmly packed
2/3 cup shortening, chilled
1/4 cup ice water

Preheat oven to 350°F.

Combine the flour, salt, and cheese in a large bowl. Using a pastry blender or 2 knives, cut in shortening until the mixture resembles a coarse meal. Sprinkle ice water over the meal, a tablespoon at a time, tossing with a fork until a dough is formed.

Place on a floured surface and roll out very thin to 1/8 inch. Cut 4-inch circles out of the dough. Drape the circles over the underside cups of a muffin tin. Leave an empty space between the circles so that the dough has room to bake, and the circles are not crowded.

Press gently with your hand, conforming the dough to the cup shape. Prick with a fork.

Bake for 10 to 15 minutes or until the cup is starting to brown on the outside. To allow for spacing, you will have to do at least 2 batches. Cool on a rack.

The shells can be stored in an airtight container for at least 2 days.

NOTE: The tarts will look prettier if you use a cutter with a crimped edge when cutting out the circles.

Red Cabbage and Bacon Vinaigrette

MAKES 2 1/2 CUPS.

2 cups grated red cabbage
4 strips crispy bacon, crumbled
2 thinly sliced scallions
1/2 cup cider vinegar
1/4 cup vegetable oil
1 tablespoon sugar
2 teaspoons bacon drippings
1 teaspoon celery seed
Salt (to taste)
Freshly ground pepper (to taste)
1 ounce Swiss cheese, cut into 12 thin strips (optional)

Combine the cabbage, bacon, and scallions in a medium-size bowl. Toss well.

In a small microwaveable bowl, combine the rest of the ingredients, except the salt and pepper and cheese. Heat the dressing in a microwave on high for 1 1/2 minutes.

Stir the dressing and pour over the slaw. Season with salt and pepper. Toss to combine.

The slaw can be served at room temperature or chilled.

This will last, well covered, in the refrigerator for 3 days.

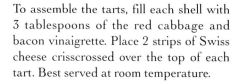

To assemble the tarts, fill each shell with 3 tablespoons of the red cabbage and bacon vinaigrette. Place 2 strips of Swiss cheese crisscrossed over the top of each tart. Best served at room temperature.

NOTE: If you don't have a microwave, heat the ingredients in a small saucepan over low heat until warm.

TURKEY AND STUFFING SANDWICHES

MAKES 24 PIECES.

12 thin slices wheat bread
Unsalted butter
6 thin slices turkey breast
6 tablespoons stuffing
6 teaspoons cranberry sauce

Spread each slice of bread with a thin coating of butter.

Lay a slice of turkey on 6 slices of bread. Spread a tablespoon of stuffing on each slice of turkey, then spoon a teaspoon of cranberry sauce over the stuffing. Top the sandwiches with the remaining bread.

Trim the crusts. Cut each sandwich into 4 pieces.

Red Cabbage and Bacon Vinaigrette Tarts.

Turkey Sandwiches with Basil Mayonnaise

MAKES 12 PIECES.

- 1 pint (16 fluid ounces) mayonnaise
- 1 cup firmly packed fresh basil leaves, washed and dried
- 2 medium cloves garlic, peeled
- Unsalted butter
- 6 thin slices white bread
- 3 thin slices leftover turkey

Put mayonnaise, basil, and garlic in a blender or a food processor fitted with the metal blade. Process until pureed, approximately 1 minute. Pour the mixture back into the mayonnaise jar. Refrigerate until chilled, at least 1 hour. This mayonnaise should keep in the refrigerator at least 2 weeks and will surely last as long as your turkey does.

To assemble the sandwiches, spread each slice of bread with a thin coating of butter. Lay a slice of turkey on 3 slices of bread. Spread 1 tablespoon of Basil Mayonnaise on each slice of turkey. Cover the sandwich with the remaining bread. Trim the crusts. Cut each sandwich into 4 pieces.

NOTE: If you cannot find fresh basil, substitute 3 tablespoons of pesto for the basil and garlic. Pesto generally can be found in the refrigerated or freezer section of most grocery stores.

Cranberry Scones

MAKES APPROXIMATELY 10 SCONES.

- 3/4 cup fresh cranberries
- 1 cup boiling water
- 2 cups flour
- 1/2 cup sugar
- 2 teaspoons baking powder
- 1 teaspoon salt
- 3 tablespoons unsalted butter, cold
- 1 egg
- 3/4 cup milk
- 1 egg yolk
- 2 tablespoons cold water

Coarsely chop the cranberries. Cover them with the boiling water and let sit for an hour. Drain off all the liquid.

Sift the dry ingredients together. Using a pastry blender or 2 knives, cut the butter into the dry ingredients until the mixture is crumbly.

Beat the egg and milk together. Pour into the dry ingredients, stirring until a dough is formed. Add the cranberries, mixing well.

Preheat oven to 350°F.

Using an ice cream scoop, form the scones, and place on a greased baking sheet.

Beat the egg yolk with the cold water. Using a pastry brush, glaze each scone with this mixture. Bake for 25 to 30 minutes or until golden brown.

Serve hot or cold with jam and clotted cream, if desired.

Gingerbread

MAKES 1 9-INCH LAYER; 6 TO 8 SLICES.

- 1/2 cup butter
- 1/2 cup plus 2 tablespoons sugar
- 2 eggs
- 1 cup dark molasses
- 2 1/2 cups sifted all-purpose flour
- 1 teaspoon cinnamon
- 1 teaspoon ground cloves
- 1 teaspoon ground ginger
- 1 teaspoon allspice
- 1 teaspoon baking soda dissolved in 1 cup boiling coffee and cooled to room temperature

Preheat oven to 350°F.

Cream the butter. Add 1/2 cup sugar, eggs, and molasses in that order, beating well after each addition.

Sift together the flour and spices. Add the flour mixture one-third at a time, alternating with the coffee, one-third at a time. Mix until smooth.

Pour into a greased 9-inch cake pan. Sprinkle the top of the batter with the remaining 2 tablespoons sugar.

Bake for 45 minutes to 1 hour. Serve hot or cold.

Cranberry Scones and Gingerbread with Fruit Sauce garnished with fruit and whipped cream.

Fruit Sauce

MAKES APPROXIMATELY 1 CUP.

1 cup sugar
1 cup unsweetened juice (apple, raspberry-apple, or cranberry-raspberry)

Combine the sugar and juice in a medium-size saucepan and heat on high until the sugar has dissolved and the mixture starts to boil.

Turn the heat down to medium and cook, stirring constantly, for 10 minutes until the mixture thickens or until 221°F is reached on a candy thermometer. Pour into a microwave-glass container. Cool, cover, and refrigerate.

The sauce can be served warm or cold.

To warm, heat in a microwave for 15 to 30 seconds. This sauce will last in the refrigerator for at least 2 weeks.

NOTE: This sauce has a tendency to become hard when it is cooled if it has been cooked just a little bit too long. To remedy this, heat in a microwave on high for 1 to 2 minutes.

If you don't have a microwave, place the container in a saucepan that is half full of hot water and heat the container over medium heat until the sauce is warm, about 15 minutes.

To serve, spoon the Fruit Sauce over each slice of Gingerbread, then place a spoonful of whipped cream on the side.

CHAPTER EIGHT

Christmas Tea

Black Forest Ham Sandwiches

Cucumber Sandwiches

Egg Mayonnaise and Watercress Sandwiches

Stilton, Walnut, and Pear Sandwiches

Jane Mudry's Christmas Cookies

Fruit and Nut Scones

Mary's Almond Mocha Cake

Darjeeling Tea (or your choice)

Serves 6.

THE HALLS ARE DECKED, THE TREE IS TRIMMED, AND CAROLERS ARE singing; holiday spirit abounds. Christmas Day is a wonderful occasion for a Tea. The decor is already in place, the ambience established; breakfast and Christmas dinner were consumed hours ago. A Tea is the perfect answer for those who grow peckish as evening draws nigh.

A Christmas Day Tea is very easy to put together. The baking can be done in advance with the rest of your holiday baking. The sandwiches can be prepared in the morning, wrapped well, and placed in the refrigerator until needed. One hour before the Tea, prepare the clotted cream (this gives it time to set and chill). When you are ready to serve, place the sandwiches and desserts on platters, set out the tea things, warm the scones, and brew the tea.

You may find, as we have, that your guests are so delighted by Christmas Tea, that it will become a tradition in your home.

We suggest the following menu for your Tea. Use it, make substitutes, or design your own.

BLACK FOREST HAM SANDWICHES

MAKES 12 PIECES.

8 thin slices dark bread
Unsalted butter
4 slices Black Forest ham
Honey mustard

Spread the top and bottom of each slice of bread with a thin coating of butter.

On 4 slices of the bread, place a ham slice, folding the ham to conform to the bread size and keeping in mind that the crusts will be trimmed off. Spread a thin coating of honey mustard on each slice of ham. Top each sandwich with the remaining bread. Trim the crusts. Cut each sandwich into 3 parallel pieces.

CUCUMBER SANDWICHES

MAKES 12 PIECES.

6 thin slices white bread
Unsalted Butter
1/2 medium cucumber, peeled and thinly sliced
Salt (to taste)
Pepper (to taste)

Spread each slice of bread with a thin coating of butter. Place the cucumber slices on 3 slices of bread, making sure the bread is well covered (approximately 6 to 8 slices of cucumber per piece of bread). Season each sandwich with salt and pepper. Cover with the remaining slices of buttered bread. Trim the crusts. Cut each sandwich into 4 pieces.

EGG MAYONNAISE AND WATERCRESS SANDWICHES

MAKES 12 PIECES.

2 hard-boiled eggs
1 1/2 tablespoons mayonnaise
3 tablespoons cream cheese at room temperature
1/8 cup watercress, washed and picked from stems
Salt (to taste)
Pepper (to taste)
4 thin slices white bread
Unsalted butter
4 thin slices wheat bread

Finely chop the hard-boiled eggs. Whisk the mayonnaise and cream cheese together until smooth. Add this mixture to the eggs and mix until well blended. Fold in the watercress. Season with salt and pepper.

Spread each slice of the white bread with a thin coating of butter. Spread the egg salad evenly on the bread. Butter the wheat bread and place a slice on top of each sandwich. Trim the crusts. Cut each sandwich into 3 parallel pieces.

STILTON, WALNUT AND PEAR SANDWICHES

MAKES 12 PIECES.

¼ pound English Stilton cheese
½ cup walnuts
½ ripe pear, cored
6 thin slices wheat bread
Unsalted butter

Crumble the cheese and let it soften. While the cheese is softening, toast the walnuts under the broiler for approximately 8 to 10 minutes or until golden brown. Cool and chop very fine.

Slice the pear into 12 thin slices.

Spread each slice of bread with a thin coating of butter.

Divide the cheese equally among 3 slices of the bread and spread it gently. Sprinkle a heaping tablespoon of walnuts over the cheese. Place 4 slices of the pear on each sandwich. Top each sandwich with the remaining bread slices, pressing down firmly.

Trim the crusts. Cut each sandwich into 4 pieces.

Decorated Christmas Cookies (see recipe on page 66).

JANE MUDRY'S CHRISTMAS COOKIES

MAKES 1 TO 1 1/2 DOZEN COOKIES.

Cookie Dough

- **1 cup unsalted butter**
- **1/2 cup sugar**
- **1 egg**
- **2 teaspoons vanilla**
- **2 1/2 cups sifted all-purpose flour**
- **1/2 teaspoon baking powder**
- **1/8 teaspoon salt**

Frosting

- **1 tablespoon unsalted butter**
- **1 1/2 cups confectioner's sugar**
- **1/2 teaspoon vanilla**
- **Milk**

Preheat oven to 350°F.

To make the cookies, cream the butter and sugar together. Add the egg and vanilla and mix well. Sift together the dry ingredients and slowly add to the butter mixture. Combine until a dough is formed. If the dough is too wet, add up to an additional 1/2 cup of flour. Put one-quarter of the dough onto a floured surface. Sprinkle the top of the dough with flour. Using a rolling pin, roll out the dough until it is 1/8-inch thick. Cut out desired shapes with cookie cutters. Repeat this procedure until all the dough has been used.

Bake on ungreased cookie sheets for 8 to 10 minutes or until lightly browned on the edges. Cool and frost.

To prepare the frosting, cream together the butter and sugar. Add the vanilla and mix well. Pour in milk, a teaspoon at a time, until you have a spreadable consistency. Frost the cooled cookies and decorate.

This recipe can be made several hours before the cookies, but should be kept in the refrigerator. You will have to allow time for the frosting to soften for use.

FRUIT AND NUT SCONES

MAKES APPROXIMATELY 12 SCONES.

- **3 cups flour**
- **1/4 cup sugar**
- **1/2 teaspoon salt**
- **1 tablespoon baking powder**
- **5 tablespoons unsalted butter**
- **2 eggs**
- **1 1/4 cups milk**
- **1/2 cup walnuts, chopped medium-fine**
- **1/4 cup currants**
- **1 egg yolk**
- **2 tablespoons cold water**

Preheat oven to 350°F.

Sift the dry ingredients together. Using a pastry blender or 2 knives, cut the butter into the dry ingredients until crumbly. Beat the eggs and milk together. Combine the walnuts with the currants. Pour the egg mixture into the dry ingredients, stirring until a dough is formed. Fold in the walnuts and currants.

Using an ice cream scoop, form the scones and place on a greased baking sheet. Beat the egg yolk with the cold water. Using a pastry brush, glaze each scone with this mixture. Bake for 20 minutes, or until golden brown. Serve hot or cold with jam and clotted cream.

MARY'S ALMOND MOCHA CAKE

SERVES 12.

Cake

- **2 teaspoons vanilla**
- **2 teaspoons water**
- **4 large eggs**
- **1/2 cup sugar**
- **1 teaspoon salt**
- **1 cup sifted all purpose flour**
- **6 tablespoons melted unsalted butter, cooled to room temperature**

Frosting

- **4 teaspoons instant coffee granules**
- **6 teaspoons hot milk**
- **2 1/2 sticks unsalted butter**
- **4 cups confectioner's sugar**
- **2 teaspoons vanilla**

Decorations

- **2 1/2 cups sliced, blanched almonds**
- **Confectioner's sugar**

To make the cake, preheat oven to 325°F.

Butter and flour a 9-inch cake pan.

Mix the vanilla and water together. Combine the eggs, sugar, salt, and vanilla mixture in a bowl and beat on high in a mixer until the batter is white and very thick. (When you lift your beaters from the bowl, the batter should fall in thick folds.)

Gently fold in the flour, then the butter, making sure both are totally incorporated. Do not stir.

Pour into the prepared cake pan and bake for 35 to 40 minutes. The cake is done when it is golden brown and springs to the touch.

Invert the cake onto a rack. When the cake has cooled completely, split it into 2 equal layers.

To make the frosting, dissolve the granules in the hot milk. Cream the butter and sugar until smooth. Mix in the vanilla. Beat in the hot milk and coffee until the frosting is creamy. If necessary, use more milk. Refrigerate the frosting until it becomes firm and spreadable. Frost.

To frost and decorate the cake, first toast the almonds in a hot oven until they are a light golden brown. Cool.

Place 1 layer of the cake on a serving dish. Cover the top of this layer with 1 to 1½ cups of the frosting, spreading evenly. Top this with the second layer and press gently.

Frost the top and sides of the cake with the remaining frosting. Starting at the bottom, press the almond slices into the cake, overlapping the almonds on top of each other, until you reach the top. Continue the same procedure with the top of the cake until all but a 3-inch circle in the center is covered.

Roughly crush the remaining almonds and sprinkle this on the uncovered section. You may find it necessary to place the cake in the refrigerator from time to time while you are decorating with the almonds, because the butter frosting may become too soft and difficult to work with.

Once the cake is completely covered with almonds, dust the top lightly with confectioner's sugar.

Almond Mocha Cake.

CHAPTER NINE

Easter Tea

Clove Chicken Puffs

Deviled Eggs

Timothy's Chicken Liver Pâté on Toast Rounds

Watercress Sandwiches

Lemon Crisps

Chocolate-Dipped Strawberries

Date-Nut Scones

Fabergé Carrot Cake

Lady Londonderry Tea (or your choice)

Serves 6.

EASTER CELEBRATES NEW LIFE. IT IS A RECOGNITION OF REBIRTH AND flowering and it symbolizes that life comes from life. There can be no more perfect symbol of this regeneration than that of the egg. The egg is the primary Easter symbol in many cultures and is expressed in accordance with their traditions. Some make braided egg breads, some prefer to express themselves in chocolate; the Ukrainians create beautiful eggs using wax dyes and allegorical motifs; and Fabergé raised the egg to its ultimate expression with jewels and precious metals.

Keeping the egg in mind, we created our Easter Tea with deviled eggs as the starting point and extended it to the chicken, keeping the first course and dessert "all in the family." Beyond the Easter symbolism, we included foods that make us think of the freshness of spring. There is a lightness to this Tea that won't interfere with a lamb or ham dinner that may be the traditional main meal in your home on Easter day.

As with many of our other Teas, most of the preparatory work can be done in advance. So don your bonnet and then, in the late afternoon or early evening, make this Easter different by having a Tea.

CLOVE CHICKEN PUFFS

MAKES 12 PUFFS.

Miniature Cream Puff Shells (Pâté à Choux)

MAKES APPROXIMATELY 12 SHELLS.

1/2 cup water
4 tablespoons salted butter
1/2 cup all-purpose flour
2 eggs

Preheat oven to 350°F.

Combine the water and butter in a medium-size saucepan. Bring to a boil. When the butter has melted, turn heat down to low and pour the flour into the pan all at once. Beat the mixture until well combined and the batter comes away from the sides of the pan. Remove from heat.

Break 1 egg into the batter and beat until smooth and glossy. Repeat with the second egg. Drop the batter, by rounded teaspoons, onto a greased baking sheet. Bake for 45 minutes or until puffed and golden. Cool.

These are best if made the day you plan to use them, but they can be stored in a dry, airtight container overnight.

Clove Chicken Salad

MAKES 6 CUPS.

Salad

1 cup walnuts
4 cups cooked chicken, medium diced
4 thinly sliced scallions
1 medium green bell pepper, medium diced
1 cup golden or brown raisins
1 teaspoon ground cloves
1/2 teaspoon salt
1/4 teaspoon minced fresh ginger

Dressing

1 1/2 cups mayonnaise
2 teaspoons ground cloves
2 tablespoons honey
2 tablespoons apple cider vinegar
1/2 cup milk

To make the salad, coarsely chop the walnuts. Combine the rest of the ingredients in a large bowl.

In another bowl, whisk together the dressing ingredients. Pour the dressing over the salad and toss to combine, making sure the salad is well mixed. Place in the refrigerator until well chilled, approximately 2 to 3 hours.

To assemble the puffs, cut the top off each shell two-thirds of the way up from the bottom. If necessary, remove the excess dough from the center. Fill the bottom of the shell with 3 tablespoons of Clove Chicken Salad. Replace the tops of each puff. Refrigerate until serving.

Deviled Eggs decorated and garnished with vegetables.

Deviled Eggs

MAKES 12 HALVES.

6 large eggs, hard-boiled and peeled
6 teaspoons minced sweet pickles
2 1/2 teaspoons minced scallions
1/2 cup mayonnaise
Salt (to taste)
Pepper (to taste)
Paprika

Cut the eggs in half lengthwise; reserve the halved egg whites.

Place the yolks in a small bowl and mash. Add the pickles and scallions to the mashed yolk, blending with a fork.

Using a fork, whip in the mayonnaise. Season with salt and pepper.

Using either a spoon or a pastry tube, refill the egg whites with the mixture, dividing equally between the 12 halves.

Sprinkle paprika over the top of each egg. Chill and serve. The eggs will not last for more than 24 hours.

VARIATION: Add 1/2 teaspoon curry powder (or to taste) to the egg mixture. Fill and chill as directed.

TIMOTHY'S CHICKEN LIVER PÂTÉ ON TOAST ROUNDS

MAKES 6 ROUNDS.

This pâté recipe has evolved over several years and is the best we have ever tasted.

2 medium onions, coarsely chopped
4 cloves garlic, coarsely chopped
3 tablespoons olive oil
8 tablespoons lightly salted butter
1 pound chicken livers, rinsed in cold water and drained
1 teaspoon dried rosemary
2 tablespoons sherry
1 hard-boiled egg, finely chopped
½ cup walnuts, finely chopped
Salt (to taste)
Pepper (to taste)
3 thin slices white bread
Butter
2 pitted black olives

Sauté the onions and garlic in the olive oil and 2 tablespoons of the butter until translucent. Add the chicken livers and rosemary, cooking on high heat until the livers are lightly browned and most of the liquid has evaporated. Cool to room temperature.

When the liver mixture has cooled, put it into a blender or food processor fitted with the metal blade and purée. Add the sherry and remaining butter to the pureed mixture. Purée again.

Place the pureed mixture in a bowl and fold in the egg and walnuts. The mixture should be the consistency of a thin paste. If it is too thick, add more sherry, 1 tablespoon at a time, to thin. Season with salt and pepper. At this point the pâté can be placed in a mold if you choose to do so. Whether you use a mold or not, put the mixture in the refrigerator until thoroughly chilled. This pâté freezes beautifully, so it can be made well in advance of any party.

To assemble, cut 2 2½-inch rounds from each slice of bread with a cookie cutter. Toast the rounds. Lightly butter each round. Spread 1 generous tablespoon of the Pâté on each round, swirling the spoon as you do so. Cut each olive into three equal pieces. Top each round with an olive piece.

VARIATION:
Put the pâté in a pastry bag and pipe it onto the rounds. You may need to use more pâté depending on the size of the nozzle you choose.

WATERCRESS SANDWICHES

MAKES 12 PIECES.

6 thin slices white bread
Unsalted butter
½ bunch watercress, approximately 20 stems, washed, dried, and leaves picked from stem
Salt (to taste)
Pepper (to taste)

Spread each slice of bread with a thin coating of butter.

Divide the watercress between three slices of bread. Season with salt and pepper. Cover the sandwiches with the remaining bread slices, pressing down firmly.

Trim the crusts. Cut each sandwich into 4 pieces.

NOTE: Some people prefer to chop the watercress leaves and spread them on the sandwiches; the option is yours.

CHOCOLATE-DIPPED STRAWBERRIES

MAKES 12 PIECES.

6 to 8 ounces semisweet chocolate
12 large strawberries, washed and dried

Melt the chocolate in the top half of a double boiler. Gently holding the hull, dip the strawberries into the chocolate until two-thirds of the strawberry is covered. Place the strawberries on a wax paper–covered plate and refrigerate until set, about ½ to 1 hour.

These can be made 24 hours in advance and covered with plastic wrap once the chocolate has set. Leftovers will last for at least 2 days, covered and refrigerated.

LEMON CRISPS

MAKES APPROXIMATELY 3 DOZEN CRISPS.

- **3/4 cup confectioner's sugar**
- **2/3 cup unsalted butter, at room temperature**
- **1/4 cup fresh lemon juice**
- **2 tablespoons grated lemon zest**
- **1 3/4 cups all-purpose flour**

In a medium-size bowl, beat the sugar and butter until light and fluffy. Add the lemon juice and zest, beating until blended. Gradually add the flour, beating until smooth. Cover with plastic wrap and refrigerate until chilled, approximately 1 hour.

Preheat oven to 325°F.

Lay the dough on a lightly floured surface. Roll it out until it is about 1/8-inch thick. Cut out with a 2-inch heart or circle cutter and place on an ungreased cookie sheet 1 inch apart. Bake for 20 to 25 minutes or until slightly golden brown around the edges. Cool. Store in an airtight container. These crisps will stay fresh for a week and freeze wonderfully for up to 2 months.

Plate of Lemon Crisps and Chocolate Dipped Strawberries with fruit and mint candy.

DATE-NUT SCONES

MAKES APPROXIMATELY 10 SCONES.

- **2 cups flour**
- **1/4 cup sugar**
- **2 teaspoons baking powder**
- **1 teaspoon salt**
- **3 tablespoons unsalted butter, cold**
- **3/4 cup milk**
- **1 egg**
- **1/2 cup minced dates**
- **1/2 cup chopped walnuts**
- **1 egg yolk**
- **2 tablespoons cold water**

Preheat oven to 350°F.

Sift the dry ingredients together. Using a pastry blender or 2 knives, cut the butter into the dry ingredients until the mixture is crumbly. Beat the milk and egg together. Pour into the dry ingredients and stir until well blended. Add the dates and nuts, stirring until they are incorporated into the mixture.

Prepare a flat surface by flouring it well (the dough will be slightly wet and will absorb the flour quickly). Place the dough on the flat surface. Knead briefly (once or twice) and pat the dough until it is 3/4-inch thick. Cut out the scones with a 2 1/2-inch biscuit center and place on a greased baking sheet.

Beat the egg yolk with the cold water. Using a pastry brush, glaze each scone with this mixture. Bake for 25 to 30 minutes or until golden brown.

Serve hot or cold, with jam and clotted cream, if desired.

FABERGÉ CARROT CAKE

MAKES 1 EGG CAKE

Cream Cheese Frosting

MAKES APPROXIMATELY 4 TO $4\frac{1}{2}$ CUPS.

- **1 pound cream cheese, at room temperature**
- **$\frac{1}{2}$ cup unsalted butter, at room temperature**
- **1 tablespoon vanilla**
- **1 1-pound box confectioner's sugar**

In a large bowl, cream the cream cheese and butter until light and fluffy. Beat in the vanilla until well blended. Add the sugar, beating until frosting is formed. Refrigerate the frosting until chilled and firm.

Carrot Egg Cake

MAKES 1 CAKE

- **2 cups all-purpose flour**
- **1 teaspoon baking powder**
- **1 teaspoon baking soda**
- **1 teaspoon salt**
- **1 teaspoon cinnamon**
- **1 teaspoon nutmeg**
- **$1\frac{1}{2}$ cups vegetable oil**
- **$1\frac{3}{4}$ cups sugar**
- **4 eggs, at room temperature**
- **$3\frac{1}{2}$ cups grated carrot, approximately $1\frac{1}{2}$ to 2 pounds**
- **1 cup finely chopped walnuts**

Preheat oven to 325°F.

In a medium-size bowl, combine the dry ingredients and spices. Sift the mixture once.

In a larger bowl, beat the oil and sugar until blended.

Add the eggs, one at a time, beating well.

Add the dry ingredients and beat until well incorporated. Blend in the carrots and nuts.

Prepare 1 set of egg cake pans by coating well with cooking spray. Set the egg halves on their stands and place on a baking sheet. Pour the batter into the egg pans, dividing evenly between the 2 pans. Gently put the baking sheet into the oven.

Bake the cakes for approximately 45 minutes to 1 hour or until a toothpick inserted in the center comes out clean. Cool in the pans.

To assemble the cakes, slice a thin layer off the bottom of 1 Carrot Cake egg half. (This will create balance and allow the cake to stand.) Place the one-half egg cake layer on a large plate or platter. Spread $\frac{3}{4}$ cup of Cream Cheese Frosting on the top of the half. Now place the other half of the cake on top, creating a whole egg.

To frost and decorate, decide what color you want the egg to be. Create the color using approximately $1\frac{1}{2}$ cups of Cream Cheese Frosting and food coloring. Frost the entire egg with this color, smoothing it as you frost.

Put $\frac{3}{4}$ cup Cream Cheese Frosting in a small bowl. Drop green and yellow food coloring into the frosting at a ratio of 3 green drops to 1 yellow drop to create a pistachio green color.

Put this mixture in a pastry tube, fitted with a tip appropriate to your design. Pipe a latticework or basket-weave pattern over the entire egg.

Put $\frac{1}{2}$ cup Cream Cheese Frosting in a bowl. Add yellow and red drops of food coloring to the frosting at a ratio of 3 red drops to 1 yellow drop to create a salmon color.

Pipe small flower designs at the point where the basket-weave lines intersect.

Chill the cake until the designs have set, approximately 2 to 3 hours.

NOTE: This frosting must be very cold to work well. Return both pastry bag and cake to the refrigerator as necessary.

Decorate the cake any way you want. Another example is to frost the cake in white. Do the basket-weave or latticework pattern in green. Put candied violets in the spaces between the lines and candy silver balls where the lines intersect.

For a nice finishing touch, surround the finished egg with fake grass. Sprinkle jelly beans on the grass for added color, or, for an elegant touch, lay small spring flowers on the grass.

Decorated Fabergé Carrot Cake.

CHAPTER TEN

RUSSIAN TEA

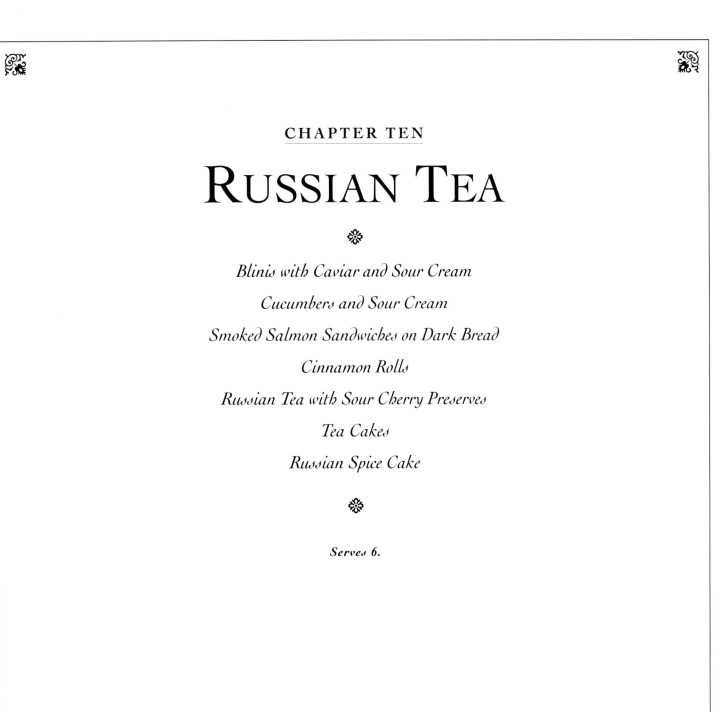

Blinis with Caviar and Sour Cream

Cucumbers and Sour Cream

Smoked Salmon Sandwiches on Dark Bread

Cinnamon Rolls

Russian Tea with Sour Cherry Preserves

Tea Cakes

Russian Spice Cake

Serves 6.

THERE IS A MYSTERY AND FRAGRANCE ABOUT RUSSIA THAT ALWAYS captures our imaginations. It is a land of great palaces, balalaikas being strummed, Fabergé eggs, and caviar; a culture where the exoticism of the East blends with the strength and practicality of the West. This is most apparent in their food. The Russian bill of fare is a hardy one, where breads, soups, and fish provide the sustenance needed to survive the fierce climate.

There are some foods that always make us think of Russia. Blinis with caviar, smoked salmon on dark bread, and richly flavored cakes, all of which are in our Russian Tea menu. The rest of the menu was designed to complement these foods and to help complete a sense of the spicy elegance that is so Russian to us.

While we do suggest that you plan on serving at least two blinis to each guest, we don't tell you how much caviar to use or what kind to buy. In a perfect world, large spoonfuls of Beluga would be ideal, but you may have to temper what is ideal with what is financially practical. And, while we do tell you how to serve tea with preserves, if you think your guests would prefer the more conventional tea with milk, the substitution will work fine. Finally, should you wish to have scones, use the Walnut Scones (recipe on page 40) in place of the Cinnamon Rolls.

This is not a Tea for the middle of summer; late fall or winter is best. If you can, arrange to time the baking of the Cinnamon Rolls with the arrival of your guests. A warm house filled with this aroma will tempt their appetites and establish a mood that will put your Tea on the road to success.

BLINIS WITH CAVIAR AND SOUR CREAM

MAKES APPROXIMATELY 30 BLINIS.

1 cup milk
1/2 package active dry yeast, approximately 1/2 tablespoon
4 large eggs, separated
1 cup sifted buckwheat flour
1/2 cup white flour
1 tablespoon sugar
1/2 teaspoon salt
3 tablespoons unsalted butter, melted and cooled to room temperature
3 tablespoons clarified butter (see NOTE)
Caviar
Sour cream
Chopped fresh dill

Pour the milk into a small saucepan. Scald, then cool to lukewarm. Add the yeast to the milk, stirring until dissolved. Let sit for 10 minutes.

Meanwhile, in a large bowl, beat the egg yolks until thick, approximately 3 to 5 minutes.

Combine the flours, sugar, and salt. Beat into the egg yolks. Add the melted butter, stirring to incorporate. Pour in the yeast mixture, stirring until blended.

Cover the bowl with a clean towel or plastic wrap. Set in a warm place to rise until doubled in size, approximately 1 1/2 hours.

When the batter has doubled in size, beat the egg whites in a separate bowl until stiff. Fold the egg whites into the batter.

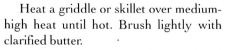

Heat a griddle or skillet over medium-high heat until hot. Brush lightly with clarified butter.

Make small pancakes by pouring 1 tablespoon of batter onto the griddle, and spreading slightly with a spoon. Cook for approximately 1 minute or until top is bubbly. Turn the blini over with a spatula and cook for about an additional 30 seconds. Keep in a warm oven while you make the remaining blinis. Brush the griddle with clarified butter as needed.

Blinis are always best if made fresh. If necessary, you can refrigerate them, well wrapped, for up to 3 days. Reheat in a microwave oven on high for 15 seconds or in a warm 325°F oven, covered, for approximately 10 minutes.

To assemble the blinis, place them on a serving tray or arrange them on individual plates.

Using a wooden or bone spoon (metal will react against the caviar) place the caviar in the center of each warm blini. Place a slightly smaller amount of sour cream to the side of the caviar. Lightly sprinkle the sour cream with fresh dill.

We suggest at least 2 blinis per guest. Arrange them so they slightly overlap.

NOTE: When clarifying butter what you are doing is separating the fat from the milk product. To do this, heat the butter in a small saucepan until melted. Skim the foam off the top. Pour out the clear yellow liquid, being careful to leave behind the white sediment on the bottom. The yellow liquid is the clarified butter.

CUCUMBERS AND SOUR CREAM

MAKES 12 PIECES.

4 finely sliced scallions
8 tablespoons sour cream
Salt (to taste)
2 large cucumbers, approximately 7 inches in circumference, peeled
Freshly ground pepper

Mix the scallions and sour cream together. Season with salt.

From the widest parts of the cucumber, cut 6 1-inch thick slices. Using a melon baller, scoop a small amount from the center of each slice.

Fill the scooped-out cucumber slices with the sour cream mix, using approximately 2 teaspoons per slice. Grind the pepper over the slices.

Refrigerate until serving.

SMOKED SALMON SANDWICHES ON DARK BREAD

MAKES 12 PIECES.

2 tablespoons unsalted butter
1/2 teaspoon capers
3 thick slices pumpernickel bread
6 ounces thinly sliced smoked salmon
Chopped fresh dill

Using a fork, mash together the butter and the capers until they are blended and the butter is soft.

Divide this mixture between the 3 slices of bread and spread evenly. Lay 2 ounces of smoked salmon on each slice of bread.

Sprinkle fresh dill over the top of each sandwich.

Cut each sandwich into 4 pieces.

Cinnamon Rolls served with tea.

CINNAMON ROLLS

MAKES APPROXIMATELY 15 ROLLS.

1 1-pound loaf frozen bread dough
10 tablespoons unsalted butter
$^1/_2$ cup light brown sugar
$^1/_2$ cup sugar
$1^1/_2$ teaspoons cinnamon
$^1/_4$ teaspoon ground cloves
$^3/_4$ cup walnut pieces
2 tablespoons honey

Prepare a 12-by-8-by-2-inch baking pan by coating it with cooking spray.

Thaw the dough according to the package instructions. While the bread is thawing, make a paste of 6 tablespoons of the butter, the sugars, and the spices. Melt the remaining butter.

Lay the thawed bread on a lightly floured surface and roll out to a rectangle measuring approximately 15 by 18 inches. Spread the sugar paste evenly on the dough, making sure the entire rectangle is covered. Sprinkle the walnut pieces over the dough.

Starting at one of the 15-inch sides, roll the dough up tightly to form a round tube. Seal the seam along the length of the tube by pinching the dough. Drizzle half the melted butter into the prepared pan. Cut 1-inch slices from the dough tube. Lay slices in the pan, being careful not to crowd them. Cover the baking dish with a cloth and let rise in a warm place until doubled in size, approximately 1 hour.

Preheat oven to 375°F.

Drizzle the remaining melted butter over the uncooked rolls. Do the same with the honey. Bake in the preheated oven for 30 to 45 minutes, or until golden brown and the filling is bubbly. Let sit for 10 minutes. Invert the pan onto a serving platter or plate. The sugary bottom will now be on top.

Serve warm or at room temperature. These rolls reheat beautifully in a microwave on high for 30 seconds or in a 325°F oven, covered with foil, for 10 to 15 minutes.

RUSSIAN TEA WITH SOUR CHERRY PRESERVES

Sour cherry preserves
1 pot freshly brewed Russian Tea
Sugar cubes
Thin lemon slices, cut in half (optional)

Place 1 teaspoon of sour cherry preserves in the bottom of each teacup, making sure each cup gets at least 1 whole cherry. Pour the tea over the preserves. Serve.

If you want to be truly authentic, use tea glasses that sit in metal stands.

The Russian tradition is to hold a sugar cube between the teeth as you drink the tea. This is not an absolute rule, but we would advise against putting sugar in the cup and stirring. The preserves sweeten the tea and the idea is to drink it with the cherry surprising the palate at the end. Stirring would disturb this. If you'd like a little extra flavor, add a thin slice of lemon to the drink.

Russian Tea with Sour Cherry Preserves.

TEA CAKES

MAKES APPROXIMATELY
3 TO 4 DOZEN CAKES.

1 cup unsalted butter, at room temperature
$4\frac{1}{2}$ cups confectioner's sugar
$1\frac{1}{2}$ teaspoons vanilla
2 cups all-purpose flour
$\frac{1}{2}$ teaspoon salt
$\frac{3}{4}$ cup finely chopped walnuts

Preheat oven to 350°F.

Cream butter in a food processor fitted with the metal blade.

Add $\frac{3}{4}$ cup of the sugar and vanilla and process until mixed.

Add flour and salt. Process until blended, but do not overwork. Pour in the nuts and pulse just until they are evenly distributed.

Remove dough from food processor and roll into 1-inch balls. Place the balls on an ungreased cookie sheet and bake until firm and starting to brown on the bottom. Remove from oven.

Carefully roll the hot cookies in confectioner's sugar. Let cool, then roll again.

Stored in an airtight container, these should last 2 weeks.

RUSSIAN SPICE CAKE

MAKES 1 9-INCH LAYER CAKE.

Spice Cake

MAKES 2 9-INCH LAYERS.

$2\frac{1}{2}$ cups self-rising cake flour
2 teaspoons cinnamon
$\frac{1}{2}$ teaspoon nutmeg
$\frac{1}{2}$ teaspoon ground ginger
$\frac{1}{2}$ teaspoon ground cloves
1 teaspoon baking soda
$\frac{1}{2}$ cup shortening (such as Crisco)
4 tablespoons butter
$\frac{3}{4}$ cup firmly packed light brown sugar
$\frac{1}{2}$ cup sugar
2 eggs
1 cup sour cream
$\frac{1}{2}$ cup milk
$\frac{3}{4}$ cup chopped walnuts, medium chopped
$\frac{3}{4}$ cup currants

Preheat oven to 350°F. Grease 2 9-inch cake pans.

Sift the flour with the rest of the dry ingredients and set aside.

In a large bowl, cream the shortening and butter. Add the sugars, beating until light and fluffy. Add the eggs 1 at a time, beating for 1 minute after each egg. Add the flour mixture, one-half at a time, alternating with half of the sour cream until all has been beaten and blended. Pour in the milk and beat until well combined. Add the nuts and currants, beating only to blend thoroughly.

Pour the batter into the prepared cake pans, dividing evenly. Bake for 25 to 35 minutes or until cakes are golden brown and a toothpick inserted in the center comes out clean. Remove to cake racks and cool.

Two-Cream Frosting

MAKES APPROXIMATELY
$3\frac{1}{2}$ TO 4 CUPS.

$\frac{1}{2}$ pound cream cheese, at room temperature
6 tablespoons butter, at room temperature
$\frac{1}{3}$ cup sour cream
1 teaspoon vanilla
1 1-pound box confectioner's sugar
1 cup walnut pieces

In a medium-size mixing bowl, blend the cream cheese and butter until light and fluffy. Add the sour cream and vanilla. Pour in the sugar and beat until frosting is formed. This frosting can be made a day or two in advance, but should be brought to room temperature for easier frosting.

To assemble the cake, place 1 layer on a plate or serving platter. Spread 1 cup of Two-Cream Frosting on the top. Place the second layer over the first. Frost the top and sides of the cake. Sprinkle the walnut pieces over the top. Chill until the frosting sets, approximately 2 hours. Set out $\frac{1}{2}$ hour before serving. Protected with plastic wrap, this cake will stay fresh 3 to 5 days.

Russian Spice Cake decorated with cherries.

CHAPTER ELEVEN

CHINESE TEA

Chinese Pancakes filled with Shredded Chicken in Peanut Sauce

Crescent Moon Melon Slices

Almond Cakes

Sweet and Crunchy Walnuts

Baby Shrimp with Cashews

Sautéed Chinese Vegetables

Oolong Tea (or your choice)

Serves 6.

OVER THE CENTURIES, CHINA HAS GENEROUSLY SHARED THE GIFTS AND benefits of its culture with the rest of the world. The Chinese have given us silk, porcelain, paper, gunpowder, firecrackers, and pasta. China has given us philosophy and blessed us with tea.

Legend has it that the Chinese emperor Shen Nung (28th century B.C.) discovered tea by accident. He always drank boiled water as a way of protecting himself from the prevalent illnesses of the time. One day his servants built the fire for his water using the branches of a nearby tree. Some of the leaves from the branches floated into the boiling water, and the fragrance released caught the emperor's attention. He sipped the hot liquid and was delighted by the flavor. That first sip flowered into tea-drinking ceremonies and traditions that steadily increased in popularity.

We wanted to do a Tea with an Asian flavor. We chose China because their foods are easily adaptable to the Western tea ceremony and it is appropriate to reflect the taste of tea's parent culture.

The pancakes are a wonderful alternative to sandwiches. We suggest you place the fillings on three separate platters surrounded by the pancakes. Be sure to have plenty of pancakes as the fillings go a long way and this combination is very popular. Let the guests fill and make their own pancakes.

The almond cakes are a combination of East and West. They are lighter than most Chinese desserts, many of which are boiled, but forgo the frosted cakiness of the West.

This Tea is simpler and lighter in style than the other Teas in this book, but equally as elegant. Keep this in mind as you arrange your table. One suggestion is to place the pancakes on one side of the tea table and the sweets on the other, with flowers and your teapot occupying the middle. Drinking the delicate oolong tea out of thin China cups is a lovely addition. Play some quiet music in the background. All of this will create an atmosphere of peace and serenity that the Chinese love and your guests will appreciate as an escape from our often hectic world.

FILLED CHINESE PANCAKES

MAKES 18 PANCAKES.

1 1/4 cups flour
1 teaspoon salt
1/2 cup boiling water
Sesame oil

In a medium-size bowl, combine flour and salt. Pour the boiling water into the bowl and stir until a dough is formed. Knead the dough for 10 minutes. Place in a bowl, cover with a cloth, and set in a warm place for 45 minutes.

Shape the dough into a tube approximately 9 inches long. Cut into 18 equal 1/2-inch thick pieces. Roll the pieces into balls. Keep the balls you are not using immediately covered with a damp paper towel. Flatten 2 of the balls at a time into small "pancakes." Place a drop of sesame oil on each pancake and spread evenly over the top. Press the 2 pancakes together, oiled sides touching, to create 1. Roll out the dough until it is very thin and approximately 7 inches in diameter.

Heat a heavy skillet until hot. Rub a small drop of sesame oil onto the bottom of the skillet. Place a pancake in the hot skillet and cook for 30 seconds. Turn the pancake over. When it has puffed, separate the 2 pancakes using your fingers. This is hot work, so be careful.

Place the pancakes on a plate and cover with a damp cloth while you cook the others. If you are eating immediately, spoon filling into the center of the pancake. Fold the bottom flap over the filling. Fold over the sides. If you plan on having the meal later, keep them covered,

unfilled, in plastic wrap and reheat in a microwave, 6 at a time (covered loosely with plastic wrap), for 30 seconds on high or until warm. If you don't have a microwave, wrap the pancakes in a wet dish towel and warm in a 350°F oven for 8 to 10 minutes or until hot.

NOTE: It may be easier for you to simply buy pancakes at your local Chinese restaurant and reheat them.

Baby Shrimp with Cashews

MAKES APPROXIMATELY 3 CUPS.

4 tablespoons chicken broth
2 tablespoons soy sauce
2 tablespoons dry sherry
1 teaspoon cornstarch
1 teaspoon sugar
1 tablespoon sesame oil
4 scallions, finely sliced
1 pound raw baby shrimp, shelled, washed, and dried
1 cup roasted cashews

In a small bowl, combine the chicken broth, soy sauce, sherry, cornstarch, and sugar.

Heat a heavy skillet until very hot. Pour in sesame oil. When the oil is hot, add scallions and cook for 1 minute. Put the shrimp in the skillet and cook until pink, about 3 minutes. Pour in sauce. Cook until thick. Add the cashews and cook until hot, about 1 to 2 minutes. Spoon the filling into a Chinese pancake. Fold the pancake and serve.

Filled Chinese Pancakes.

Shredded Chicken in Peanut Sauce

MAKES 3 CUPS.

1 medium clove garlic
1 teaspoon fresh ginger slices
1/6 cup sesame oil
1/4 cup vegetable oil
1 tablespoon chili oil (optional)
1 tablespoon honey mustard
3 tablespoons rice vinegar
2 tablespoons soy sauce
4 tablespoons creamy peanut butter
Juice of 1 orange
3 cups cooked chicken, shredded
1/2 cucumber, julienned

Place the garlic, ginger, and oils in a blender or food processor fitted with the metal blade. Process until the garlic and ginger are pureed. Add the mustard, vinegar, soy sauce, and peanut butter. Process until all the ingredients are well blended. Pour in the orange juice and pulse until completely incorporated. Pour the peanut sauce over the chicken and toss until well combined.

Spoon the filling into a Chinese pancake. Garnish with cucumber. Fold the pancake and serve.

If you are making this filling in advance, refrigerate. Bring the filling back to room temperature before serving.

Sautéed Chinese Vegetables

MAKES APPROXIMATELY 2 1/2 TO 3 CUPS.

1 teaspoon plus 1 tablespoon sesame oil
1 egg, beaten
3 tablespoons chicken broth
3 tablespoons soy sauce
1 tablespoon sugar
1/2 teaspoon cornstarch
1 tablespoon vegetable oil
1 large clove garlic, minced
2 scallions, cut into 4-inch pieces and julienned
1 1/2 cups thinly sliced shiitake mushrooms
1 medium carrot, cut in half and julienned
1/2 cup fresh bean sprouts
1/2 cup bamboo shoots
1 cup thinly sliced Chinese cabbage
Plum or hoisin sauce

Heat 1 teaspoon sesame oil in a heavy skillet or wok until very hot.

Pour in beaten egg. Cook until firm. Turn over and cook for an additional minute. Remove to a plate and cut into very thin slices.

In a small bowl, combine chicken broth, soy sauce, sugar, and cornstarch. Set aside.

Heat 1 tablespoon each of sesame oil and vegetable oil in the skillet or wok until very hot.

Add garlic and cook for 30 seconds. Add the rest of the vegetables, sautéing for 5 minutes over high heat or until they start to lose their crunch.

Pour in reserved sauce and cook for an additional 3 minutes. Add egg, tossing well. Cook until egg is warmed. Spoon the filling onto a Chinese pancake. Top with plum or hoisin sauce. Fold the pancake and serve.

CRESCENT MOON MELON SLICES

MAKES 6 SLICES.

1/2 small honeydew melon
2 tablespoons plum wine, schnapps, or your favorite fruit liqueur

Remove all seeds and membrane from the melon half. Sprinkle the wine or liqueur over the melon. Cover with plastic wrap and refrigerate until chilled, 1 to 2 hours.

When ready to serve, cut the melon half into equal slices. Arrange on a plate. (If you have flowers, place a few in the center of the plate and arrange the melon slices around the flowers.)

Crescent Moon Melon Slices garnished with Sweet and Crunchy Walnuts and pineapple slices.

Decorated Almond Cakes.

ALMOND CAKES

MAKES APPROXIMATELY
1 DOZEN CAKES.

- **4 jumbo egg whites, at room temperature**
- **1/2 cup superfine sugar**
- **1 cup finely ground almonds**
- **1 cup self-rising cake flour**
- **2 teaspoons almond extract**
- **12 blanched almonds**
- **1/4 cup honey**

Preheat oven to 325°F. Coat a 12-cup cupcake tin with cooking spray.

In a large mixing bowl, beat the egg whites until they form soft peaks. Gradually add the sugar and continue beating until very stiff. Carefully fold in the ground almonds, then the flour, until both are completely incorporated. Gently mix in the almond extract.

Spoon the batter into the prepared cupcake tin. There should be enough batter to reach the rim of each cup. Place a blanched almond on top of each cup of batter. Bake for approximately 20 to 25 minutes or until the cakes are puffed, firm, and golden brown. Remove the tin from the oven and rest on a cooling rack.

Heat the honey in a microwave on high for 30 to 45 seconds or until hot and very fluid. (If you don't have a microwave, heat the honey in a small saucepan over low heat until hot.) Brush the honey lightly on the hot cakes. Let the cakes cool in the tin, then remove. The cakes are best served within 24 hours.

SWEET AND CRUNCHY WALNUTS

MAKES 1 CUP.

- **1 cup walnut halves**
- **1 cup water**
- **1/4 cup sugar**
- **1/4 cup light Karo syrup**
- **2 1/2 tablespoons unsalted butter**

Place the walnuts in a small saucepan, cover with water, and bring to a boil. Boil for 1 minute. Remove from heat and drain off all water.

Pour the sugar and Karo syrup over walnuts. Stir well and return to the heat. Bring the mixture to a boil. Turn down heat and simmer for 10 minutes. One and a half minutes before the walnuts are ready, melt butter in a skillet and heat until hot.

Using a slotted spoon, remove walnuts from syrup, leaving as much syrup in the saucepan as possible. Add the walnuts to the butter and cook over medium-high heat until brown and crispy.

Using a slotted spoon, remove walnuts from the skillet, leaving as much of the drippings in the skillet as possible.

Spread the walnuts over a plate and let cool. If any excess caramelized sugar clings to the walnuts, simply break it off after they have cooled.

Stored in an airtight container, the walnuts should last at least a week.

NOTE: If after the walnuts have cooled you find them slightly greasy, lay them on a sheet of paper towel, cover with another sheet of paper towel, and pat gently.

YELLOW

CHAPTER TWELVE

CHILDREN'S TEA

Miniature Pita Pizzas

Peanut Butter and Jelly Sandwiches

Ham Sandwiches

Toll House Cookies

Cream Scones

Ice Cream Cone Cakes

Queen Mary (or your choice) Tea and Milk

Serves 6.

Oh, grown-ups cannot understand,
and grown-ups never will,
how short the way to fairyland
across the purple hill.
ALFRED NOYES

CHILDREN LOVE TEAS. THEY FIND MAGIC IN THEM AND ARE PREPARED TO be on their best behavior. Theirs is the remarkable ability to slip from the everyday and enter into the spirit of the occasion.

Children like having their sandwiches cut into small shapes and having the choices a Tea presents. The interesting thing about children at a Tea is that they only take as much as they can eat.

Naturally, we gear the Teas to suit their tastes, what children we know like, and what we liked as children. Pizzas and peanut butter and jelly sandwiches are standard favorites. The carrot and celery sticks are for the sake of mothers. As carrot and celery sticks are self-descriptive, we don't give a recipe. Do include the scones in your Tea. Children like them and will show you their thanks by politely trying them with both the cream and jam. The Toll House Cookies are such a favorite classic, nothing further need be said. The cone cakes were a fad in the 1950s. We had completely forgotten about them until a friend reminded us. The novelty alone entices children, and we remember being charmed. One additional tip if the children are drinking tea, substitute honey for sugar; they prefer it.

Keep in mind that it will make for a more comfortable Tea if you accommodate the china and seating arrangements to the children's size.

Finally, it's not necessary to have a special occasion for a children's Tea. Many of our friends do it once a week as a way of creating and sharing a special time with their children.

MINIATURE PITA PIZZAS

MAKES 6 PIZZAS.

6 tablespoons pizza sauce
6 1-ounce miniature pitas
1/2 cup grated mozzarella cheese
6 teaspoons grated parmesan cheese

Preheat broiler.

Spread 1 tablespoon of sauce on each pita. Sprinkle 4 teaspoons of mozzarella over the sauce on each pita. Sprinkle 1 teaspoon of parmesan cheese on each pita.

Using a spatula, place the pitas on an ungreased baking sheet. Place the baking sheet under the hot broiler and cook until the cheese is melted and crispy, approximately 3 to 5 minutes. Serve warm.

VARIATION: Most children prefer plain cheese pizza. If you wish, add additional toppings of your choice.

NOTE: Be careful not to put too much mozzarella on the pitas or the cheese will slide off.

Nutritious carrot and celery sticks.

PEANUT BUTTER AND JELLY SANDWICHES

MAKES 12 PIECES.

6 thin slices white bread
Unsalted butter
3 tablespoons creamy peanut butter
3 tablespoons jelly or jam

Spread each slice of bread with a thin coating of butter.

Spread 1 tablespoon of peanut butter on each of 3 slices of bread. Spread 1 tablespoon of jelly on each of the remaining 3 slices of bread. Top the peanut butter slices with the jelly slices.

Trim the crusts. Cut each sandwich into 4 pieces.

NOTE: A fun idea for children is to use cookie cutters to cut out sandwiches that have different shapes or characters, such as stars and angels. Make the sandwiches first and then do the cutting. The thinness of the sandwich will adapt itself to cutting very easily.

One word of caution: Depending on the size of your cutters, you may have to adjust the number of sandwiches you make so that each child gets 2 pieces (if your cutters are large, 1 would do). Doing your sandwiches this way also increases probable waste, which may be a factor.

HAM SANDWICHES

MAKES 12 PIECES.

6 thin slices wheat bread
Unsalted butter
3 slices boiled ham, approximately 3 ounces
Mustard

Spread each slice of bread with a thin coating of butter. Lay a slice of ham on 3 slices of bread, folding the ham to conform to the size of the bread. Spread a smear of mustard on each slice of ham. Cover the bread with the remaining 3 slices. Trim the crusts. Cut each sandwich into 4 pieces.

NOTE: Please refer to note on page 95 (peanut-butter sandwiches) for directions on cutting the sandwiches into different shapes.

TOLL HOUSE COOKIES

MAKES 2 1/2 DOZEN COOKIES.

1 cup plus 2 tablespoons all-purpose flour
1/2 teaspoon baking soda
1/2 teaspoon salt
1/2 cup unsalted butter, softened
6 tablespoons sugar
6 tablespoons firmly packed brown sugar
1/2 teaspoon vanilla extract
1 egg
1 6-ounce package (1 cup) semisweet chocolate morsels
1/2 cup chopped nuts

Preheat oven to 375°F.

In a small bowl, combine flour, baking soda, and salt. Set aside.

In a large bowl, combine butter, sugars, and vanilla extract.

Beat until creamy. Beat in egg. Gradually add flour mixture. Stir in chocolate morsels and nuts. Drop by rounded measuring tablespoons onto an ungreased cookie sheet.

Bake 9 to 11 minutes or until the cookies are brown on the edges. Cool and serve.

CREAM SCONES

MAKES APPROXIMATELY 10 SCONES.

2 cups flour
1/4 cup sugar
1 tablespoon baking powder
1 teaspoon salt
3 tablespoons unsalted butter, cold
1 egg
1 1/4 cups heavy cream
1 egg yolk
2 tablespoons cold water

Preheat oven to 350°F. Grease a baking sheet and set aside.

Sift the dry ingredients together. Using a pastry blender or 2 knives, cut in the butter until the mixture is crumbly.

Beat the egg and heavy cream together. Pour into the dry ingredients and stir until well blended.

Prepare a flat surface by flouring it well (the dough will be slightly wet and will absorb the flour quickly). Place the dough on the flat surface. Pat the dough down with your hands until it is 3/4-inch thick. Cut out the scones with a 2 1/2-inch biscuit cutter and place on a greased baking sheet.

Beat the egg yolk with the cold water. Using a pastry brush, glaze scones with this mixture.

Bake for 25 to 30 minutes or until golden brown.

Serve hot or cold with jam and Clotted Cream, if desired.

Cream Scones with Clotted Cream and jam.

ICE CREAM CONE CAKES

MAKES 6 CONES.

- 6 Nabisco™ Comet cones
- 1 1/2 cups Grandma Paradis' Quickie Chocolate Cake batter
- 1 cup Easy Yellow Cake batter
- Buttercream Frosting
- 3 maraschino cherries
- Sprinkles

Preheat oven to 350°F.

Place the 6 empty cones upright in a cupcake tin.

Fill 3 cones with 1/2 cup each of the chocolate cake batter, then fill the remaining cones with 1/3 cup each of the yellow cake batter.

Place the muffin tin carefully in the oven and bake for 25 to 30 minutes or until the cake has puffed up firm and golden brown. Remove from oven and cool.

Frost the top of each cone cake with 2 tablespoons of Buttercream Frosting, swirling the knife (or spoon) as you go. Cut the cherries in half and place on top, cut-side down. Cover generously with sprinkles.

Grandma Paradis' Quickie Chocolate Cake

MAKES 1 THIN 9-INCH LAYER OR 2 1/2 CUPS BATTER.

- 3/4 cup sugar
- 1 egg
- 2 tablespoons shortening (such as Crisco)
- 1 teaspoon baking soda dissolved in 1/2 cup buttermilk
- 1/2 teaspoon salt
- 1 cup all-purpose flour
- 1 1/2 teaspoons vanilla
- 1/4 cup unsweetened cocoa dissolved in 1/4 cup boiling water
- Confectioner's sugar

Preheat oven to 350°F. Grease a 9-inch cake pan and set aside.

Mix all ingredients except the cocoa and confectioner's sugar in a bowl. Beat for 1 minute.

Add the cocoa and beat for 2 minutes or until batter is smooth. Pour batter into cake pan.

Bake for 30 to 35 minutes or until cake is firm and springs back to the touch. Cool in pan. Remove to a plate and dust with confectioner's sugar.

NOTE: If using this recipe for the Ice Cream Cone Cakes, do *not* bake the batter until it has been poured into the cones.

Easy Yellow Cake

MAKES 2 9-INCH LAYERS OR 4 CUPS BATTER.

- 1/2 cup shortening (such as Crisco), at room temperature
- 1 cup sugar
- 2 eggs
- 2 cups all-purpose flour
- 1/2 teaspoon salt
- 2 teaspoons baking powder
- 1 cup milk
- 1/2 teaspoon vanilla

Preheat oven to 350°F. Grease 2 9-inch cake pans and set aside.

Cream the shortening. Gradually add the sugar and continue to cream. Add the eggs, 1 at a time, beating after each addition.

Sift the dry ingredients together. Add the dry ingredients (1/3 at a time) alternating with the milk, to the creamed mixture. Beat until smooth. Pour in vanilla and mix well. Divide batter between the 2 cake pans.

Bake for 30 to 35 minutes or until cake is golden and springs back to the touch.

NOTE: If using this recipe for the Ice Cream Cone Cakes, do *not* bake the batter until it has been poured into the cones.

Brightly decorated Ice Cream Cone Cakes.

Buttercream Frosting

MAKES $1\frac{1}{3}$ CUPS, ENOUGH TO FROST 6 CONES.

6 tablespoons butter, softened
2 cups confectioner's sugar
1 teaspoon vanilla
2 tablespoons hot milk

Cream the butter and sugar until smooth. Mix in the vanilla. Beat in the hot milk until the frosting is creamy. Place in the refrigerator so that the frosting becomes firm and spreadable.

This frosting is best when made close to frosting time.

NOTE: The cake part of dessert can be baked the day before, wrapped in wax paper or plastic wrap. Use any leftover cake batter to make cupcakes.

CHAPTER THIRTEEN

Chocolate Lover's Tea

Prosciutto and Explorateur Cheese Sandwiches

Smoked Turkey and Chutney Sandwiches

Sliced Chicken Sandwiches

Chocolate Dipped Shortbread Hearts

Chocolate-Chip Scones

Chocolate Delight Cake

White Chocolate Dipped Fruit

Chocolate Truffles

Irish Breakfast Tea (or your choice)

Serves 6.

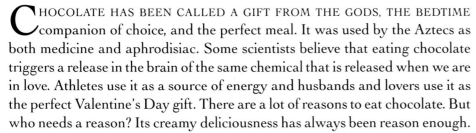

CHOCOLATE HAS BEEN CALLED A GIFT FROM THE GODS, THE BEDTIME companion of choice, and the perfect meal. It was used by the Aztecs as both medicine and aphrodisiac. Some scientists believe that eating chocolate triggers a release in the brain of the same chemical that is released when we are in love. Athletes use it as a source of energy and husbands and lovers use it as the perfect Valentine's Day gift. There are a lot of reasons to eat chocolate. But who needs a reason? Its creamy deliciousness has always been reason enough.

Not everyone is a chocolate devotee. Some, a minority, no doubt, have little or no use for it. If that is the case, then this Tea is not for them. It is for those who glory and revel in the dark delight; those who appreciate an afternoon of unrestrained pleasure.

This is a rich Tea and it is absolutely meant to be so. It is not one you would have every week or even every month. Rather, it suits a very special occasion when you and your guests have decided to forget about calories and simply enjoy yourselves.

For variety we have added a touch of spice to the sandwiches. We like the way spicy foods and chocolate play off one another.

Serve clotted cream with this Tea just as with every other. Some hardy guests have even been known to have a spoon of it with their cake, so you might consider making extra.

Have fun with this. Use some of your own chocolate favorites if you wish, and give in to an afternoon of sybaritic pleasure.

PROSCIUTTO AND EXPLORATEUR CHEESE SANDWICHES

MAKES 12 PIECES.

6 thin slices white bread
Unsalted butter
3 ounces Explorateur cheese, at room temperature
2 ounces thinly sliced prosciutto, approximately

Spread each slice of bread with a thin coating of butter.

Spread a thin layer of cheese on 3 slices of bread. Lay a slice of prosciutto on the cheese, folding the prosciutto to conform to the size of the bread. Cover the 3 sandwiches with the remaining bread.

Trim the crusts. Cut each sandwich into 4 pieces.

SMOKED TURKEY AND CHUTNEY SANDWICHES

MAKES 12 PIECES.

6 thin slices wheat bread
Unsalted butter
3 slices smoked turkey, approximately 3 ounces total
3 teaspoons chutney of your choice (we use mango)

Spread each slice of bread with a thin coating of butter. Lay a slice of turkey on 3 slices of bread. Spread a teaspoon of chutney on each slice of turkey. Top the bread with the remaining slices. Trim the crusts. Cut each sandwich into 4 pieces.

SLICED CHICKEN SANDWICHES

MAKES 12 PIECES.

6 thin slices white bread
Unsalted butter
6 ounces cooked chicken breast, thinly sliced
Salt (to taste)
Pepper (to taste)

Spread each slice of bread with a thin coating of butter. Divide the chicken slices (2 ounces per sandwich) between 3 pieces of bread. Salt and pepper each sandwich. Cover each sandwich with the remaining bread. Trim the crusts. Cut each sandwich into 4 pieces.

CHOCOLATE DIPPED SHORTBREAD HEARTS

MAKES APPROXIMATELY 4 DOZEN COOKIES.

- **1 pound unsalted butter**
- **1 cup sugar**
- **4 cups flour**
- **8 ounces semisweet chocolate**

Preheat oven to 375°F.

Cream butter. Add sugar gradually. Add flour, making sure it is well mixed, but don't overwork. Pat out the dough on a lightly floured board until it is about 3/4-inch thick. Using a 2-inch heart-shaped cookie cutter, cut out hearts and place on an ungreased cookie sheet. Cook 15 to 20 minutes or until cookies are golden brown on the edges. Watch the first few batches closely and lower oven to 350°F or 325°F if they cook too quickly.

Place baked cookies on a rack to cool. Melt the chocolate in a microwave-proof container for about 45 seconds per square, depending on the oven. (If you don't have a microwave oven, melt the chocolate in the top of a double boiler that has been coated with cooking spray until the chocolate liquidizes.) Dip half the heart into the melted chocolate so that you have a black and white effect.

Lay dipped hearts on a plate covered with wax paper. Place plate in the refrigerator 1 hour or until chocolate has set.

Store the hearts in a cool, dry container with sheets of wax paper between the layers. Undipped hearts can be frozen up to 2 months, providing they are well wrapped.

Chocolate Dipped Shortbread Hearts garnished with flowers.

CHOCOLATE CHIP SCONES

MAKES APPROXIMATELY 10 SCONES.

- **2 cups flour**
- **1/4 cup sugar**
- **2 teaspoons baking powder**
- **1 teaspoon salt**
- **3 tablespoons unsalted butter**
- **1 egg**
- **3/4 cup milk**
- **1/2 cup chocolate morsels**
- **1 egg yolk**
- **2 tablespoons cold water**

Preheat oven to 350°F.

Sift the dry ingredients together. Using a pastry blender or 2 knives, cut in the butter until crumbly.

Beat the egg and milk together. Pour into the dry ingredients, stirring until a dough is formed. Add the chocolate chips, combining well.

Using an ice cream scoop, form the scones and place on a greased baking sheet.

Beat the egg yolk with the cold water. Using a pastry brush, glaze each scone with this mixture.

Bake for 25 to 30 minutes or until golden brown.

Serve hot or cold with jam and Clotted Cream, if desired.

Chocolate Delight Cake garnished with flowers.

CHOCOLATE DELIGHT CAKE

A DARK, RICH CAKE WITH AN EVEN darker, richer frosting. This cake is a chocolate lover's delight.

MAKES 1 10-INCH TUBE CAKE.

Dark Chocolate Cake

- **4 ounces unsweetened chocolate**
- **1 tablespoon instant coffee granules**
- **2 cups cake flour**
- **2 teaspoons baking soda**
- **1/2 teaspoon salt**
- **1/2 pound butter, at room temperature**
- **1 1/2 cups packed dark brown sugar**
- **3 eggs, at room temperature**
- **2 teaspoons vanilla**
- **1/2 cup buttermilk**
- **1/2 cup boiling water**

Preheat oven to 350°F. Grease a 10-inch tube cake pan and set aside.

Melt the chocolate and coffee together in the top half of a double boiler or microwave. Cool to room temperature.

Combine the flour, baking soda, and salt. In a large bowl, cream the butter and sugar. Add the eggs to the butter and sugar mixture 1 at a time, beating until well mixed. Pour in the vanilla, beating an additional 30 seconds. Add the cooled chocolate and coffee and beat until well blended.

Spoon in one-third of the flour mixture and 1/4 cup of buttermilk, beating until mixed. Repeat.

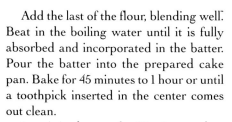

Add the last of the flour, blending well. Beat in the boiling water until it is fully absorbed and incorporated in the batter. Pour the batter into the prepared cake pan. Bake for 45 minutes to 1 hour or until a toothpick inserted in the center comes out clean.

Let sit in the pan for 10 minutes, then turn out onto a serving plate or platter. Cool completely.

Chocolate Ganache

MAKES APPROXIMATELY 3/4 CUP, ENOUGH TO FROST 1 10-INCH CAKE.

6 ounces semisweet chocolate
1/2 cup heavy cream

Break the chocolate into small bits. (You can put it in a food processor fitted with the metal blade and process until it is very finely chopped.) Put the chocolate into a medium-size bowl.

Heat the cream to boiling point. Whisk the hot cream into the chocolate and continue whisking until the chocolate is melted and blended with the cream.

Let sit, covered, until it reaches room temperature.

NOTE: This frosting can sit out on your counter, covered, overnight, and still be good for use. Do not refrigerate, for it will become hard.

To frost the cake, spoon 1/4 cup of the Chocolate Ganache around the top of the cake, letting it drip down the sides.

Using a knife, spread the ganache so that the entire cake has a very thin coating. Put cake in the refrigerator and chill until the ganache starts to set, approximately 45 minutes. Remove from refrigerator and frost with the remaining ganache until the cake is coated with a thick, even layer.

Chill until set, approximately 1 1/2 hours. This cake is best served at room temperature.

Just before serving, decorate the top of the cake with small, fresh flowers or the decorations of your choice.

WHITE CHOCOLATE DIPPED FRUIT

MAKES APPROXIMATELY 12 PIECES OF FRUIT.

7 ounces white chocolate for dipping
6 large navel orange sections, excess pith and membrane removed
6 large strawberries, washed and dried

Melt the white chocolate in the top half of a double boiler. Holding the orange sections at the top, dip each slice into the chocolate until two-thirds of the slice is covered. Place the fruit on a wax paper-covered plate.

Gently holding the hull, dip the strawberries into the chocolate until two-thirds of each strawberry is covered. Place the strawberries on the plate.

Refrigerate the fruit until the chocolate is set, approximately 1/2 to 1 hour. These should be made on the day of the Tea.

CHOCOLATE TRUFFLES

MAKES APPROXIMATELY 2 DOZEN TRUFFLES.

8 ounces semisweet chocolate
3/4 cup heavy cream
1 1/2 tablespoons rum (optional)
Powdered cocoa
Paper bonbon cups

Place the chocolate in a food processor fitted with the metal blade, or break by hand. Pulse until finely grated and transfer to a bowl.

In a saucepan, heat the heavy cream until it scalds. Pour the hot cream over the chocolate and whisk the mixture together until the chocolate is melted and both are well blended. Add the rum, if desired.

Cover the mixture and refrigerate until it has cooled and thickened, approximately 3 to 4 hours.

Using a teaspoon, place a mound of dough in the palm of your hand. Roll it into a ball, then roll in powdered cocoa until it is completely covered. Place the truffle in a bonbon cup.

NOTE: If you find it difficult to shape the truffles, add 2 tablespoons of soft butter to the mix and refrigerate until it is set.

CHAPTER FOURTEEN

Feel Better Tea

Chicken Consommé

Hot Buttered Toast

Red Egg on Toast°

Fruit Sherbet

Herbal Tea

Serves 6.

We have all suffered from a cold or flu that has made us feel as though we were at death's door. We lay on our bed feeling miserable. Then, the door would open and someone would come in bringing hot soup or tea. They would put their hand on our forehead. We'd feel a little better. The room didn't seem as dark. It's amazing how a little care and attention helps to heal.

We never can remember if it's feed a cold and starve a fever, or vice versa. Perhaps the "patient" really isn't up to having anything, but the caring a simple tea tray represents will help lift the spirits. The food *will* help. A good broth provides nourishment and the toast provides easy sustenance. The tea and sherbert soothe the throat while giving the body needed liquid.

Remember to make the tray look as appealing as possible. Put a nice cloth on it, a flower in a vase, and use a china cup for the tea. This will help both body and spirit.

Hot Buttered Toast, tea, and jam.

Hot Buttered Toast

MAKES 8 PIECES.

Unsalted butter
2 slices bread

Toast the bread. Butter it lightly. Trim the crusts. Cut each slice into 4 diagonal pieces (called toast points). Serve warm.

Red Egg on Toast

SERVES 1.

Red Egg on Toast may be served to the patient when the "crisis" has passed and something more is required. This childhood favorite is a tasty, filling, and gentle form of nourishment.

Unsalted butter
1 egg
1 slice bread
1/4 cup canned tomato soup, undiluted

Put a teaspoon of butter in a small skillet and heat on low heat until melted. Gently crack an egg into the butter and cook for 1 minute on each side.

While the egg is cooking, toast and butter a slice of bread. Place on a plate. Put the egg on the toast.

Heat the soup until hot, either in the microwave (1 minute on high) or on the top of the stove. Spoon the hot soup over the egg, making sure to cover the egg and toast entirely. Serve hot.

CHICKEN CONSOMMÉ

MAKES APPROXIMATELY 1½ CUPS.

- 4 large chicken legs (approximately 2½ pounds)
- 1 carrot, cut into 4 pieces
- 1 celery stalk, cut into 4 pieces
- 1 large clove garlic, cut into 4 pieces
- 1 medium onion, cut into 8 sections
- 1 teaspoon parsley
- ½ teaspoon rosemary
- ½ teaspoon basil
- 2 quarts cold water
- Salt (to taste)

Put the chicken, carrot, celery, garlic, and onion in a large pot. Place the herbs in the center of a 2-inch square piece of cheesecloth. Bring the corners together, creating a pouch, and twist. Tie with string to secure. Add the bag to the pot. Pour in the cold water.

Bring the mixture to a boil, then lower heat and simmer for 2 hours. Remove the cheesecloth pouch.

Pour the entire mixture through a strainer to separate the chicken and vegetables from the broth. Return the broth to the pot. Skim off and remove any apparent fat. Cook the broth on medium-high heat until reduced by half. Season lightly with salt and serve.

The consommé can be safely kept in the refrigerator for 1 week, and freezes well for at least 3 months. Once it is thawed, use within 24 hours.

Chicken Consommé, Hot Buttered Toast, and Herb Tea.

CHAPTER FIFTEEN

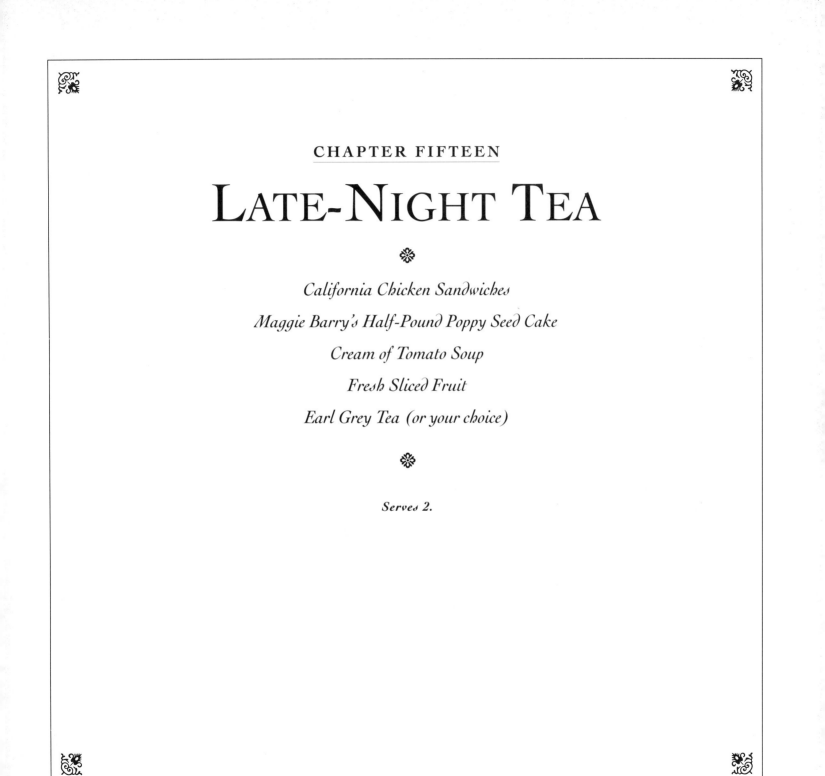

Late-Night Tea

California Chicken Sandwiches

Maggie Barry's Half-Pound Poppy Seed Cake

Cream of Tomato Soup

Fresh Sliced Fruit

Earl Grey Tea (or your choice)

Serves 2.

WE'VE DESIGNED THIS TEA FOR THOSE EVENINGS WHEN YOU ARE OUT LATE but want to create a nice meal at home with a minimum of fuss.

Both the Cream of Tomato Soup and Poppy Seed Cake can be made a day or two in advance. Slice the chicken, mix the alfalfa sprouts with the mayonnaise, and sprinkle the peeled, sliced avocado with lemon. Put them all (covered well) in the refrigerator until you need them. Wash and dry the fruit, if necessary. When you come home, assemble the sandwiches, heat the soup, and slice the fruit and cake. You're ready to serve.

A Tea such as this provides a wonderful opportunity for a dinner *à deux*. Take advantage of this opportunity and create a romantic setting. Set the table before leaving with freshly pressed linen, your nicest dishes, long-stemmed glasses for water (or wine), and candles. Buy fresh flowers and arrange them in a small vase, nothing too large, because you want to keep the setting intimate. setting intimate.

Enjoy your evening out. You'll be coming home knowing the best of it lies ahead.

CALIFORNIA CHICKEN SANDWICHES

MAKES 2 OPEN-FACED SANDWICHES.

2 thick slices pumpernickel bread
1 cup alfalfa sprouts
1/3 cup mayonnaise
1/2 small avocado
1 teaspoon fresh lemon or lime juice
6 ounces cooked chicken, thinly sliced
2 ounces Swiss or Jarlsberg cheese
1/2 teaspoon sesame seeds

Toast 1 side of the bread under a hot broiler.

Mix together the alfalfa sprouts and mayonnaise, blending well. Cut the avocado into 8 thin slices. Sprinkle the citrus juice over the avocado slices. Spread one-half of the sprouts and mayonnaise mixture on the untoasted side of each slice of bread.

Place 4 avocado slices on top of the sprouts. Divide the chicken slices between the 2 sandwiches, placing them on top of the avocado. Place 1 ounce of sliced cheese over the top of each sandwich. Sprinkle 1/4 teaspoon sesame seeds over each sandwich.

Using a spatula, put the sandwiches on a baking sheet and broil until the cheese is melted and starting to puff and brown, about 5 to 10 minutes. Serve immediately.

MAGGIE BARRY'S HALF-POUND POPPY SEED CAKE

MAKES 1 9-BY-5-BY-3-INCH LOAF.

1/2 pound unsalted butter, at room temperature
1 cup sugar
2 eggs, at room temperature
2 teaspoons vanilla
2 cups self-rising cake flour
1/2 cup milk
3 tablespoons poppy seeds

Preheat oven to 350°F. Grease a 9-by-5-by-3-inch loaf pan and set aside.

Cream the butter in a mixer until light and fluffy, about 1 minute. Pour in sugar and repeat process. Add the eggs and vanilla and beat for an additional 30 seconds. Add the flour, 1 cup at a time, beating until combined. Pour in the milk and beat until smooth. Add poppy seeds and blend. Pour batter into the prepared loaf pan, pressing down with a spoon to remove air pockets.

Bake for 45 minutes to 1 hour, or until golden brown and a toothpick inserted in the center comes out clean. Remove from oven and cool on a cake rack. When the pan is cool, remove the cake from the pan and let it sit on the cake rack until it is completely cool.

Serve plain or lightly toasted with butter and preserves.

Well wrapped, the cake will last 5 days.

California Chicken Sandwiches and Earl Grey Tea.

Cream of Tomato Soup served with Crackers.

Cream of Tomato Soup

MAKES APPROXIMATELY 4½ CUPS.

4 tablespoons plus 2 teaspoons unsalted butter
1 medium yellow onion, coarsely chopped
14 plum tomatoes (3 cups), peeled, seeded, and cut into quarters
2 cups chicken broth
½ cup heavy cream
Salt (to taste)

Melt 4 tablespoons of the butter in a large saucepan over medium-high heat until it just starts to brown. Add the onion and cook until translucent and starting to brown, about 2 minutes. Put in the tomatoes and cook until soft, about 3 minutes. Pour in the chicken broth and bring to a boil. Turn the heat down and simmer for 5 minutes.

Purée the soup in a food processor fitted with the metal blade or a blender. Return the soup to the pot and bring to a boil.

Add the heavy cream and 2 teaspoons butter, continuing to heat until the butter is melted and soup is hot. Season with salt.

This soup will stay fresh in the refrigerator 3 to 5 days; it can be frozen for up to 6 months.

FRESH SLICED FRUIT

SERVES 2.

DEPENDING ON THE SEASON, WE SUGGEST you choose one of the combinations listed below.

1/2 small honeydew melon
1 pint strawberries
or
1 fresh Bosc pear
1 ripe kiwi

Melon and Strawberries:

Early in the day of your Tea, wash and dry the strawberries. Seed the half melon and cut into 4 slices. Arrange the 4 slices of melon around the edge of a plate so it makes a circle. Place the strawberries in the middle of the plate. Cover with plastic wrap and refrigerate until needed.

Pear and Kiwi:

Just before serving, peel and cut the kiwi into 1/4-inch slices. Lay them, overlapping, in a circular pattern in the center of a plate. Cut the pear into 8 slices and cut out the center core. Lay the pear slices evenly around the plate, extending outward from the kiwi circle to create a sunburst effect.

Fresh Sliced Fruit and Maggie Barry's Half Pound Poppy Seed Cake (see recipe on page 112).

CHAPTER SIXTEEN

Bare Bones Tea

Any Combination of:

Grilled Cheese Sandwiches

"Whatever" Croques

Creamed Mushrooms

Easy Crepes

Peanut Butter and Banana Sandwiches

Cinnamon Toast Fingers

Herb Omelet

Toast Points with Jam

Black Currant Tea (or your choice)

Serves 2.

We all have had those times when someone drops by unexpectedly. We are glad to see the guest and would like to make an "occasion" of the visit, but the cupboards seem bare. What to do?

We can help. The following suggestions and recipes can be made with a minimum of fuss and waste. These simple ideas will keep you prepared for any of those times when you would like to do a little something extra. Any one of the recipes given is sufficient to provide a small Tea we call "bare bones."

Always keep some nice cookies in your cupboard. Packaged cookies generally have a long shelf life. Be sure to carefully close opened packages to ensure that the remaining cookies don't go stale. Arrange the cookies on a small plate and serve with tea.

Bake one of the pound cakes named in earlier chapters (see pages 41, 104, and 112) and store in the freezer. When you have a need for the cake, slice off what you need and return the remainder to the freezer. To thaw, let the cake sit for 10 to 15 minutes covered in plastic wrap. You can speed up the process by heating the covered cake in a microwave for approximately 15 seconds on high. A nice touch would be to toast the pound cake, butter it, and cut it into finger-size pieces.

Bake the shortbread hearts (see page 103), omitting the chocolate dipping, or any of the cookies from previous chapters, and keep them in the freezer. Take them out as needed. A short time at room temperature will quickly render them edible.

Toast Points with Jam

MAKES 8 PIECES.

Jam
2 thin slices white bread
Unsalted butter

Fill a small bowl with jam. Set the bowl in the middle of a plate.

Toast the bread and butter it well. Trim the crusts. Cut each slice into 4 diagonal pieces. Arrange the 8 toast points around the bowl of jam.

Creamed Mushrooms

MAKES 1 CUP.

Creamed mushrooms are a tasty tidbit and easy to prepare. Keeping a small can of sliced mushrooms in the cupboard is no bother—and will always come in handy.

1 3-ounce can sliced mushrooms
1 tablespoon butter or margarine
4 teaspoons flour
1/2 cup milk
Pinch nutmeg
Salt (to taste)
Pepper (to taste)

Open and drain the can of mushrooms, reserving the liquid (approximately three-eighths of a can).

Heat a small skillet over medium-low heat. Add the butter and melt until foamy. Whisk in the flour, beating until the roux is smooth. Let the roux cook until it starts to brown, approximately 1 to 2 minutes. Whisk in the reserved mushroom juice.

As the sauce starts to thicken, add the milk and beat until smooth. Spoon in the sliced mushrooms and heat until the mushrooms are hot. Add a generous pinch of nutmeg (not too much or the sauce will be bitter), and season with salt and pepper.

Serve the mushrooms hot over toast points (see page 108).

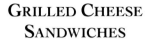

GRILLED CHEESE SANDWICHES

MAKES 8 PIECES.

KEEP BREAD AND CHEDDAR CHEESE IN the freezer and use it to make grilled sandwiches.

Unsalted butter
4 slices bread
1 cup grated cheese (just take it from the freezer and grate it)
1/8 teaspoon basil (or herb of your choice)

Coat a skillet with cooking spray. Generously butter 2 slices of bread. Lay them butter side down on the skillet.

Carefully place 1/2 cup of grated cheese on each sandwich. Sprinkle a small amount of herbs (fresh are best) on the cheese.

Butter the remaining bread slices and place on top of the grated cheese, butter side up.

Turn the flame to low. Cook the sandwiches for 3 minutes on each side or until they are golden brown. Cover the pan with a lid and let cook for an additional 2 minutes to ensure the cheese is melted.

Place on plates and cut each sandwich into 4 pieces. Serve hot.

Assorted cookies, pound cake, and tea.

Cinnamon toast can be served whole or cut into fingers.

CINNAMON TOAST FINGERS

MAKES 8 PIECES.

- 2 slices bread, preferably sliced thick
- 2 teaspoons sugar
- 1/2 teaspoon cinnamon
- Unsalted butter

Toast 1 side of the 2 bread slices under a broiler or in a toaster oven. In a small bowl, combine the sugar and cinnamon. Generously butter the untoasted sides of bread. Divide the sugar and cinnamon between the 2 toasts, sprinkling evenly over the entire surface. Return the bread to the broiler and cook until the sugar is bubbling, about 5 minutes. Remove the toast from the oven and cut each slice into 4 fingers.

NOTE: For a nice touch, take a pretty piece of linen or embroidered cloth, lay it on a small plate, pile the toast fingers on it, and bring up the corners to cover the toast and serve.

"WHATEVER" CROQUES

MAKES 8 PIECES.

YOU CAN PUT TOGETHER A CROQUE-TYPE sandwich using any bits and pieces you have in the refrigerator.

- Unsalted butter
- 4 slices bread
- 2 ounces (2 slices) whatever luncheon type meat you have available (leftover chicken or turkey work, too)
- 2 ounces (2 slices) whatever cheese you have in the refrigerator or freezer
- 2 eggs, beaten
- 2 tablespoons milk
- 2 tablespoons butter or margarine (for grilling)

Butter the 4 slices of bread. Place 1 ounce of meat and 1 ounce of cheese on 2 of the slices of bread. Top the sandwiches with the remaining bread. Set aside.

In a bowl or baking dish, mix the beaten eggs with the milk. Holding the sandwiches tightly, lay them in the egg batter.

Turn the sandwiches so that they are completely covered with egg. Let them sit in the batter while you prepare the skillet, turning them every 30 seconds or so.

Put 2 tablespoons of butter into a medium-size skillet and heat over medium-low flame. When the butter is hot and foamy, carefully lay the sandwiches in the skillet. Cook until golden brown on 1 side, about 3 to 5 minutes. Repeat on the other side.

Turn the heat down very low, cover the pan, and cook the sandwiches 1 additional minute to ensure the cheese is melted.

Place the sandwiches on plates and cut into 4 pieces. Serve hot.

Easy Crepes

MAKES APPROXIMATELY 6 CREPES.

$\frac{1}{2}$ cup all-purpose flour
1 tablespoon sugar
$\frac{1}{8}$ teaspoon salt
1 egg
$\frac{1}{2}$ cup milk
1 tablespoon melted butter or margarine, at room temperature
Vegetable oil
Butter or margarine (for spreading)
Granulated or confectioner's sugar
Preserves

In a small bowl, combine the flour, sugar, and salt. In a separate bowl beat the egg with the milk. Whisk the egg mixture into the flour mixture, beating until smooth. Pour in the melted butter and mix well until blended.

Coat a small skillet with a cooking spray. Heat the skillet over a low flame until hot, then lightly brush it with vegetable oil. It should not be necessary to repeat this process, but if the crepes start to stick, do so as necessary.

Pour $2\frac{1}{2}$ tablespoons of batter into the skillet, moving the skillet in a circular motion to spread the batter in a circle that covers the bottom of the pan.

Cook for approximately 30 seconds or until lightly browned. Turn over and cook until lightly browned, approximately 30 seconds. Remove crepe from pan. Spread lightly with butter. Roll up and keep in a warm oven while you cook the rest.

When all the crepes are cooked, place them on a warm plate. Sprinkle confectioner's or granulated sugar over the top and serve.

Your favorite fruit preserve is a lovely accompaniment to the crepes.

Herb Omelet

MAKES 2 SMALL OMELETS.

4 large eggs
4 tablespoons cold water
2 teaspoons dried herb of your choice (or 1 teaspoon fresh)
3 teaspoons butter

Break 2 eggs into a glass. Add 2 tablespoons cold water and 1 teaspoon herbs. Put $1\frac{1}{2}$ teaspoons butter into a small skillet and heat on medium-low until the butter is melted and hot.

While the butter is melting, beat the eggs with a fork. (Using a glass limits the amount of air that goes into the eggs, giving you a fluffier omelet.)

Pour the egg into the hot butter and cook, covered, until the top of the omelet is done. Slide the omelet onto a plate, folding it in half as you do. Keep the omelet in a warm oven while you repeat this process for the second omelet.

Serve hot with toast points (see page 108).

Peanut Butter and Banana Sandwiches

MAKES 8 PIECES.

Peanut butter has been an American favorite ever since George Washington Carver invented it, and it is now a staple in most homes. Combine it with banana and you get a nutritious snack that is easy to produce on the spur of the moment.

Butter
4 slices bread
4 tablespoons peanut butter
$\frac{1}{2}$ ripe banana

Spread each slice of bread with a thin coating of butter.

Evenly spread 2 tablespoons of peanut butter on 2 of the slices of bread. Cut the banana into thin slices and lay the slices on top of the peanut butter, dividing evenly. Top the sandwiches with the remaining bread.

Trim the crusts. Cut each sandwich into 4 pieces.

SOURCES

The following organizations and companies were very helpful in providing us with tea information.

BENCHLEY TEA
RD #1 178-G
Highway 34 and Ridgewood Road
Wall Township, New Jersey 07719

R. C. BIGELOW, INC.
15 Merwin Street
Norwalk, Connecticut 06856

CADBURY TYPHOO LTD
Franklin House
P.O. Box 171
Bounville, Birmingham B30 2NA
England

CELESTIAL SEASONINGS (Herbal Teas)
1780 55th Street
Boulder, Colorado 80301-2795

JACKSONS OF PICCADILLY
66-72 St. Johns Road
Clapham Junctions
London SW11 1PT
England

THOMAS J. LIPTON, INC.
800 Sylvan Avenue
Englewood Cliffs, New Jersey 07632

LYONS TETLEY LTD
325 Old Field Lande
Greenford, Middlesex UB6 0A82
England

TEA ASSOCIATION OF THE U.S.A.
230 Park Avenue
New York, New York 10169

TEA & COFFEE ASSOCIATION OF CANADA
1185 Eglinton Avenue East
Suite 101
Don Mills, Ontario
M3C 3C6

TEA COUNCIL OF CANADA
Suite 501
701 Evans Avenue
Etobicoke, Ontario
M9C 1A3

TEA COUNCIL OF THE U.S.A.
230 Park Avenue
New York, New York 10169

Sources

Photographer/KATRINA DELEON
Prop and Set Stylies/JANE PANICO-TRZECIAK
Food Stylist/MARIANNE S. TWOHIE
Special thanks for set construction/MARTIN DELEON

CHAPTER 1 / TEA THE DRINK

Metal tea canister
PANTRY AND HEARTH
121 East 35th Street
New York, NY 10016

CHAPTER 3 / A BRITISH CREAM TEA

Silver tea set, biscuit box (Scones) pastry/sandwich stand, silver tray (Tarts), and server
MICHAEL FEINBERG
225 5th Avenue
New York, NY 10001

Crystal vase
MILLER ROGASKA
225 5th Avenue
New York, NY 10001

Napkins
WOLFMAN-GOLD & GOOD CO.
116 Greene St
New York, NY 10012

Cake stand (Sponge Cake), tea cups and saucers
BARDITH
31 E 72nd Street
New York, NY 10021

CHAPTER 4 / AN AMERICAN CREAM TEA

Cups and saucers
L/S COLLECTION
225 5th Avenue
New York, NY 10001

Cake stand (Lemon Bundt Cake), tart plate, sandwich plate, napkin, napkin ring, and silver tea set
EUROMART
1-800-356-6870

CHAPTER 5 / A SOUTHERN TEA

Location
Rocky Pines
Eldred, NY 12732

Wicker table and chair
WICKERY
342 3rd Avenue
New York, NY 10010

Pedestal cake plate (Coconut Cake), pedestal compote (Scones), tart plate, ceramic platter, sandwich and cookie plate, tea pots and teacups
PORTA
225 5th Avenue
New York, NY 10001

Napkins, cake server, and ice tea glasses
WOLFMAN-GOLD & GOOD CO.
116 Greene Street
New York, NY 10012

Glass pitcher
MILLER ROGASKA
225 5th Avenue
New York, NY 10001

CHAPTER 6 / HIGH TEA

Tea set, cups, fruit bowl, glass bowl (Chutney)
BARDITH
31 East 72nd Street
New York, NY 10021

CHAPTER 7 / THANKSGIVING TEA

Chair, napkins, and metal box
PANTRY AND HEARTH
121 East 35th Street
New York, NY 10016

CHAPTER 8 / CHRISTMAS TEA

Tea set, cups, tiered sandwich plate, and small bowl
GALLERY 726
225 5th Avenue
New York, NY 10001

Silver basket, and napkin (Scones), gold candlesticks, cookie plate, and small bowl
GALLERY 320
225 5th Avenue
New York, NY 10001

Napkin
WOLFMAN-GOLD & GOOD CO.
116 Greene Street
New York, NY 10012

CHAPTER 9 / EASTER TEA

Napkin rings and cake plate
FITZ AND FLOYD
225 5th Avenue
New York, NY 10001

Sandwich plate (Catalina pattern)
Villeroy and Bach
225 5th Avenue
New York, NY 10001

Teapot, Stand, cups, saucers, ceramic rabbit, and ceramic basket
H. Lexington Collection
907 Madison Avenue
New York, NY 10021

Ceramic easter eggs
Artoria/Porcelain De Limoges
225 Fifth Avenue
New York, NY 10001

Napkin inside ceramic basket
Deborah Mallow Designs, Inc.
1261 Broadway, Suite 1010
New York, NY 10001

Catalina pattern plate (Strawberries and Lemon Crisps)
Villeroy and Bach
225 5th Avenue
New York, NY 10001

Chapter 10 / Russian Tea

Tablecloth and Napkins
Deborah Mallow Designs, Inc.
1261 Broadway, Suite 1010
New York, NY 10001

Chapter 11 / Chinese Tea

Tea pot and cups
Terri Shapiro, artist

Placemats, napkins, and basket
Pottery Barn
700 Broadway
New York, NY 10003

Chopsticks, chopstick Stands, and fan
Five Eggs
436 West Broadway
New York, NY 10012

Chapter 12 / Children's Tea

Tea pot and cups
Lynn Fisher, artist
Route 2, Box 41
Bellaire, MI 49615

Plate (Peanut Butter and Jelly Sandwich)
Pottery Barn
700 Broadway
New York, NY 10003

Children's artwork and toys
Special thanks to Alissa Trzeciak

Chapter 13 / Chocolate Lover's Tea

Plate (Truffles)
Diana White

Tea set
Sadler and Co.
225 5th Avenue
New York, NY 10001

Chapter 14 / Feel Better Tea

Bedding (quilt, pillowcase, and ruffled pillow)
Sheridan
595 Madison Avenue
New York, NY 10022

Bed tray
Wickery
342 3rd Avenue
New York, NY 10010

Honey jar and glass bowl (Preserves)
Wooden Indian Antiques
60 West 15 Street
New York, NY 10011

Vase, teapot, tea cup and saucer, silver toast holder
H. Lexington Collection
907 Madison Avenue
New York, NY 10021

Chapter 15 / Late - Night Tea

Teapot, sandwich plate, candlesticks, and pedestal plate
H. Lexington Collection
907 Madison Avenue
New York, NY 10021

Vase
Miller Rogaska
225 5th Avenue
New York, NY 10001

Chapter 16 / Bare Bones Tea

All props from private collections.

Endpapers

Brunschwig & Fils
75 Virginia Road
North White Plains, NY 10603

INDEX